ALSO BY THOMAS FRANK

One Market Under God
The Conquest of Cool
Commodify Your Dissent (coeditor)

What's the Matter with
KANSAS?

What's the Matter with
KANSAS?

How Conservatives Won the Heart of America

THOMAS FRANK

METROPOLITAN BOOKS

Henry Holt and Company | New York

Metropolitan Books
Henry Holt and Company, LLC
Publishers since 1866
115 West 18th Street
New York, New York 10011

Metropolitan Books™ is a registered
trademark of Henry Holt and Company, LLC.

Library of Congress Cataloging-in-Publication Data

Frank, Thomas, 1965–
    What's the matter with Kansas? : how conservatives won the heart
of America / Thomas Frank—1st ed.
        p.   cm.
    Includes index.
    ISBN 0-8050-7339-6
        1. Conservatism—Kansas.   2. Kansas—Politics and
government—1951–   I. Title.

F686.2.F73 2004
978.1'033—dc22   2004044824

First Edition 2004

Map by Patrick W. Welch

Printed in the United States of America

2   4   6   8   10   9   7   5   3   1

Oh, Kansas fools! Poor Kansas fools!
The banker makes of you a tool.

—Populist song, 1892

Contents

What's the Matter with
KANSAS?

Introduction

What's the Matter with America?

The poorest county in America isn't in Appalachia or the Deep South. It is on the Great Plains, a region of struggling ranchers and dying farm towns, and in the election of 2000 the Republican candidate for president, George W. Bush, carried it by a majority of greater than 80 percent.[1]

This puzzled me when I first read about it, as it puzzles many of the people I know. For us it is the Democrats that are the party of workers, of the poor, of the weak and the victimized. Understanding this, we think, is basic; it is part of the ABCs of adulthood. When I told a friend of mine about that impoverished High Plains county so enamored of President Bush, she was perplexed. "How can anyone who has ever worked for someone else vote Republican?" she asked. How could so many people get it so wrong?

Her question is apt; it is, in many ways, the preeminent question of our times. People getting their fundamental interests wrong is what American political life is all about. This species of derangement is the bedrock of our civic order; it is the foundation on which all else rests. This derangement has put the Republicans in charge of all three branches of government; it has elected presidents, senators, governors; it shifts the Democrats to the right and then impeaches Bill Clinton just for fun.

If you earn over $300,000 a year, you owe a great deal to this derangement. Raise a glass sometime to those indigent High Plains Republicans as you contemplate your good fortune: It is thanks to their self-denying votes that you are no longer burdened by the estate tax, or troublesome labor unions, or meddling banking regulators. Thanks to the allegiance of these sons and daughters of toil, you have escaped what your affluent forebears used to call "confiscatory" income tax levels. It is thanks to them that you were able to buy two Rolexes this year instead of one and get that Segway with the special gold trim.

Or perhaps you are one of those many, many millions of average-income Americans who see nothing deranged about this at all. For you this picture of hard-times conservatism makes perfect sense, and it is the opposite phenomenon—working-class people who insist on voting for liberals—that strikes you as an indecipherable puzzlement. Maybe you see it the way the bumper sticker I spotted at a Kansas City gun show puts it: "A working person that *supports* Democrats is like a chicken that *supports* Col. Sanders!"

Maybe you were one of those who stood up for America way back in 1968, sick of hearing those rich kids in beads bad-mouth the country every night on TV. Maybe you knew exactly what Richard Nixon meant when he talked about the "silent majority," the people whose hard work was rewarded with constant insults from the network news, the Hollywood movies, and the know-it-all college professors, none of them interested in anything you had to say. Or maybe it was the liberal judges who got you mad as hell, casually rewriting the laws of your state according to some daft idea they had picked up at a cocktail party, or ordering your town to shoulder some billion-dollar desegregation scheme that they had dreamed up on their own, or turning criminals loose to prey on the hardworking and the industrious. Or perhaps it was the drive for gun control, which was obviously directed toward the same end of disarming and ultimately disempowering people like you.

Maybe Ronald Reagan pulled you into the conservative swirl, the way he talked about that sunshiny, Glenn Miller America you remembered from the time before the world went to hell. Or maybe Rush Limbaugh won you over, with his daily beatdown of the arrogant and the self-important. Or maybe you were pushed; maybe Bill Clinton made a Republican out of you with his patently phony "compassion" and his obvious contempt for average, non-Ivy Americans, the ones he had the nerve to order into combat even though he himself took the coward's way out when his turn came.

Nearly everyone has a conversion story they can tell: how their dad had been a union steelworker and a stalwart Democrat, but how all their brothers and sisters started voting Republican; or how their cousin gave up on Methodism and started going to the Pentecostal church out on the edge of town; or how they themselves just got so sick of being scolded for eating meat or for wearing clothes emblazoned with the State U's Indian mascot that one day Fox News started to seem "fair and balanced" to them after all.

Take the family of a friend of mine, a guy who came from one of those midwestern cities that sociologists used to descend upon periodically because it was supposed to be so "typical." It was a middling-sized industrial burg where they made machine tools, auto parts, and so forth. When Reagan took office in 1981, more than half the working population of the city was employed in factories, and most of them were union members. The ethos of the place was working-class, and the city was prosperous, tidy, and liberal, in the old sense of the word.

My friend's dad was a teacher in the local public schools, a loyal member of the teachers' union, and a more dedicated liberal than most: not only had he been a staunch supporter of George McGovern, but in the 1980 Democratic primary he had voted for Barbara Jordan, the black U.S. Representative from Texas. My friend, meanwhile, was in those days a high school Republican, a Reagan youth who fancied Adam Smith ties and savored the writing of William F. Buckley. The dad would listen to the son spout off about Milton Friedman and the godliness of free-market capitalism, and he would just shake his head. *Someday, kid, you'll know what a jerk you are.*

It was the dad, though, who was eventually converted. These days he votes for the farthest-right Republicans he can find on the ballot. The particular issue that brought him over was abortion. A devout Catholic, my friend's dad was persuaded in the early nineties that the sanctity of the fetus outweighed all of his other concerns, and from there he gradually accepted the whole pantheon of conservative devil-figures: the elite media and the American Civil Liberties Union, contemptuous of our values; the la-di-da feminists; the idea that Christians are vilely persecuted—right here in the U.S. of A. It doesn't even bother him, really, when his new hero Bill O'Reilly blasts the teachers' union as a group that "does not love America."

His superaverage midwestern town, meanwhile, has followed the same trajectory. Even as Republican economic policy laid waste to the city's industries, unions, and neighborhoods, the townsfolk responded by lashing out on cultural issues, eventually winding up with a hard-right Republican congressman, a born-again Christian who campaigned largely on an anti-abortion platform. Today the city looks like a miniature Detroit. And with every bit of economic bad news it seems to get more bitter, more cynical, and more conservative still.

This derangement is the signature expression of the Great Backlash, a style of conservatism that first came snarling onto the national stage in response to the partying and protests of the late sixties. While earlier forms of conservatism emphasized fiscal sobriety, the backlash mobilizes voters with explosive social issues—summoning public outrage over everything from busing to un-Christian art—which it then marries to pro-business economic policies. Cultural anger is marshaled to achieve economic ends. And it is these economic achievements—not the forgettable skirmishes of the never-ending culture wars—that are the movement's greatest monuments. The backlash is what has made possible the international free-market consensus of recent years, with all the privatization, deregulation, and deunionization that are its components. Backlash ensures that Republicans will continue to be returned to office even when their free-market miracles fail and their libertarian schemes don't deliver and their "New Economy" collapses. It makes possible the policy pushers' fantasies of "globalization" and a free-trade empire that are foisted upon the rest of the world with such self-assurance. Because some artist decides to shock the hicks by dunking Jesus in urine, the entire planet must remake itself along the lines preferred by the Republican Party, U.S.A.

The Great Backlash has made the laissez-faire revival possible, but this does not mean that it speaks to us in the manner of the capitalists of old, invoking the divine right of money or demanding that the lowly learn their place in the great chain of being. On the contrary; the backlash imagines itself as a foe of the elite, as the voice of the unfairly persecuted, as a righteous protest of the people on history's receiving end. That its champions today control all three branches of government matters not a whit. That its greatest beneficiaries are the wealthiest people on the planet does not give it pause.

In fact, backlash leaders systematically downplay the politics of economics. The movement's basic premise is that culture outweighs economics as a matter of public concern—that *Values Matter Most,* as one backlash title has it. On those grounds it rallies citizens who would once have been reliable partisans of the New Deal to the standard of conservatism.[2] Old-fashioned values may count when conservatives appear on the stump, but once conservatives are in office the only old-fashioned situation they care to revive is an economic regimen of low wages and lax regulations. Over the last three decades they have smashed the welfare state, reduced the tax burden on corporations and the wealthy, and generally facilitated the country's return to a nineteenth-century pattern of wealth distribution. Thus the primary contradiction of the backlash: it is a working-class movement that has done incalculable, historic harm to working-class people.

The leaders of the backlash may talk Christ, but they walk corporate. Values may "matter most" to voters, but they always take a backseat to the needs of money once the elections are won. This is a basic earmark of the phenomenon, absolutely consistent across its decades-long history. Abortion is never halted. Affirmative action is never abolished. The culture industry is never forced to clean up its act. Even the greatest culture warrior of them all was a notorious cop-out once it came time to deliver. "Reagan made himself the champion of 'traditional values,' but there is no evidence he regarded their restoration as a high priority," wrote Christopher Lasch, one of the most astute analysts of the backlash sensibility. "What he really cared about was the revival of the unregulated capitalism of the twenties: the repeal of the New Deal."[3]

This is vexing for observers, and one might expect it to vex the movement's true believers even more. Their grandstanding leaders never deliver, their fury mounts and mounts, and nevertheless they turn out every two years to return their right-wing heroes to office for a second, a third, a twentieth try. The trick never ages; the illusion never wears off. *Vote* to stop abortion; *receive* a rollback in capital gains taxes. *Vote* to make our country strong again; *receive* deindustrialization. *Vote* to screw those politically correct college professors; *receive* electricity deregulation. *Vote* to get government off our backs; *receive* conglomeration and monopoly everywhere from media to meatpacking. *Vote* to stand tall against terrorists; *receive* Social Security privatization. *Vote* to strike a blow against elitism; *receive* a social order in which wealth is more concentrated than ever before in our lifetimes, in which workers have been stripped of power and CEOs are rewarded in a manner beyond imagining.

Backlash theorists, as we shall see, imagine countless conspiracies in which the wealthy, powerful, and well connected—the liberal media, the atheistic scientists, the obnoxious eastern elite—pull the strings and make the puppets dance. And yet the backlash itself has been a political trap so devastating to the interests of Middle America that even the most diabolical of stringpullers would have had trouble dreaming it up. Here, after all, is a rebellion against "the establishment" that has wound up abolishing the tax on inherited estates. Here is a movement whose response to the power structure is to make the rich even richer; whose answer to the inexorable degradation of working-class life is to lash out angrily at labor unions and liberal workplace-safety programs; whose solution to the rise of ignorance in America is to pull the rug out from under public education.

Like a French Revolution in reverse—one in which the sans-culottes pour down the streets demanding more power for the aristocracy—the backlash pushes the spectrum of the acceptable to the right, to the right, farther to the right. It may never bring prayer back to the schools, but it has rescued all manner of right-wing economic nostrums from history's dustbin. Having rolled back the landmark economic reforms of the sixties (the war on poverty) and those of the thirties (labor law, agricultural price supports, banking regulation), its leaders now turn their guns on the accomplishments of the earliest years of progressivism (Woodrow Wilson's estate tax; Theodore Roosevelt's antitrust measures). With a little more effort, the backlash may well repeal the entire twentieth century.[4]

As a formula for holding together a dominant political coalition, the backlash seems so improbable and so self-contradictory that liberal observers often have trouble believing it is actually happening. By all rights, they figure, these two groups—business and blue-collar—should be at each other's throats. For the Republican Party to present itself as the champion of working-class America strikes liberals as such an egregious denial of political reality that they dismiss the whole phenomenon, refusing to take it seriously. The Great Backlash, they believe, is nothing but crypto-racism, or a disease of the elderly, or the random gripings of religious rednecks, or the protests of "angry white men" feeling left behind by history.

But to understand the backlash in this way is to miss its power as an idea and its broad popular vitality. It keeps coming despite everything, a plague of bitterness capable of spreading from the old to the young, from Protestant fundamentalists to Catholics and Jews, and from the angry white man to every demographic shading imaginable.

It matters not at all that the forces that triggered the original "silent majority" back in Nixon's day have long since disappeared; the backlash roars on undiminished, its rage carrying easily across the decades. The confident liberals who led America in those days are a dying species. The New Left, with its gleeful obscenities and contempt for the flag, is extinct altogether. The whole "affluent society," with its paternalistic corporations and powerful labor unions, fades farther into the ether with each passing year. But the backlash endures. It continues to dream its terrifying dreams of national decline, epic lawlessness, and betrayal at the top regardless of what is actually going on in the world.

Along the way what was once genuine and grassroots and even "populist" about the backlash phenomenon has been transformed into a stimulus-response melodrama with a plot as formulaic as an episode of *The O'Reilly Factor* and with results as predictable—and as profitable—as Coca-Cola advertising. In one end you feed an item about, say, the menace of gay marriage, and at the other end you generate, almost mechanically, an uptick of middle-American indignation, angry letters to the editor, an electoral harvest of the most gratifying sort.

My aim is to examine the backlash from top to bottom—its theorists, its elected officials, and its foot soldiers—and to understand the species of derangement that has brought so many ordinary people to such a self-damaging political extreme. I will do so by focusing on a place where the political shift has been dramatic: my home state of Kansas, a reliable hotbed of leftist reform movements a hundred years ago that today ranks among the nation's most eager audiences for bearers of backlash buncombe. The state's story, like the long history of the backlash itself, is not one that will reassure the optimistic or silence the cynical. And yet if we are to understand the forces that have pulled us so far to the right, it is to Kansas that we must turn our attention. The high priests of conservatism like to comfort themselves by insisting that it is the free market, that wise and benevolent god, that has ordained all the economic measures they have pressed on America and the world over the last few decades. But in truth it is the carefully cultivated derangement of places like Kansas that has propelled their movement along. It is culture war that gets the goods.

From the air-conditioned heights of a suburban office complex this may look like a new age of reason, with the Web sites singing each to each, with a mall down the way that every week has miraculously anticipated our subtly shifting tastes, with a global economy whose rich rewards just keep flowing, and with a long parade of rust-free Infinitis purring down the streets of beautifully manicured planned communities. But on closer inspection the country seems more like a panorama of madness and delusion worthy of Hieronymous Bosch: of sturdy blue-collar patriots reciting the Pledge while they strangle their own life chances; of small farmers proudly voting themselves off the land; of devoted family men carefully seeing to it that their children will never be able to afford college or proper health care; of working-class guys in midwestern cities cheering as they deliver up a landslide for a candidate whose policies will end their way of life, will transform their region into a "rust belt," will strike people like them blows from which they will never recover.

PART I:

Mysteries of the
Great Plains

Chapter One

The Two Nations

In the backlash imagination, America is always in a state of quasi–civil war: on one side are the unpretentious millions of authentic Americans; on the other stand the bookish, all-powerful liberals who run the country but are contemptuous of the tastes and beliefs of the people who inhabit it. When the chairman of the Republican National Committee in 1992 announced to a national TV audience, "We are America" and "those other people are not," he was merely giving new and more blunt expression to a decades-old formula. Newt Gingrich's famous description of Democrats as "the enemy of normal Americans" was just one more winning iteration of this well-worn theme.

The current installment of this fantasy is the story of "the two Americas," the symbolic division of the country that, after the presidential election of 2000, captivated not only backlashers but a sizable chunk of the pundit class. The idea found its inspiration in the map of the electoral results that year: there were those vast stretches of inland "red" space (the networks all used red to designate Republican victories) where people voted for George W. Bush, and those tiny little "blue" coastal areas where people lived in big cities and voted for Al Gore. On the face of it there was nothing really remarkable about these red and blue blocs, especially since in terms of the popular vote the contest was essentially a tie.

Still, many commentators divined in the 2000 map a baleful cultural cleavage, a looming crisis over identity and values. "This nation has rarely appeared more divided than it does right now," moaned David Broder, the *Washington Post*'s pundit-in-chief, in a story published a few days after the election. The two regions were more than mere voting blocs; they were complete sociological profiles, two different Americas at loggerheads with each other.

And these pundits knew—before election night was over and just by looking at the map—what those two Americas represented. Indeed, the explanation was ready to go before the election even happened.[1] The great dream of conservatives ever since the thirties has been a working-class movement that for once takes *their* side of the issues, that votes Republican and reverses the achievements of working-class movements of the past. In the starkly divided red/blue map of 2000 they thought they saw it being realized: the old Democratic regions of the South and the Great Plains were on their team now, solid masses of uninterrupted red, while the Democrats were restricted to the old-line, blueblood states of the Northeast, along with the hedonist left coast.*

I do not want to minimize the change that this represents. Certain parts of the Midwest were once so reliably leftist that the historian Walter Prescott Webb, in his classic 1931 history of the

---

*The handful of midwestern states that also went Democratic did not fit easily into this scheme, and so were rarely taken into account by commentators.

region, pointed to its persistent radicalism as one of the "Mysteries of the Great Plains." Today the mystery is only heightened; it seems inconceivable that the Midwest was ever thought of as a "radical" place, as anything but the land of the bland, the easy snoozing flyover. Readers in the thirties, on the other hand, would have known instantly what Webb was talking about, since so many of the great political upheavals of their part of the twentieth century were launched from the territory west of the Ohio River. The region as they knew it was what gave the country Socialists like Eugene Debs, fiery progressives like Robert La Follette, and practical unionists like Walter Reuther; it spawned the anarchist IWW and the coldly calculating UAW; and it was periodically convulsed in gargantuan and often bloody industrial disputes. They might even have known that there were once Socialist newspapers in Kansas and Socialist voters in Oklahoma and Socialist mayors in Milwaukee, and that there were radical farmers across the region forever enlisting in militant agrarian organization with names like the Farmers' Alliance, or the Farmer-Labor Party, or the Non-Partisan League, or the Farm Holiday Association. And they would surely have been aware that Social Security, the basic element of the liberal welfare state, was largely a product of the midwestern mind.

Almost all of these associations have evaporated today. That the region's character has been altered so thoroughly—that so much of the Midwest now regards the welfare state as an alien imposition; that we have trouble even believing there was a time when progressives were described with adjectives like *fiery*, rather than *snooty* or *bossy* or *wimpy*—has to stand as one of the great reversals of American history.

So when the electoral map of 2000 is compared to that of 1896—the year of the showdown between the "great commoner," William Jennings Bryan, and the voice of business, William McKinley—a remarkable inversion is indeed evident.

Bryan was a Nebraskan, a leftist, and a fundamentalist Christian, an almost unimaginable combination today, and in 1896 he
swept most of the country outside the Northeast and upper Midwest, which stood rock-solid for industrial capitalism. George
W. Bush's advisers love to compare their man to McKinley,[2] and
armed with the electoral map of 2000 the president's fans are
able to envisage the great contest of 1896 refought with optimal
results: the politics of McKinley chosen by the Middle America
of Bryan.

From this one piece of evidence, the electoral map, the pundits simply veered off into authoritative-sounding cultural proclamation. Just by looking at the map, they reasoned, we could
easily tell that George W. Bush was the choice of the plain people, the grassroots Americans who inhabited the place we know
as the "heartland," a region of humility, guilelessness, and,
above all, stout yeoman *righteousness*. The Democrats, on the
other hand, were the party of the elite. Just by looking at the map
we could see that liberals were sophisticated, wealthy, and materialistic. While the big cities blued themselves shamelessly, the
land knew what it was about and went Republican, by a margin
in square miles of four to one.[3]

The attraction of such a scheme for conservatives was powerful and obvious.[4] The red-state narrative brought majoritarian
legitimacy to a president who had actually lost the popular vote.
It also allowed conservatives to present their views as the philosophy of a region that Americans—even sophisticated urban
ones—traditionally venerate as the repository of national virtue,
a place of plain speaking and straight shooting.

The red-state/blue-state divide also helped conservatives perform one of their dearest rhetorical maneuvers, which we will
call the *latte libel*: the suggestion that liberals are identifiable by
their tastes and consumer preferences and that these tastes and
preferences reveal the essential arrogance and foreignness of lib-

eralism. While a more straightforward discussion of politics might begin by considering the economic interests that each party serves, the latte libel insists that such interests are irrelevant. Instead it's the places that people live and the things that they drink, eat, and drive that are the critical factors, the clues that bring us to the truth. In particular, the things that *liberals* are said to drink, eat, and drive: the Volvos, the imported cheese, and above all, the lattes.*

The red-state/blue-state idea appeared to many in the media to be a scientific validation of this familiar stereotype, and before long it was a standard element of the media's pop-sociology repertoire. The "two Americas" idea became a hook for all manner of local think pieces (blue Minnesota is only separated by one thin street from red Minnesota, but my, how different those two Minnesotas are); it provided an easy tool for contextualizing the small stories (red Americans love a certain stage show in Vegas, but blue Americans don't) or for spinning the big stories (John Walker Lindh, the American who fought for the Taliban, was from California and therefore a reflection of blue-state values); and it justified countless *USA Today*–style contemplations of who we Americans really are, meaning mainly investigations of the burning usual—what we Americans like to listen to, watch on TV, or buy at the supermarket.

---

*The state of Vermont is a favorite target of the latte libel. In his best-selling *Bobos in Paradise,* David Brooks ridicules the city of Burlington in that state as the prototypical "latte town," a city where "Beverly Hills income levels" meet a Scandinavian-style social consciousness. In a TV commercial aired in early 2004 by the conservative Club for Growth, onetime Democratic presidential candidate Howard Dean, the former governor of Vermont, is reviled by two supposedly average people who advise him to "take his tax-hiking, government-expanding, latte-drinking, sushi-eating, Volvo-driving, *New York Times*–reading, body-piercing, Hollywood-loving, left-wing freak show back to Vermont, where it belongs."

Red America, these stories typically imply,[5] is a mysterious place whose thoughts and values are essentially foreign to society's masters. Like the "Other America" of the sixties or the "Forgotten Men" of the thirties, its vast stretches are tragically ignored by the dominant class—that is, the people who write the sitcoms and screenplays and the stories in glossy magazines, all of whom, according to the conservative commentator Michael Barone, simply "can't imagine living in such places." Which is particularly unfair of them, impudent even, because Red America is in fact the *real* America, the part of the country where reside, as a column in the Canadian *National Post* put it, "the original values of America's founding."

And since many of the pundits who were hailing the virtues of the red states—pundits, remember, who were conservatives and who supported George W. Bush—actually, physically lived in blue states that went for Gore, the rules of this idiotic game allowed them to present the latte libel in the elevated language of the confession. David Brooks, who has since made a career out of projecting the liberal stereotype onto the map, took to the pages of *The Atlantic* magazine to admit on behalf of *everyone who lives in a blue zone* that they are all snobs, toffs, wusses, ignoramuses, and utterly out of touch with the authentic life of the people.

> We in the coastal metro Blue areas read more books and attend more plays than the people in the Red heartland. We're more sophisticated and cosmopolitan—just ask us about our alumni trips to China or Provence, or our interest in Buddhism. But don't ask us, please, what life in Red America is like. We don't know. We don't know who Tim LaHaye and Jerry B. Jenkins are. . . . We don't know what James Dobson says on his radio program, which is listened to by millions. We don't know about

Reba and Travis. . . . Very few of us know what goes on in Branson, Missouri, even though it has seven million visitors a year, or could name even five NASCAR drivers. . . . We don't know how to shoot or clean a rifle. We can't tell a military officer's rank by looking at his insignia. We don't know what soy beans look like when they're growing in a field.[6]

One is tempted to dismiss Brooks's grand generalizations by rattling off the many ways in which he gets it wrong: by pointing out that the top three soybean producers—Illinois, Iowa, and Minnesota—were in fact blue states; or by listing the many military bases located on the coasts; or by noting that when it came time to build a NASCAR track in Kansas, the county that won the honor was one of only two in the state that went for Gore. Average per capita income in that same lonely blue county, I might as well add, is $16,000, which places it well below Kansas and national averages, and far below what would be required for the putting on of elitist or cosmopolitan airs of any kind.[7]

It's pretty much a waste of time, however, to catalog the contradictions[8] and tautologies[9] and huge, honking errors[10] blowing round in a media flurry like this. The tools being used are the blunt instruments of propaganda, not the precise metrics of sociology. Yet, as with all successful propaganda, the narrative does contain a grain of truth: we all know that there *are* many aspects of American life that are off the culture industry's radar; that vast reaches of the country *have* gone from being liberal if not radical to being stoutly conservative; and that there *is* a small segment of the "cosmopolitan" upper middle class that considers itself socially enlightened, that knows nothing of the fine points of hayseediana, that likes lattes, and that opted for Gore.

But the "two nations" commentators showed no interest in examining the mysterious inversion of American politics in any systematic way. Their aim was simply to bolster the stereotypes using whatever tools were at hand: to cast the Democrats as the party of a wealthy, pampered, arrogant elite that lives as far as it can from real Americans; and to represent Republicanism as the faith of the hardworking common people of the heartland, an expression of their unpretentious, all-American ways just like country music and NASCAR. At this pursuit they largely succeeded. By 2003 the conservative claim to the Midwest was so uncontested that Fox News launched a talk show dealing in culture-war outrage that was called, simply, *Heartland*.

What characterizes the good people of Red America? Reading through the "two Americas" literature is a little like watching a series of Frank Capra one-reelers explaining the principles of some turbocharged Boy Scout Law:

A *red-stater is humble*. In fact, humility is, according to reigning journalistic myth, the signature quality of Red America, just as it was one of the central themes of George W. Bush's presidential campaign. "In Red America the self is small," teaches David Brooks. "People declare in a million ways, 'I am normal.'" As evidence of this modesty, Brooks refers to the plain clothing that he saw residents wearing in a county in Pennsylvania that voted for Bush, and in particular to the unremarkable brand names he spotted on the locals' caps. The caps clearly indicate that the people of Red America enjoy trusting and untroubled relationships with Wal-Mart and McDonald's; ipso facto they are humble.

John Podhoretz, a former speechwriter for Bush the Elder, finds the same noble simplicity beneath every adjusto-cap. "Bush Red is a simpler place," he concludes, after watching people at play in Las Vegas; it's a land "where people mourn the death of NASCAR champion Dale Earnhardt, root lustily for their teams, go to church, and find comfort in old-fashioned verities."

When the red-staters themselves get into the act, composing lists of their own virtues, things get bad fast. How "humble" can you be when you're writing a three-thousand-word essay claiming that all the known virtues of democracy are sitting right there with you at the word processor? This problem comes into blinding focus in a much-reprinted red-state blast by the Missouri farmer Blake Hurst that was originally published in *The American Enterprise* magazine. He and his fellow Bush voters, Hurst stepped forward to tell the world, were *humble, humble, humble, humble!*

> Most Red Americans can't deconstruct post-modern literature, give proper orders to a nanny, pick out a cabernet with aftertones of licorice, or quote prices from the Abercrombie and Fitch catalog. But we can raise great children, wire our own houses, make beautiful and delicious creations with our own two hands, talk casually and comfortably about God, repair a small engine, recognize a good maple sugar tree, tell you the histories of our towns and the hopes of our neighbors, shoot a gun and run a chainsaw without fear, calculate the bearing load of a roof, grow our own asparagus . . .

And so on.

On the blue side of the great virtue divide, Brooks reports, "the self is more commonly large." This species of American can be easily identified in the field by their constant witty showing off: *They think they are so damn smart.* Podhoretz, a former Republican speechwriter, remember, admits that "we" blue-staters "cannot live without irony," by which he means mocking everything that crosses our path, because "we" foolishly believe that "ideological and moral confusion are signs of a higher consciousness." Brooks, who has elsewhere ascribed the decline of the Democratic Party to its snobbery,[11] mocks blue-staters for eating at fancy restaurants and shopping in small, pretentious stores instead of at Wal-Mart, retailer to real America. He actually finds a poll in which 43 percent of liberals confess that they "like to show off," which he then tops with another poll in which 75 percent of liberals describe themselves as "intellectuals." Such admissions, in this company, are tantamount to calling yourself a mind-twisting communist.

Which was, according to that Canadian columnist, precisely what liberals were, as one could plainly see from the famous electoral map. While humble red-state people had been minding their own business over the years, "intellectuals educated at European universities" were lapping up the poisonous teachings of Karl Marx, then returning to "dominate our universities," where they "have condemned America's values and indoctrinated generations of students in their collectivist ideals." Thus the reason that liberals rallied to Al Gore was the opportunity to advance "collectivism." (Podhoretz, for his part, claims liberals liked Gore because he was so witty!)

A *red-stater*, meanwhile, *is reverent*. As we were repeatedly reminded after the election, red-state people have a better relationship with God than the rest of us. They go to church regularly. They are "observant, tradition-minded, moralistic," in Michael Barone's formulation. Liberals of the coasts, meanwhile, are said to be "unobservant, liberation-minded, relativistic."

But don't worry; *a red-stater is courteous, kind, cheerful*. They may be religious, but they aren't at all pushy about it. The people David Brooks encountered in that one county in Pennsylvania declined to discuss abortion with him, from which he concludes that "potentially controversial subjects are often played down" throughout Red America. Even the preachers he met there are careful to respect the views of others. These fine people "don't like public scolds." They are easygoing believers, not interested in taking you on in a culture war. Don't be frightened.

A red-stater is loyal. This is the part of the country that fills the army's ranks and defends the flag against all comers. While the European-minded know-it-alls of blue land waited only a short time after 9/11 to commence blaming America for the tragedy, the story goes, sturdy red-staters stepped forward unhesitatingly to serve their country one more time. For Blake Hurst of Missouri, this special relationship with the military is both a matter of pride ("Red America is never redder than on our bloodiest battlefields") and a grievance—you know, the usual one, the one you saw in *Rambo,* the one where all the cowards of the coasts stab the men of red land in the back during the Vietnam War.

But above all, *a red-stater is a regular, down-home working stiff,* whereas a blue-stater is always some sort of pretentious paper shuffler. The idea that the United States is "two nations" defined by social rank was first articulated by the labor movement and the historical left. The agrarian radicals of the 1890s used the "two nations" image to distinguish between "producers" and "parasites," or simply "the robbers and the robbed," as Sockless Jerry Simpson, the leftist congressman from Kansas, liked to put it. The radical novelist John Dos Passos used the phrase to describe his disillusionment with capitalist America in the twenties, while the Democratic presidential candidate John Edwards has recently made a point of reviving the term in its original meaning.[12] For the most part, however, the way the "two Americas" image is used these days, it incorporates all the disillusionment, all the resentment, but none of the leftism. "Rural America is pissed," a small-town Pennsylvania man told a reporter from *Newsweek* in 2001. Explaining why he and his neighbors voted for George Bush, he said: "These people are tired of moral decay.

They're tired of everything being wonderful on Wall Street and terrible on Main Street." Let me repeat that: they're voting *Republican* in order to *get even with Wall Street*.

This is not yet the place to try to sort out the tangled reasoning that leads a hardworking citizen of an impoverished town to conclude that voting for George W. Bush is a way to strike a blow against big business, but it is important to remind ourselves of the context. During the decade that was then ending, the grand idea that had made the pundits gawk and the airwaves sing had been the coming of a New Economy, a free-market millennium in which physical work was as obsolete as the sundial. It was the age of the "knowledge worker," we were told, the heroic entrepreneur who was building a "weightless" economy out of "thin air." Blue-collar workers, meanwhile, were the ones who "didn't get it," fast-fading relics of an outmoded and all-too-material past. Certain celebrated capitalist thinkers even declared, at the height of the boom, that blue collars and white collars had swapped moral positions, with workers now the "parasites" free-loading on the Olympian labors of management.[13]

The red-state/blue-state literature simply corrected this most egregious excess of the previous decade, rediscovering the nobility of the average worker and reasserting the original definitions of *parasite* and *producer*.[14] What was novel was that it did so in the service of the very same free-market policies that characterized the hallucinatory nineties. The actors had put away their laptops and donned overalls, but the play remained the same.

Consider, in this connection, the "two nations" story that appeared in *American Handgunner,* which tells us how the 9/11 terrorist attack brought home the truth to one "self-described 'Blue' American in New York City." As she stood "alongside other New York 'intellectuals'" watching the construction workers and firefighters do their job, she realized that those tired men and women passing in trucks make it all happen. They are the ones who do the actual work of running the country. They cause the electricity to flow, the schools to be built, the criminals to be arrested and society to run seamlessly. She realized, with a blazingly bright lightbulb of awareness flashing in her mind, she didn't know how to change a tire, grow tomatoes, or where electricity comes from.

This deracinated white-collar worker cast her mind back over her "power lunches" and other pretentious doings and suddenly understood that "she had no real skills." No lightbulb flashes to remind her that the rescue and construction workers were *also* from a blue state and probably voted for Gore. Instead, we are told, she has become a humbler person, a red-stater in attitude if not in place of residence. The tale then ends with an exhortation to get out there and vote.

Blake Hurst, the Missouri farmer who is so proud of being humble, also chimes in on this theme, pointing out in *The American Enterprise* that "the work we [red-staters] do can be measured in bushels, pounds, shingles nailed, and bricks laid, rather than in the fussy judgments that make up office employee reviews." But there's something fishy about Hurst's claim to the mantle of workerist righteousness, something beyond the immediate fishiness of a magazine ordinarily given to assailing unions and saluting the Dow now printing such a fervent celebration of blue-collar life. Just being familiar with the physical world shouldn't automatically make you a member of the beaten-down producer class any more than does living in a state that voted for George W. Bush. Indeed, elsewhere Hurst describes himself not as a simple farmer but as the co-owner of a family business overseeing the labors of a number of employees, employees to whom, he confides, he and his family "don't pay high wages." Hurst has even written an essay on that timeless lament of the boss, the unbelievable laziness of workers today.[15] This man may live in the sticks, but he is about as much a blue-collar toiler as is Al Gore himself.

Perhaps that is why Hurst is so certain that, while there is obviously a work-related divide between the two Americas—separating them into Hurst's humble, producer America and the liberals' conceited, parasite America—it isn't the scary divide that Dos Passos wrote about, the sort of divide between workers and bosses that might cause problems for readers of *The American Enterprise*. "Class-consciousness isn't a problem in Red America," he assures them; people are "perfectly happy to be slightly overweight [and] a little underpaid."

David Brooks goes even further, concluding from his field-work in Red America that the standard notion of class is flawed. Thinking about class in terms of a hierarchy, where some people occupy more exalted positions than others, he writes, is "Marxist" and presumably illegitimate. The correct model, he suggests, is a high school cafeteria, segmented into self-chosen taste clusters like "nerds, jocks, punks, bikers, techies, druggies, God Squadders," and so on. "The jocks knew there would always be nerds, and the nerds knew there would always be jocks," he writes. "That's just the way life is." We choose where we want to sit and whom we want to mimic and what class we want to belong to the same way we choose hairstyles or TV shows or extracurricular activities. We're all free agents in this noncoercive class system, and Brooks eventually concludes that worrying about the problems faced by workers is yet another deluded affectation of the blue-state rich.[16]

As a description of the way society works, this is preposterous. Even by high school, most of us know that we won't be able to choose our station in life the way we choose a soda pop or even the way we choose our friends. But as a clue into the deepest predilections of the backlash mind, Brooks's scheme is a revelation.[17]

What divides Americans is *authenticity*, not something hard and ugly like economics. While liberals commit endless acts of hubris, sucking down lattes, driving ostentatious European cars, and trying to reform the world, the humble people of the red states go about their unpretentious business, eating down-home foods, vacationing in the Ozarks, whistling while they work, feeling comfortable about who they are, and knowing they are secure under the watch of George W. Bush, a man they love as one of their own.

Chapter Two

Deep in the Heart
of Redness

As long as America loves authenticity, my home state of Kansas is going to be symbolically preeminent. Whatever the standard for measuring salt-of-the-earthness happens to be at the moment—the WPA social realism of the thirties or the red-state theories of today's conservatives—Kansas is going to rank high. It may not do too well by other measurements, but in the quest for symbols of down-home, stand-pat, plainspoken, unvarnished, bedrock American goodness Kansas has everyone else beat. If it's 100 percent Americanism we're looking for, Kansas delivers 110 percent. If it's the down-to-earth stoicism of Nixon-voting Middle Americans that's being celebrated, somebody will point out that Kansas is the most middling of all possible American places, the exact center of the continental United States, in fact. The vortex of the nation, in Allen Ginsberg's phrase. Kansas is deepest Reagan country, the heart of the heartland, the roots of the grass, the reddest of red states.

Kansas is what New York City is not: a guileless, straight-talking truth-place where people are unaffected, genuine, and attuned to the rhythms of the universe. "I loved Kansas City!" Ann Coulter exclaimed to an interviewer in New York. "It's like my favorite place in the world. Oh, I think it is so great out there. Well, that's America. It's the opposite of this town. They're Americans, they're so great, they're rooting for America. I mean, there's so much common sense!"[1]

Coulter is embracing a literary myth of long standing when she enthuses this way. Like Peoria or Muncie, Kansas figures in literature and film as a stand-in for the nation as a whole, the distilled essence of who we are. "The Kansan," wrote John Gunther in 1947, is "the most average of all Americans, a kind of common denominator for the entire continent."[2] Kansas is "Midway, USA"; it's the setting for countless Depression-era documentary photographs; it's the home of the bright boy in the mailroom who wants to be a player on Wall Street. It's where Dorothy wants to return. It's where Superman grows up. It's where Bonnie and Clyde steal a car and Elmer Gantry studies the Bible and Russian ICBMs destroy everything and the overchurched antihero of *An American Tragedy* learns the sinful ways of the world.

The state has an undeniable instinct for the average in real life, too. It is anti-exotic, familiar even if you've never been there. As a tourist destination, Kansas ranks dead last among the states[3] but it remains a popular proving ground for test marketers of every kind. It has been a prolific birthplace of chain restaurants—Pizza Hut, White Castle, and Applebees, to name a few[4]—and it supplies the nation with anchormen, comedians, and actors of wholesome visage and accent inoffensive. Kansas City* is the home of Hallmark Cards and the nation's very first

---

*Kansas City proper is in Missouri, but its metropolitan area sprawls across the state line, incorporating the much smaller Kansas City, Kansas, and the

suburban shopping center. Thanks to its unerring sense for the middle, the state is a politician producer of the first rank, a reliable wellspring of down-home statesmen.[5]

Its averageness has also made Kansas a symbol of squareness in the vast world of commodified dissent, the place that actors announce they're "not in anymore" when they chew an especially minty kind of gum or walk into a room where there's a lot of people with xtreme hairdos. Recall the late-eighties T-shirts that sneered, "New York—It Ain't Kansas." Or think back to those teen-rebellion movies in which the stern Kansas elders forbid dancing and all the bored farm kids long to escape to Los Angeles, where they can be themselves and adopt the lifestyle of their choice.

In politics, however, where Americans worship at the shrine of the unaffected common man, averageness allows Kansans to present themselves as something of an aristocracy. Regardless of the social position they actually enjoy, they are all to the farmhouse born. Even bankers and oilmen, if they come from Kansas, carry with them the coveted authenticity of the real American: they speak automatically with the vox populi, and they strut upon the national stage with all the virtuous self-assurance that once belonged to the horny-handed sons of toil. Thus Senator Sam Brownback, a member of one of the wealthiest families in the state and a stalwart friend of the CEO class, refers to himself on the floor of Congress as a "farmboy from Parker, Kansas." Thus Bob Dole, that consummate Washington insider, opened his 1996 presidential campaign by complaining that "our leaders have grown too isolated from places like Topeka—embarrassed by the values here."

But nice warm averageness has not always been the framing

---

affluent suburbs of Johnson County, Kansas. Today about a third of the metro area's population lives in Kansas.

myth here. A century ago the favorite stereotype of Kansas was not the land of normality but the freak state.[6] The place crawled with religious fanatics, crackpot demagogues, and alarming hybrids of the two, such as the murderous abolitionist John Brown, who is generally regarded as the state's patron saint, and the rabid prohibitionist Carry A. Nation, who expressed her distaste for liquor by smashing saloons with a hatchet. Kansas was a violent and a radical and maybe even a crazy place both by nature and by the circumstances of its founding. The state was initially settled by eastern abolitionists and free-soilers who came there to block Missourians from moving westward—in other words, to contain the "slave power" by armed force; before long the unique savagery of the border war they fought put Kansas in headlines around the world. Dodge City and Abilene, famed for picturesque cowboy homicides, are found there as well, as are a good proportion of the nation's tornadoes and, in the twentieth century, its dust storms, which obliterated farms and carried the topsoil of the entire region off into the wild blue yonder. Early accounts of the state even tell of settlers driven insane by the constant howling of the wind.

Politically, Kansas is what the marketing boys call an "early adopter," a state where the various ideological nostrums of the day—from Free Love to Prohibition, utopian communism to the John Birch Society—were embraced quickly and ardently. In the thirties the state almost elected as its governor a beloved radio doctor who claimed to restore virility by transplanting goat testicles into humans.

But its periodic bouts of leftism were what really branded Kansas with the mark of the freak. Every part of the country in the nineteenth century had labor upheavals and protosocialist reform movements, of course. In Kansas, though, the radicals kept coming out on top. It was as though the blank landscape prompted dreams of a blank-slate society, a place where institutions might be remade as the human mind saw fit. Maps of the state from the 1880s show a hamlet (since vanished) called Radical City; in nearby Crawford County the town of Girard was home to the *Appeal to Reason,* a socialist newspaper whose circulation was in the hundreds of thousands. In that same town, in 1908, Eugene Debs gave a fiery speech accepting the Socialist Party's nomination for president; in 1912 Debs actually carried Crawford County, one of four he won nationwide. (All were in the Midwest.) In 1910 Theodore Roosevelt signaled his own lurch to the left by traveling to Kansas and giving an inflammatory address in Osawatomie, the onetime home of John Brown.[7]

The most famous freak-out of them all was Populism, the first of the great American leftist movements.* Populism tore through other states as well—wailing all across Texas, the South, and the West in the 1890s—but Kansas was the place that really distinguished itself by its enthusiasm. Driven to the brink of ruin by years of bad prices, debt, and deflation, the state's farmers came together in huge meetings where homegrown troublemakers like Mary Elizabeth Lease exhorted them to "raise less corn and more hell." The radicalized farmers marched through the small towns in day-long parades, raging against what they called the "money power." And despite all the clamor, they still managed to take the state's traditional Republican masters utterly by surprise in 1890, sweeping the small-town slickers out of office and ending the careers of many a career politician. In the decade that followed they elected Populist governors, Populist senators, Populist congressmen, Populist supreme court justices, Populist

---

*Spelled with an uppercase *P*, *Populism* refers to the specific movement associated with the Farmers' Alliance and the People's Party in the late nineteenth century. Spelled with a lowercase *p*, *populism* denotes a more general political style that emphasizes class antagonism and the nobility of the common man.

city councils, and probably Populist dogcatchers, too; men of strong ideas, curious nicknames, and a colorful patois.

The Pops' demands don't look all that crazy today: they wanted various farm programs, state ownership of railroads, a graduated income tax to pay for it all, and a silver or even a paper currency. At the time, however, they were damned by the respectable for their radicalism. *New York Times* writers did not, for example, find in them the very embodiment of unpretentious "red-state" Americanness. On the contrary; they were reviled by such newspapers for their bumpkin assault on free-market orthodoxy. The most vicious pummeling, though, came from one of their own: William Allen White, the Emporia editor later renowned as the voice of small-town America, who savaged the Populists in an 1896 essay titled "What's the Matter with Kansas?" The piece is a classic of political clock-cleaning. Mounting the platform of Republican respectability, White, a gifted lyricist of business ambition, blamed the Kansas radicals for ruining the state's economy with their cynical attitudes and heretical economics.

> Oh, this is a state to be proud of! We are a people who can hold up our heads! What we need is not more money, but less capital, fewer white shirts and brains, fewer men with business judgment, and more of those fellows who boast that they are "just ordinary clodhoppers, but they know more in a minute about finance than John Sherman"; we need more men . . . who hate prosperity, and who think, because a man believes in national honor, he is a tool of Wall Street.[8]

The essay was picked up by the McKinley campaign and reprinted in vast numbers for use against William Jennings Bryan. It made White an instant Republican superstar.

Other observers saw in the movement's giant meetings and plainspoken style the markings of a "religious crusade." Populism was, as one Kansan put it, a "pentecost of politics in which a tongue of flame set upon every man, and each spake as the spirit gave him utterance."[9] This is not far distant from how the Populists saw their movement: as a sort of revelation, a moment when an entire generation of "Kansas fools" figured out that they'd been lied to all their lives. Whether it was Republicans or Democrats in charge, they believed, mainstream politics were a "sham battle" distracting the nation from its real problem—corporate capitalism.

One of Populism's first electoral victims was the then-famous U.S. senator John J. Ingalls, whom the state legislature tossed out amid the deluge of 1890 to make way for a man whose beard dangled all the way to his waist. Stunned by his misfortune, Ingalls handed down a classic denunciation of crazy Kansas.

> For a generation, Kansas has been the testing-ground for every experiment in morals, politics, and social life. Doubt of all existing institutions has been respectable. Nothing has been venerable or revered merely because it exists or has endured. Prohibition, female suffrage, fiat money, free silver, every incoherent and fantastic dream of social improvement and reform, every economic delusion that has bewildered the foggy brains of fanatics, every political fallacy nurtured by misfortune, poverty and failure, rejected elsewhere, has here found tolerance and advocacy.[10]

Today the two myths are one. Kansas may be the land of averageness, but it is a freaky, militant, outraged averageness. Kansas today is a burned-over district of conservatism where the backlash propaganda has woven itself into the fabric of everyday life. People in suburban Kansas City vituperate against the sinful cosmopolitan elite of New York and Washington, D.C.; people in rural Kansas vituperate against the sinful cosmopolitan elite of Topeka and suburban Kansas City. Survivalist supply shops sprout in neighborhood strip-malls. People send Christmas cards urging their friends to look on the bright side of Islamic terrorism, since the Rapture is now clearly at hand.

Under the state's simple blue flag are gathered today some of the most flamboyant cranks, conspiracists, and calamity howlers the Republic has ever seen. The Kansas school board draws the guffaws of the world for purging state science standards of references to evolution. Cities large and small across the state still hold out against water fluoridation, while one tiny hamlet takes the additional step of requiring firearms in every home. A prominent female politician expresses public doubts about the wisdom of women's suffrage, while another pol proposes that the state sell off the Kansas Turnpike in order to solve its budget crisis. Impoverished inhabitants of the state's most scenic area fight with fanatical determination to prevent a national park from opening up in their neighborhood, while the rails-to-trails program, regarded everywhere else in the union as a harmless scheme for family fun, is reviled in Kansas as an infernal design on the rights of property owners. Operation Rescue selects Wichita as the stage for its great offensive against abortion, calling down thirty thousand testifying fundamentalists on the city, witnessing and blocking traffic and chaining themselves to fences. A preacher from Topeka travels the nation advising Americans to love God's holy hate, showing up wherever a gay person has been in the news to announce that "God Hates Fags." Survivalists and secessionists dream of backyard confederacies out on the lone prairie; schismatic Catholics declare the pope himself to be insufficiently Catholic; Posses Comitatus hold imaginary legal proceedings, sternly prosecuting state officials for participating in actual legal proceedings; and homegrown terrorists swap conspiracy theories at a house in Dickinson County before screaming off to strike a blow against big government in Oklahoma City.

In its implacable bitterness Kansas holds up a mirror to the rest of us. If this is the place where America goes looking for its national soul, then this is where America finds that its soul, after stewing in the primal resentment of the backlash, has gone all sour and wrong. If Kansas is the concentrated essence of normality, then here is where we can see the deranged gradually become normal, where we look into that handsome, confident, reassuring, all-American face—class president, quarterback, Rhodes scholar, bond trader, builder of industry—and realize that we are staring into the eyes of a lunatic.

According to the backlash vision of America as it's supposed to be, people in places like Kansas are part of one big authentic family, basking in the easy solidarity of patriotism, hard work, and the universal ability to identify soybeans in a field. But of course this isn't the case. All over America, in the red states as well as the blue, different communities support different industries and experience dramatically different fates. And in Kansas, true to its reputation as a microcosm of America, you can find each of the basic elements of the American economic mix. In the wealthy Kansas City suburbs of Johnson County, "creative" white-collar types develop business strategies over lattes. In Wichita, unionized blue-collar workers manufacture airplanes. Way out west in Garden City, low-wage immigrant workers kill cows. And in between, farmers struggle to make a living on the most fertile and productive land in the world.

Let us begin our survey of the state with the Kansans who suffer no derangement, the people who know precisely where

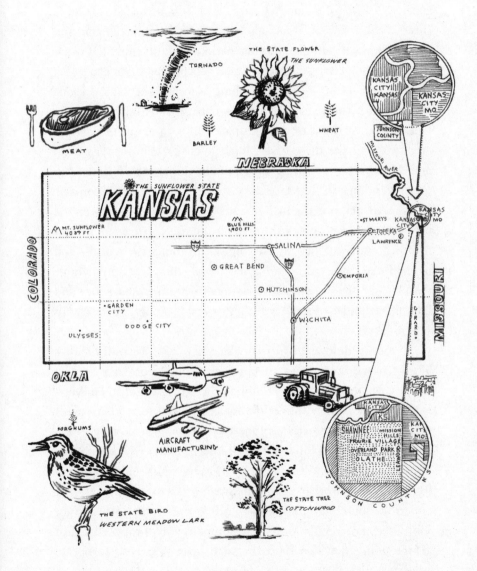

MEAT

TORNADO

BARLEY

THE STATE FLOWER
THE SUNFLOWER

WHEAT

KANSAS CITY KANSAS

KANSAS CITY MO.

JOHNSON COUNTY

NEBRASKA

☀ THE SUNFLOWER STATE

KANSAS

COLORADO

MT. SUNFLOWER 4039 FT

BLUE HILLS 1,900 FT

ST MARYS

KANSAS CITY

KANSAS CITY MO

MISSOURI RIVER

SALINA

TOPEKA

LAWRENCE

GREAT BEND

EMPORIA

HUTCHINSON

GARDEN CITY

DODGE CITY

WICHITA

ULYSSES

GIRARD

MISSOURI

OKLA

AIRCRAFT MANUFACTURING

SORGHUMS

THE STATE BIRD
WESTERN MEADOW LARK

THE STATE TREE
COTTONWOOD

KANSAS CITY KS

SHAWNEE   MISSION HILLS
PRAIRIE VILLAGE
OVERLAND PARK
OLATHE   LEAWOOD

KAN CITY MO

JOHNSON COUNTY KS

their interests lie and who go directly about getting what they want. In 2003, as it happens, the tastes, habits, and deeds of this species of Kansan came under intense media scrutiny, thanks to three local corporate scandals. Just as the *affaires* Enron and WorldCom were enlightening the nation about the mischief made by its CEO class, so three similar corporate disasters, on a slightly smaller scale, were teaching Kansans the same lessons about their own, homegrown elites—and, incidentally, about the true nature of the economic climate that conservatism has created. Each of the three cases, like the larger scandals of Enron and WorldCom, involved a quasi–public utility whose leadership had taken long pulls from the bubbling bong of New Economy theory. At each one the bosses, always heralded as geniuses, had invented elaborate plans for freeing themselves from the humdrum of public service and setting out to mulct the world—and in each case these plans collapsed for all the usual, predictable reasons, while workers and customers screamed and Mom and Pop Shareholder discovered they weren't going to retire in Hawaii after all.

In the windblown city of Topeka, the tale concerns the state's largest power company, an outfit that once bore the humble name Western Resources. Humility, though, was not to be Western's destiny. When this outfit looked in the mirror, it saw a *player.* So after almost a century spent playing the boring, regulated utility game, in the mid-nineties Western brought to Topeka one David Wittig, a flashy mergers-and-acquisitions man from Salomon Brothers, the Wall Street brokerage house, and set out to do some merging and acquiring, preferably in fields not subject to state regulation.[11] The company even proposed a deal at one point in which the debt piled up in all these corporate adventures would stay with the plodding public utility back in Topeka, where those plodding Kansas ratepayers could pay it off, while Wittig himself would run the sexy unregulated acquisitions. You know the routine: socialize the risk, privatize the profits.[12] Along the road to this moment of enlightenment the organization picked up a "chief strategic officer," a stable of company jets, and a new name: Westar.

Westar never quite made it to player status. Its acquisitions turned out to be ill-advised, and shares in the company, which are widely held in Kansas, fell 73 percent from their 1998 highs. Wittig himself, however, became Topeka's player-in-chief. He continued to pull down millions of dollars in compensation even while the company's share price plummeted and employees were laid off to reduce costs. Wittig routinely flew to Europe and the Hamptons on company jets; he spent $6.5 million decorating the company's executive suite to plans drawn up by Marc Charbonnet, a celebrated New York interior designer;* he even bought the old mansion of hometown hero Alf Landon and had it conspicuously renovated by this same Charbonnet. At the same time Westar's board was purged of dissenters and somehow prevented from entering the extravagant new offices.[13] When Wittig finally left the company in 2002, thanks to an embarrassing but unrelated money-laundering charge (the president of a Topeka bank had approved a $1.5-million loan to Wittig, which amount he then lent back to the bank president), local headlines screamed that he might walk away with some $42.5 million *more* in cumulative compensation.

Just across the state line in Missouri, a similar story was unfolding. This one involved a power company whose original, unassuming name had been Missouri Public Service . . . which it had upgraded to Utilicorp, and then, breaking the surly bonds of

---

*This is not a small sum in a city like Topeka. For example, Jayhawk Tower, one of the city's most notable landmarks, is appraised for only $1.6 million. Wittig could theoretically have purchased it four times over for the price of his office decorating scheme.

meaning altogether, to Aquila. The idea of public service was jet-tisoned too, as Aquila prepared for the great competitive utopia to come by acquiring utilities around the country and overseas, by investing heavily in fiber optics (there could never be too much fiber optics!), and by setting up a freewheeling energy trading operation where it sought to replicate the spectacular success then being enjoyed by Enron, that idol of the manage-ment gurus. At Aquila the resident geniuses were brothers Robert and Richard Green, who took turns sitting in the CEO's chair. And then came the familiar stages of disaster: the bonds downgraded to junk; the massive layoffs; the share price plum-meting 96 percent; and the public revelation that Richard Green had pulled down $21.6 million during the years of the collapse while Robert took home $19 million, plus an additional $7.6-million severance package when he walked away from the wreckage. Let the regulators clean it up.[14]

Then there is Sprint, the familiar provider of cell-phone and long-distance service, which started life as a small-town Kansas phone company called United Telecommunications. The free-market revolution of the nineties ballooned this sleepy local out-fit into a telecom superpower, a titan in the most fabled New Economic field of them all. By 1999, Sprint was the largest employer in the Kansas City area and was building a colossal corporate campus in the Johnson County suburb of Overland Park that would incorporate 3.9 million square feet of office space, sixteen parking garages, and its own zip code. This was typical of the industry. In the world of the telecoms everything was bigger. The sums pocketed by those on the winning side of this great capitalist awakening were beyond comprehension, while the rhetoric buoying them up was otherworldly, awestruck, utopian—remember? The abolition of distance. The "visionary" CEOs. The "telecosm." Unfortunately, all that money and all that idolatry encouraged what now seems to have been a staggering amount of fraud and overconstruction.[15]

On a different level stood Sprint. Here the master of the whirl was William T. Esrey, a Kansas City native beloved by business journalists. Esrey's greatest moment was also the climax of the telecom bubble—the proposed 1999 merger with WorldCom that, at $129 billion, would have been the largest of all time, and that would naturally have required Sprint to move to WorldCom's hometown. The national media turned somersaults saluting Esrey for engineering the triumph. What he really engineered, though, was a prominent place in the rogues' gallery of personal financial gluttony. As a condition of the deal, he and his top lieutenants were granted stupendous helpings of stock options—$311 million worth between Esrey and Ronald LeMay, his right-hand man—whether regulators allowed the merger to go through or not.[16]

Kansas Citians were stunned. Not so much by the stock options, which were considered sort of normal in those CEO-worshiping days, but by the prospect of the city's largest employer packing up and disappearing. The threat was especially menacing in the smiling suburb of Overland Park, where the corporate way is almost a religion and where Sprint's massive "campus" was nearing completion. Were these the wages of "leadership," of "excellence," of deregulation? Would the suburb's southern reaches, which had been redesigned to please the telecom giant, now become a New Economy ghost town? Who would fill those parking garages, bid up the values of those gated communities, play on all those designer golf courses?*

---

*Look on the bright side, counseled Jerry Heaster, the *Kansas City Star*'s veteran business columnist. After all, "Kansas City can take pride in having provided an environment in which a company could be nurtured to the point of fetching the highest acquisition price in the history of corporate mergers."[17]

As we all know, federal regulators nixed the deal, saving Overland Park's Republican ass. Esrey and his posse still got their paper millions, as per their plan. But between late 1999 and the summer of 2002, Sprint shareholders saw the value of their holdings shrivel by 90 percent as the telecom rapture gave way to reality. By the beginning of 2003, Sprint had laid off more than seventeen thousand workers. WorldCom, meanwhile, confessed to accounting fraud on a scale previously unknown and then went bankrupt. The final act came in February 2003, when the tax shelters in which Esrey and LeMay had stashed their loot were called into question by the IRS. The two, it was revealed, had never sold the shares they received back in 1999, and now they were liable for a bubble-era tax bill in a distinctly austere time. Sprint responded to their plight by firing them.

At the time of their corporate stardom, Bill Esrey of Sprint and Bob Green of Aquila both lived in Mission Hills, Kansas, a small suburb of Kansas City. David Wittig, for his part, grew up in the next suburb to the south, while Ronald LeMay lived a few blocks to the east. Green's slate-roofed neoclassical manse is in fact only a few minutes' walk from Esrey's turreted Norman chateau, which in turn is situated next door to the rustic French manor of Irvine Hockaday, a retired Hallmark executive who sat on the boards of both men's companies. Scattered nearby are the homes of the owners of H&R Block, Hallmark, and Marion Merrell Dow, plus the slightly less imposing estates of various regional bank chieftains, press lords, and the ubiquitous suburban developers. Even the governor of Kansas lived here for a

---

Heaster's wisdom is worth recalling years later, as the New Economy hangover slowly wears off. Utilities don't exist to serve cities: *cities serve utilities,* and the public's highest hope is that the casino of capitalism will someday fetch them up a gullible boob who will pay a premium for the operation thus "nurtured."

while in the nineties, in a suburban house less than one block from the Missouri line.

Out-of-town papers typically refer to the Kansas City "business community" as *close-knit*. David Brooks might say that Kansas City's owners are just people who like to sit together in life's cafeteria at what happens to be a very small, very well-stocked table. The correct description for them, however, is *elite*. In fact, this is the very word used by the local business magazine, which publishes a special "Power Elite" feature each year in which fawning essays about the nature of powerfulness accompany a list ranking the great men's relative puissance, in the same way that other magazines rank restaurants or movies or cars.

Mission Hills is a graphic illustration of what elites are about. Its two square miles of rolling, landscaped exquisiteness house a population of about thirty-six hundred with a median annual household income of $188,821, making it by far the richest town in Kansas and, indeed, one of the richest in the country.[18] Combined with the surrounding towns, it generates more money in individual contributions to the two political parties than does the rest of Kansas put together.[19] But to call it a town, while technically correct, is misleading. Mission Hills has three country clubs and a church but no businesses of any kind. Its population is about the same as that of the two blocks surrounding my apartment in Chicago. It doesn't have buses, commuter trains, or even proper sidewalks, in most places. What it has are mansions, modern and colonial, whimsical and sober, ensconced in vast, carefully maintained lawns that roll tastefully to the horizon.

Mission Hills is obviously not representative of all of Kansas, but it is my family's home, my little town on the prairie, and it will serve us far better as an introduction to the way life is lived in the mysterious Midwest than would a thousand sentimental meditations on the noble red versus the arrogant blue. When Mission Hills was built after World War I, it was merely an extension of the upscale section of Kansas City known as the Country Club District. All the rest of that glamorous area, including the famous Country Club Plaza, the world's first suburban shopping center, was in Missouri. Mission Hills was the name given to the little bit of the development that spilled over State Line Road into Johnson County, Kansas. There was almost nothing to the south or west of Mission Hills in those days; for purposes of water and mail delivery, the suburb was treated as though it were part of Kansas City, Missouri.[20]

When my family moved to Mission Hills at the tail end of the bull market of the sixties, it was a suburb where doctors and lawyers rubbed elbows with CEOs; where one found Pontiacs and riding lawn mowers and driveway basketball courts and even the occasional ranch house with an asphalt roof. There were also, of course, the original inhabitants whose grand old houses were now overgrown with vines and invisible from the street thanks to shrubbery and weeds that had been neglected for years. In their picturesque decay these dark palaces became a source of morbid fascination to my brothers and me in the troubled seventies. Even as children we knew these houses were relics of a dead past, a time when people had servants and gardeners and hand-built cars. In our own age of loss and decline it was prohibitively expensive simply to heat them, let alone tend their vast lawns. We followed the progress of a nearby creek as it slowly undercut a heavy stone gazebo, some millionaire's folly from that lost age, until after one rainstorm nothing was left but ruins. As late as 1987, the largest house in Mission Hills, an eleven-thousand-square-foot English-baronial layout that had been the home of the man who invented the Eskimo Pie, sat forlornly on the real estate market for months, unable to find a buyer.[21]

I recount all this not to downplay the suburb's affluence but only to note that it was affluence of a very different character than we see today. Nobody mows their own lawn in Mission Hills anymore, and only a foot soldier in its armies of gardeners would park a Pontiac there. The doctors who lived near us in the seventies have pretty much been gentrified out, their places taken by the bankers and brokers and CEOs who have lapped them repeatedly on the racetrack of status and income. Every time I paid Mission Hills a visit during the nineties, it seemed another of the more modest houses in our neighborhood had been torn down and replaced by a much larger edifice, a three-story stone chateau, say, bristling with turrets and porches and dormers and gazebos and a three-car garage. The dark old palaces from the twenties sprouted spiffy new slate roofs, immaculately tailored gardens, remote-controlled driveway gates, and sometimes entire new wings. One grand old pile down the street from us was fitted with shiny new gutters made entirely of copper. A new house a few doors down from Esrey's spread is so large it has *two* multicar garages, one at either end.

These changes are of course not unique to Mission Hills. What has gone on there is normal in its freakishness. You can observe the same changes in Shaker Heights or La Jolla or Winnetka or Ann Coulter's hometown of New Canaan, Connecticut. They reflect the simplest and hardest of economic realities: The fortunes of Mission Hills rise and fall in inverse relation to the fortunes of ordinary working people. When workers are powerful, taxes are high, and labor is expensive (as was the case from World War II until the late seventies), the houses built here are smaller, the cars domestic, the servants rare, and the overgrown look fashionable in gardening circles. People read novels about eccentric English aristocrats trapped in a democratic age, sighing sadly for their lost world.

When workers are weak, taxes are down, and labor is cheap (as in the twenties and again today), Mission Hills coats itself in shimmering raiments of gold and green. Now the stock returns are plush, the bonus packages fat, the servants affordable, and the suburb finds that the princely life isn't dead after all. It builds new additions and new fountains and new Italianate porches overlooking Olympic-sized flower gardens maintained by shifts of laborers. People read books about the glory of empire. The kids get Porsches or SUVs when they turn sixteen; the houses with asphalt roofs discreetly disappear; the wings that were closed off are triumphantly reopened, and all is restored to its former grandeur. Times may be hard where you live, but here events have yielded a heaven on earth, a pleasure colony out of the paintings of Maxfield Parrish.

For my own family, this has not been an entirely happy series of developments. While it's soothing to have a neighbor who buzzes around the block in a Ferrari Superamerica, the plutocratization of Mission Hills has pushed the Franks the other way. My father's unpretentious house is now valuable only for the lot that it sits on—his friends call it "the teardown"—and knowing this has pretty much drained his enthusiasm for maintaining it. The city has actually sent him notices warning him to keep the lawn mowed. It's that kind of place.

Growing up in Mission Hills, you quickly learn the boundaries and customs of the local notables: the local prep school attended by all the CEOs' kids, the snob colleges they all plan to attend in a few years, the family businesses they stand to inherit, the private police forces they maintain, the superexclusive country club they all belong to—which country club, by the way, was also the designated polling place for our corner of Mission Hills, the place where we had to go to vote, despite the fact that a good many people in the neighborhood would never be permitted to join.

You also learn that many of your friends' rich dads are in prison. Epidemic white-collar crime is the silent partner of the suburb's contentment, the ugly companion of its tranquil domesticity and the earnest flattery of its courtiers. In addition to disgraced CEOs like Esrey and Green, Mission Hills is the home of numerous smaller-scale thieves, embezzlers, tax evaders, real estate frauds, and check forgers. Even the kids are often thuglets: At the age of ten I was threatened by a switchblade-wielding lad who is today the president of a prestigious local bank. At the age of nineteen I watched a gang of Kansas City's most privileged, in their uniform madras shorts and polo shirts, snort cocaine at a party in some local grandee's sprawling Tudor-baronial pile. Growing up here teaches the indelible lesson that wealth has some secret bond with crime—also with drug use, bullying, lying, adultery, and thundering, world-class megalomania.

When I discovered that Mission Hills had been laid out by the same landscape architects responsible for River Oaks in Houston, the home of Ken Lay and other Enron execs, I began to suspect that tastefully wooded lawns were somehow the culprit, turning good men bad with their mysterious sylvan whisperings. But the prominence of the criminal element here is more likely due to Kansas's unlimited homestead exemption, which allows those declaring bankruptcy to keep their residence. Naturally, people preparing to go under wanted the priciest houses available, and thus Mission Hills became a magnet for the legally challenged from all across the region. That, plus the borderline criminality of capitalism itself, a condition that has rudely impressed itself on much of the world in the last few years.

Until World War II there was little development in Johnson County, Kansas, beyond Mission Hills. That suburb was then the very edge of the city, a semirural retreat for Kansas City's wealthy. But from that tiny affluent acorn a mighty suburban forest has since grown. The change occurred quite suddenly in the years after the war. As they did in so many places, cheap federal loans made possible an instant suburban metropolis, mile after mile of ranch homes and split-levels and shopping malls thrown up by heroic developers in just a few years.

The second stage of the Johnson County boom, also as in most of suburban America, was triggered by the school desegregation ruling of 1954 and fueled by white flight out of Kansas City. Its third phase, in the eighties and nineties, came when corporate Kansas City packed up and moved its operations out to the Johnson County suburbs, where its top executives already lived. Today suburbs radiate across Johnson County from Mission Hills for fifteen miles to the south and the west, nearly eclipsing Kansas City proper and altering the complexion of the entire state of Kansas. Altogether Johnson County now houses more than 450,000 souls, making it the largest metropolitan area in the state.[22]

The result has been one of the country's most extreme cases of low-density sprawl.[23] When I was in high school, our neighbors worked, shopped, and viced in Kansas City, Missouri; today they all drive in the other direction. A long way in the other direction: by the end of the nineties the metropolitan area's center of gravity had shifted to the most peripheral point of the Kansas suburbs. The largest of the suburbs, the aforementioned Overland Park, began to dream of rivaling Kansas City itself. It built hotels and a convention center, hoping to siphon even more sustenance away from the gasping metropolis; it slapped up shopping malls at a dizzying pace; it constructed a new office district, complete with runty glass mini-skyscrapers, at the southernmost point of settlement; and it platted out subdivisions without end, a raw, wood-shingled fortification stretching over the hills as far as the eye could see. And, as noted, it convinced Sprint to choose this locale for its sixteen-parking-garage "campus."

Today, Johnson County is a vast suburban empire, a happy, humming confusion of freeways and malls and nonstop construction; of identical cul-de-sacs and pretentious European street names and overachieving school districts and oversized houses constructed to one of four designs. By all the standards of contemporary American business civilization, it is a great success story. It is the wealthiest county in Kansas by a considerable margin,[24] and the free-market rapture of the New Economy nineties served it well, scandals notwithstanding. Telecom and corporate management were the right businesses to be in, and Johnson County's population grew by almost 100,000 over the course of the decade, an unflagging stream of middle-class humanity to fill its office parks and to absorb the manufactured bonhomie of its Fuddruckers and TGI Fridays. Johnson County is also one of the most intensely Republican places in the nation. Registered Republicans outnumber Democrats here by more than two to one. Of Johnson County's twenty-two representatives in the Kansas house, only one is a Democrat.

Back in the eighties, the journalist Richard Rhodes nailed the place with just two words: *Cupcake Land*.[25] To the irritation of local leaders, the nickname has stuck. Cupcake Land is a metropolis built entirely according to the developer's plan, without the interference of angry proles or ethnic pols as in nearby Kansas City. Cupcake Land encourages no culture but that which increases property values; supports no learning but that which burnishes the brand; hears no opinions but those that will further fatten the cupcake elite; tolerates no rebellion but that expressed in haircuts and piercings and alternative rock. You know what it's like even though you haven't been there. Smooth jazz. Hallmark cards. Applebees. Corporate Woods. Its greatest civic holiday is the turning-on of the

Christmas lights at a nearby shopping center—an event so inspirational to the cupcake mind that the mall thus illuminated has been rendered in paint by none other than Thomas Kinkade.

I myself witnessed Cupcake Land's dynamic recent growth episodically, coming back to visit every six months or so from a nineteenth-century city where people lived in apartments and dragged their groceries home in two-wheeled wire carts. Seeing it this way magnified Johnson County's strangeness: every time I returned, the developers had leapfrogged farther into the countryside, clicking off the once-unimaginable distances (119th Street! 143rd Street!) the way the Dow ascends past this or that landmark valuation. There was always some new suburban oddity to observe, some superlative to register, some combination church-mall to gawk at. I remember my astonishment when, driving around in 1996 after exploring an outer-ring development called Patrician Woods, I happened upon a Dean & DeLuca grocery store, a luxury chain previously found mainly in New York City, now holding down a corner opposite a plowed field. Even more bizarre: the budding "lifestyle center" of which it was part was called Town Center Plaza, despite being a full twenty miles from downtown Kansas City.

I am the strange one, though, for being astonished by all this. While dining recently at 40 Sardines, probably the finest restaurant in the KC area despite being situated in a mall built where corn grew only a few years ago, I quizzed employees and other patrons and discovered that they had all recently moved here from the corporate suburbs of other big cities. They saw nothing odd about finding, in what had so recently been farmland, this dimly lit postmodern palace, with its whimsical pebble-encrusted bar and its selection of foie-gras and duck-prosciutto appetizers. The people of Cupcake Land approve of age when talking about wine and cheese; they expect their cities to be brand-new.

. . .

The only other part of Kansas that had a winning formula for the New Economy years was at the other end of the state, the area around Garden City, a remote town on the treeless western plains. Johnson County is an anomaly, people believe, but Garden City is the future, the only real-world model for how the rest of the state can grow. Everyone in Kansas says this. I myself heard it from a U.S. senator.

There are no Dean & DeLucas in Garden City, though. This is cattle country, the other end of the food chain. The other end of the world.

They call places like Garden City "rural boomtowns." When you're there, you keep coming across the slogan "Just Plain Success." And from a statistical angle its accomplishments do look impressive. Thanks to Garden City and the nearby towns of Liberal and Dodge City, Kansas was the biggest beef-packing state in the country through most of the last decade. Today those three towns in far-western Kansas have a "daily slaughter capacity" of some twenty-four thousand cattle, and they produce fully 20 percent of the beef consumed in the United States.[26] I am a great eater of beef, and so I suppose this is something to be proud of.

But it is profoundly misleading to describe all these things in this old-fashioned way—as though Garden City were "cow butcher to the world," some miniature Chicago resourceful Kansans have hewn out of the barren prairie. These are things that have been done *to* Kansas and Garden City, and *to* remote towns all across the Great Plains. The only actors with real power in this situation are the companies that build the slaughterhouses and call the shots: Tyson (known universally by its former name, IBP, for Iowa Beef Packers), the unmelodious ConAgra (known universally by its former name, Monfort), and the even less melodious Cargill Meat Solutions (known universally by its former name, Excel). And these entities, in turn, claim their every move is dictated by the remorseless demands of the market. There are ranchers aplenty but few rugged individualists out here anymore; today Garden City and Dodge City are caught on the steel hooks of economic logic as surely and as haplessly as are the cows they hack so industriously apart.

The single most important element of that logic is, as always, the demand for cheap labor. From that simple imperative springs nearly everything that has happened here over the last twenty-five years. Beginning in the sixties the big thinkers of the meat biz figured out ways to routinize and de-skill their operations from beginning to end. Not only would this allow them to undercut the skilled, unionized butchers who were then employed by grocery stores, but it would also let them move their plants to the remotest part of the Great Plains, where they could ditch their unionized big-city workers and save on rent. By the early nineties this strategy had put the century-old stockyards in Chicago and Kansas City out of business altogether. As with every other profit-maximizing entity, the industry's ultimate preference would probably be to have done with this expensive country once and for all and relocate operations to the third world, where it could be free from regulators, trial lawyers, and prying journalists. Sadly, for the packers, they are prevented from achieving that dream by various food regulations. So instead they bring the workers here, employing waves of immigrants from Southeast Asia, Mexico, and points south.

There were other advantages for the packers in moving to distant and isolated towns. In the big cities, they had always been conspicuous targets for reformers and reporters; you couldn't pass through Chicago without catching a whiff of the stockyards and being instantly reminded of *The Jungle*. On the High Plains the packers are just about the only game in town. And they use their power accordingly. They threaten to close down a plant if they don't get their way on some issue or other. They play towns off against one another the way pro sports franchises do. Who will give the packers the biggest tax abatement? Who will vote the fattest bond issue? Who will let them pollute the most?

The stories about Garden City that appear in the national media tend to focus on all the town's non-anglophone residents and to marvel with enthusiasm on finding such "vibrant" multiculturalism out here on the lone prairie. And I suppose this is very liberal of them. Just like the conservative champions of Red America, however, the larger media generally shrinks from examining the brutal economic processes that make it all happen. The area around Garden City is a showplace of industrialized agriculture: vast farms raise nothing but feed corn despite the semiarid climate; gigantic rolling irrigation devices pump water from a subterranean aquifer and make this otherwise unthinkable crop possible; feedlots the size of cities transform the corn into cowflesh; and the windowless concrete slaughterhouses squat silently on the outskirts of town, harvesting the final product. Take a drive through the countryside here, and you will see no trees, no picturesque old windmills or bridges or farm buildings, and almost no people. When the aquifer dries up, as it someday will—its millions of years of collected rainwater spent in just a few decades—you will see even less out here.

One thing you do see these days are the trailer-park cities, dilapidated and unpaved and rubbish-strewn, that house a large part of Garden City's workforce. Confronted with some of the most advanced union-avoidance strategies ever conceived by the mind of business man, these people receive mediocre wages for doing what is statistically the most dangerous work in industrial America. Thanks to the rapid turnover at the slaughterhouses, few of them receive health or retirement benefits. The "social costs" of supporting them—education, health care, law enforcement—

are "externalized," as the scholarly types put it, pushed off onto the towns themselves, or onto church groups and welfare agencies, or onto the countries from which the workers come. With constant speedup of the line and with the cold temperatures of the plant, one angry worker told me, "After ten years, people walk like they're sixty or seventy years old."

This is economic growth, yes, but it is the sort of growth that makes a city *less* wealthy and *less* healthy as its population increases.[27] Nor does the situation improve much as the decades pass. It has been twenty years now since the packers first moved to Garden City, and two anthropologists who have studied the region now warn of a "permanent breakdown" in middle-class life; of a strategy of development that forever puts a town, despite its best efforts, "at the mercy of the meat industry's insatiable appetite for cheap labor and the social turmoil that follows from it."[28]

Driving to Garden City, which is far from any interstate highway and well beyond the reach of my cell-phone service, I was reminded of one of those New Economy parables that some computer company used to run on TV back in the nineties: A bright and eager junior executive is shown driving a hardened old senior executive far out into the countryside. On the way the old guy gripes about the price of doing business in Manhattan. Once out in the middle of nowhere, though, the kid's dream is explained to him: New communications technology makes Manhattan irrelevant! This isn't the boondocks; this is the *frontier*— the land of opportunity. The old fellow's eyes light up as he gets it; he leaps and yips, a veritable cowboy. Out here, the businessman's century-long wage-and-tax nightmare is over. Out here he is his own master once again, a Wyatt Earp unencumbered by grandstanding aldermen or grievance-filing shop stewards or fancy intellectuals.

Driving back from Garden City, after taking in its brooding

slaughterhouses and its unearthly odors and the feeder lots that sprawl over the landscape like some post-Apocalyptic suburb of death, I was reminded of another parable, one that the Kansas Populists used to talk about: the frontier as a site of ghastly, spectacular plunder. Buffalo carcasses littering the ground, cattle ranchers shooting down the Indians, corporations moving whole populations around the globe, farmers exhausting the land, railroads taking the farmers for all they're worth—free-market economics in full and unrestrained effect.

Viewed from Mission Hills, this is a social order that delivers quaint slate roofs, copper gutters, and gurgling fountains in elegant traffic islands; viewed from Garden City, it is an order that brings injury and infection and death by a hundred forms of degradation; rusting playgrounds for the kids, shabby decaying schools, a lifetime of productiveness gone in a few decades, and depleted groundwater, too. The anthropologists caution us in their sober way about a recipe for "growth" that blandly accepts a permanent impoverished class,[29] but the people of Mission Hills are unfazed. They may be too polite to say it aloud, but they know that poverty rocks. Poverty is profitable. Poverty makes stocks go up and labor come down.

Two hundred miles east of Garden City lies Wichita, Kansas, a metropolis of 340,000 that is to civil aviation what Detroit used to be to automobiles. Maps of what is called the Air Capital are crisscrossed with the landing fields of the various manufacturers: Boeing, Cessna, Learjet, and Beechcraft* each build planes there, and McConnell Air Force Base keeps the sky filled at all hours with KC-135s and the occasional B-52. As the aircraft

---

*Cessna is now owned by Textron, Learjet is owned by Bombardier, and Beechcraft is now known as Raytheon.

industry's fortunes have risen and fallen, so have those of Wichita: The city's population exploded during World War II, as the defense contracts rolled in and the Boeing B-29s roared off for the Pacific. In the fifties and sixties Wichita built B-47s and B-52s; in later years it produced Boeing 737s and contributed elements to the company's other jetliners.

Histories of Wichita tend to focus on the promethean efforts of its business leaders, marveling at how they conjured up a thriving city from the bare prairie.[30] Viewed from the ground, however, the place looks very different. Wichita is a deeply blue-collar town, a city where manufacturing is still the largest sector of the local economy and just about the only place in the state with a strong union presence.

Until quite recently Wichita enjoyed the sort of blue-collar prosperity that is only a dim memory in places like Cleveland and Pittsburgh. Wichita is in trouble today, following the aircraft industry into a sharp nosedive, but in its fundamentals the place is still intact, its factories still open for business. The huge Boeing plant that sprawls for several city blocks is the largest private employer in Kansas. Entire neighborhoods are populated with Boeing workers, union members with excellent benefits and wages good enough to allow them to afford the sort of ranches or split levels that would elsewhere be the prerogative of white-collar types only. Wichita is the kind of city where the newspaper runs editorials about the Haymarket martyrs on Labor Day and where an election for the state legislature might well pit a maintenance man against a pipe fitter.

If you are, like me, a fan of American middleness, Wichita is your kind of place: an El Dorado of hamburger stands, alliterative city slogans, pork tenderloin sandwiches, souped-up trucks, old-school diners, bowling alleys, and steakhouses with Spandex-clad waitresses. And, above all, churches. Many, many churches: COGICs, Assemblies of God, Foursquare Gospels, and every known variant of charismatic. The titles of upcoming sermons, displayed on signs outside these many churches, are enough to keep a collector of sacred kitsch occupied for hours: "Put on your spiritual running shoes"; "An R$_x$ for spiritual pain." Even labor unions here have Bibles specially printed with their logo. Then there's the dark side, the trucks plastered with huge, graphic photos of broken fetuses that occasionally wander the city. And the cryptic side, the message that appeared through the steam on my bathroom mirror at the Wichita Hyatt, after I had let the hot water run for a few minutes: "Knight in God's Armor." I imagined a delegate to a pro-life gathering, reeling in some sort of saintly ecstasy, scrawling it there with his finger so it hovered over his head while he shaved.

Michael Carmody, the editor of a Wichita weekly, likens the town to a depression in the middle of the country that catches the pop culture runoff from everywhere else, a place where dead fads collect and build up and never really evaporate. "People think Camaros are still cool here," he tells me. The keenest observers of this freakishly average place were the Embarrassment, an early-eighties indie-rock outfit who may well have been the greatest rock band of them all. (They were, without a doubt, the finest ever produced by Kansas.) According to red-state myth, people out here are supposed to shun wit and cynicism on the grounds that these are symptoms of pseudosophisticated coastal liberalism, but the Embarrassment were as arch and melodic as anything that came out of the East Village in the same period, with their songs about thrift-store shopping, TV preachers, polyester clothes, sitcom reruns, and, of course, cars.

> *Scott's Trans Am has the windows down*
> *But he's in a jam when the girl's around.*
> *He yells, "Hey! Get out of my way!"*
> *"I haven't had any sex all day."*

The nineties were a bad decade for Wichita, just as they were for cities all over that still relied on manufacturing and skilled workers for their prosperity. The problem wasn't so much the end of the cold war, although that obviously took a toll; it was that companies like Boeing had fastened their eyes on a vision of themselves as "virtual corporations," shedding the old-fashioned baggage of gigantic plants and armies of employees. Throwing around words like *flexibility* and *competitiveness*, they subcontracted and "outsourced," they asked cities to bid against one another for new projects, they moved production overseas, and they picked fights with their unions. Between 1999 and 2002, the main union representing Boeing workers nationally lost nearly a third of its membership to layoffs; in Wichita, the number was closer to half.

The terrorist attacks of September 2001 made the situation worse, as the airlines reeled and orders for Boeing jetliners dried up overnight. Besides New York, the Air Capital may well have been the city most affected by the catastrophe. Boeing took the opportunity to shed even more union workers, informing Wichita that, this time, the jobs wouldn't be coming back even when times got better. In the summer of 2003, unemployment in Wichita passed 7 percent and foreclosures on homes spiked as these disasters reverberated through the local economy.

There were so many closed shops in Wichita when I visited in 2003 that you could drive for blocks without ever leaving their empty parking lots, running parallel to the city streets past the shut-down sporting goods stores and toy stores and farm implement stores. Once I simply stopped my car for several minutes in the middle of what my map claimed to be a busy Wichita thoroughfare; there was nobody around. Along Douglas Avenue, the city's main drag, there used to be a famous sign that arched over the throngs, crowing "Watch Wichita Win"; these days the street is lined with bronze statues of average people, apparently so it doesn't look quite so eerily empty.

As for the rest of the state, nobody even bothers to try papering over what's happened; it's pretty much in free fall. I have even heard people justify what goes on in Garden City by reasoning that, well, it's better than what's gone on everywhere else in rural Kansas. It's better than having no economy at all.

Walk down the main street of just about any farm town in the state, and you know immediately what they're talking about: this is a civilization in the early stages of irreversible decay.

I was startled the first time I took such a stroll. I hadn't spent much time in small-town Kansas since the early eighties, and when I reminisced about the place, it always compared pretty favorably to the South Side Chicago neighborhood I have inhabited since then. I always thought of small-town Kansas the way you're supposed to think of it: friendly folks ambling slowly down the old brick sidewalks, little kids singing in the school, average people in rambling Victorian houses listening attentively to the radio broadcast of the high school football game. Maybe my recollections were too idealized; maybe Chicago's high-speed gentrification (and its systematic expulsion of the poor) over the intervening years has thrown me off. Either way, in the desolation sweepstakes, Chicago has nothing on Kansas anymore.

Main Streets here are vacant, almost as a rule; their grandiose stone facades are crumbling and covered up with plywood—rotting plywood, usually, itself simply hung and abandoned fifteen years ago or whenever it was that Wal-Mart came to town.

The one business that consistently survives here, whether you're in Osawatomie or El Dorado, is junk stores. This is what people do on Main Street nowadays: they sell old stuff that in a more prosperous era would have gone to the Salvation Army or the trash. Leftover yarn. A bourbon bottle shaped like a CB radio. A box of *National Geographics*. Whom they sell it *to* remains a mystery. In each of the dozen or so Main Street junk stores I visited, I was clearly one of the only customers to come through all day.

If a Kansas town was once big enough to support shopping malls, you will find derelict buildings of the 1970s in addition to derelict buildings of the 1870s. You will find vast acres of crumbling asphalt surrounding former JCPenneys, which are either thrift stores now as well or else closed down altogether.

And you will start to wonder where the people are. To judge from the activity on the streets, every day looks like a Sunday or a holiday or 5 a.m. Go ahead, park anywhere; yours will be the only car on the block.

Indeed, over two-thirds of Kansas counties lost population between 1980 and 2000, some by as much as 25 percent. I am told that there are entire towns in the western part of the state getting by on Social Security; no one is left there but the aged. There are no doctors, no shoe stores. One town out here even sold its public school on eBay. Kansas dwindles in significance with each passing decade as its congressional delegation and electoral vote are steadily whittled away.

The town where this feeling of dissipation struck me most powerfully was Emporia, a place once famous as the home of the author and newspaperman William Allen White. In our grandparents' day White was a nationally known figure, a confidant of presidents, a winner of the Pulitzer Prize, and the unofficial spokesman of small-town America. White's signature literary offering, at least in his early days, was the droll vignette of village life; portraits of a Middle America that was easygoing and contented, industrious, tidy, crime-free, and wise in its humility. Kansas was so bountiful, White called it "the garden of the world." All that it demanded of life was a chance to work hard, play fair, and show 'em what we were made of here in the heartland.

White is pretty much forgotten today, even in Kansas (a Republican official in Emporia told me he had never heard of the man before moving there), but in the architecture of Emporia's decaying downtown you can still discern traces of his booster heyday. The 1880 building with its twelve-foot-high second-story windows; the elegant Presbyterian church, built to serve an army of prosperous faithful: Here in crumbling brick are all the dead dreams of all the dead generations of small-town Kansas businessmen—so eager to put on a clean shirt and a positive attitude and to get in the game. They were going to get their town noticed by the august financiers in the big cities; they were going to draw in population and sell bonds and make improvements and raise a family and see their town rise in the world.[31] Sure, they were. Just you watch Wichita win.

Here is what I saw in the two hours when I wandered around Emporia on an October day some ninety-eight years after William Allen White published *In Our Town:* houses made of painted particleboard; a facade on Commercial Street composed of untreated two-by-fours, nailed one next to the other; imposing brick homes with every window frame empty and grass three feet high in the yard; tumbledown apartment buildings with sprayed-on stucco and peeling veneer; bungalows with porches in midcollapse and flimsy plastic wrap instead of glass; prefabricated steel utility buildings interspersed with residences; stone-slab sidewalks grown so craggy and broken they can't be used; a rain gutter jutting from a house like a bone from a broken arm; a window air conditioner abandoned in the middle of a weedy lawn. And wafting faintly above it all, as if from the PA system at some nearby public swimming pool, the eternal classic rock of the 1970s—Led Zeppelin, Van Halen, Rush. For some reason I kept thinking of what Sam Walton or one of our other modern robber barons would say to the town's faithful, optimistic founders: *So you wanted to be capitalists, eh?*

While I was absorbing all this bedragglement, a parade passed by. It was homecoming at Emporia State University, and the various leaders of the Kansas Republican Party were along for the ride. A fraternity boy in an enormous black cowboy hat shouted out to his best gal:

He: Where's my sweatshirt?
She (lifting sweatshirt to flash him): It's right here, bitch.

There's a reason you probably haven't heard much about this aspect of the heartland. This kind of blight can't be easily blamed on the usual suspects like government or counterculture or high-hat urban policy. The villain that did this to my home state wasn't the Supreme Court or Lyndon Johnson, showering dollars on the poor or putting criminals back on the street. The culprit is the conservatives' beloved free-market capitalism, a system that, at its most unrestrained, has little use for small-town merchants or the agricultural system that supported the small towns in the first place. Deregulated capitalism is what has allowed Wal-Mart to crush local businesses across Kansas and, even more important, what has driven agriculture, the state's raison d'être, to a state of near collapse.

"The U.S. is experiencing the greatest farm loss numbers since the mid-1980s," says the National Family Farm Coalition.[32] Talk to just about any farmer in Kansas, and you will find him extremely pessimistic about his livelihood. Except for the owners of the very largest spreads, farmers simply cannot make a profit. Kansas has only about half as many farms as it did in 1950; those that remain continue to grow. A few are getting big; most are getting out.

As usual, there are many factors at work in the latest farm crisis, among them (at least in Kansas) a severe drought in 2001 and 2002. But the main cause is the five or six huge agribusiness conglomerates that buy raw materials from farmers and process and package them for export or for sale in grocery stores. People who have never lived in a farm state often think of all agriculture interests as essentially identical: farmers and agribusiness all want the same things, they believe. But in reality the interests of the two are more like those of the chicken and Colonel Sanders of backlash lore. And Colonel Sanders has been on an unbroken winning streak now for twenty-some years, with farm legislation, trade policy, and a regulatory climate all crafted to strengthen the conglomerates while weakening farmers. For shareholders and upper management of companies like Archer Daniels Midland (ADM) and Tyson, the result has been miraculous, a heaven on earth. For towns like Emporia, it has been ruinous.

Ironically, the farm is where Americans learned their first lessons in the pitfalls of laissez-faire economics a hundred years ago. Farming is a field uniquely unsuited to the freewheeling whirl of the open market. There are millions of farmers, and they are naturally disorganized; they can't coordinate their plans one with another. Not only are they easily victimized by powerful middlemen (as they were by the railroads in the Populists' day), but when they find themselves in a tough situation—when, say, the price they are getting for wheat is low—farmers do not have the option of cutting back production, as every other industry does. Instead, each of those millions of farmers works harder, competes better, becomes more efficient, cranks out more of the commodity in question . . . and thus makes the glut even worse and pushes the prices still lower. This is called an "overproduction trap," and it can only be overcome by a suspension of competition through government intervention. Such intervention is what the Populists and the farmers' unions fought for decades to secure; it finally came with the New Deal, which brought price supports and acreage set-asides and loan guarantees.

For agribusiness, however, farm overproduction is the ideal situation. From their perspective, lower farm prices means higher profits and even greater power in the marketplace. Overproduction and all-out competition between farmers are thus to be encouraged by all available political means.

While farmers are naturally disorganized, agribusiness moves in the opposite direction: like all industries, it seeks always to merge and acquire and choke off competition. And, also like other industries, it was finally permitted to do these things in the deregulatory climate of the Reagan-Clinton era. In the eighties, according to William Heffernan, a sociologist at the University of Missouri, agriculture experts generally agreed that if four companies controlled over 40 percent of market share in a given field, it was no longer competitive. Today, however, Heffernan estimates, the four largest players process 81 percent of the beef, 59 percent of the pork, and 50 percent of the chicken produced in the United States. The same phenomenon is at work in grain: the largest four process 61 percent of American wheat, 80 percent of American soybeans, and either 57 percent or 74 percent of American corn, depending on the method.[33] It is no coincidence that the internal motto of Archer Daniels Midland, the grain-processing giant notorious for its political clout and its price-fixing, is reported to be "the competitor is our friend and the customer is our enemy."[34]

Agribusiness had acquired most of this stranglehold by the mid-nineties, but farmers were not yet totally in their grasp, thanks to the various farm programs enacted in the thirties. This escape route was closed off in 1996 under the ironically named Freedom to Farm Act, which effectively terminated certain price supports, threw all acreage open to cultivation, and generally brought a close to the New Deal system of agriculture regulation. It also launched the nation's remaining farmers into a desperate overproduction spiral, a frantic race to compete in which the devil, as usual, takes the hindmost. Written by Kansas senator Pat Roberts and supported by the other Republican members of the state's delegation, Freedom to Farm was one of the many bold deregulatory initiatives that marked the New Economy era; farmers, it was believed, now had the tools to compete effectively on the free market. Everything was different now. They didn't need the government telling them what to do (that farmers had themselves demanded the New Deal programs was forgotten by then); they could grow whatever they wanted in whatever quantities and trust to the market to give them a fair price.[35] Markets were great. Markets made everything jake.

But it turned out those bummer economic laws of the old days hadn't gone away after all. Farmers began producing food at maximum capacity, and farm prices plummeted, no longer supported by what were called "non-recourse loans." From a high of over $6.50 in 1996, the average price of a bushel of wheat (the dominant crop in Kansas) fell to $2.25 in 1999, the same price that it had fetched in the disaster years of the mid-eighties. At such a rate, failure was inevitable for everyone except the largest and most efficient farms. In fact, the crisis got so bad so fast that the federal government resumed making massive payouts to farmers in order to stop the bleeding—not as price supports this time, but simply on the basis of production, so that the larger farms, the ones that needed the money the least, got the most. In Kansas in 2000 and 2001, such federal handouts were actually greater than what farmers earned from farming itself.[36]

For ADM, Cargill, ConAgra, and the rest of the food trust, Freedom to Farm couldn't have been better if they had written the law themselves. The processor or feedlot operator now paid substantially less for his wheat and corn than what it cost to *grow* the wheat and corn; for his finished goods he continued to charge shoppers at the grocery store the same price as before.[37] The problem of fending off complete collapse in farm country, meanwhile, was shouldered by the government.[38] Bruce Larkin, a state legislator and farmer from northeastern Kansas, is blunt about the results. Freedom to Farm, he says, is "a license to a couple of multinational grain companies to steal the product produced by the farmers." The gigantic subsidies handed out since the law was passed in 1996 are merely "an indirect taxpayer subsidy to large-scale corporations and livestock operations."

Thinking in grander historical terms, the agricultural journalist A. V. Krebs finds in Freedom to Farm an exact antithesis to the Populist revolt that swept Kansas in the 1890s. This was the end of the century-long battle, the point of total defeat for the little guy, the moment where "corporate agribusiness finally realized their dream of robbing family farmers of their nearly last vestiges of that economic power first conceived and asserted by the agrarian Populists a century earlier."[39]

The admirers of farm deregulation—and there are plenty of them, in economics departments as well as the Bush administration's Department of Agriculture—see in it not some hideous power grab but a heroic "restructuring" of the food industry. This is "vertical integration," a more flexible and a far more efficient food-delivery system than the fragmented, disorganized, heavily subsidized system of the past. Cargill, ADM, and the rest of the giants are bringing order out of chaos; if we finally have to say good-bye to the Jeffersonian fantasy of the family farm—if we have to transform the prosperous farmer into a sharecropper[40] and turn the countryside into an industrialized wasteland and destroy the small towns—maybe it's all for the best.

Chapter Three

God, Meet Mammon

One thing unites all these different groups of Kansans, these millionaires and trailer-park dwellers, these farmers and thrift-store managers and slaughterhouse workers and utility executives: they are almost all Republicans. Meatpacking Garden City voted for George W. Bush in even greater numbers than did affluent Johnson County.[1] The blue-collar, heavily unionized city of Wichita used to be one of the few Democratic strongholds in the state; in the nineties it became one of the most consistently conservative places of them all, a mighty fortress in the wars over abortion, evolution, loose interpretation of the Constitution, and water fluoridation.

Not too long ago, Kansas would have responded to the current situation by making the bastards pay. This would have been a political certainty, as predictable as what happens when you touch a match to a puddle of gasoline. When business screwed the farmers and the workers—when it implemented monopoly strategies invasive beyond the Populists' furthest imaginings—when it ripped off shareholders and casually tossed thousands out of work—you could be damned sure about what would follow.

Not these days. Out here the gravity of discontent pulls in only one direction: to the right, to the right, farther to the right. Strip today's Kansans of their job security, and they head out to become registered Republicans. Push them off their land, and next thing you know they're protesting in front of abortion clinics. Squander their life savings on manicures for the CEO, and there's a good chance they'll join the John Birch Society. But ask them about the remedies their ancestors proposed (unions, antitrust, public ownership), and you might as well be referring to the days when knighthood was in flower.

The ills described here—depopulation, the rise of the food trust, the general reorganization of life to favor the wealthy—have been going on for ten to twenty years now. Nobody denies that they have happened, that they're still happening. Yet Kansas, that famous warrior for justice, how does it react? Why, Kansas looks its problems straight in the eye, sets its jaw, rolls up its sleeves—and charges off in exactly the wrong direction.

It's not that Kansas isn't angry; rage is a bumper crop here, and Kansas has produced enough fury to give every man, woman, and child in the country apoplexy. The state is in rebellion. The state is up in arms. It's just that the arms are all pointing away from the culprit.

Kansans just don't care about economic issues, gloats Republican senator Sam Brownback, a man who believes the cause of poverty is spiritual rather than "mechanistic."[2] Kansans have set their sights on grander things, like the purity of the nation. Good wages, fair play in farm country, the fate of the small town, even the one we live in—all these are a distant second to evolution, which we will strike from the books, and public education, which we will undermine in a hundred inventive ways.

Hear as our leaders square off against the issues of the day.

What afflicts us is a "crisis of the soul," wails Wichita congressman Todd Tiahrt. What motivates us, says a leader of the state's
largest anti-abortion group, is disgust with the "immoral dec-
adence in society." "We in America and we here in Kansas are
in a moral crisis," thunders the state's conservative Galahad,
David Miller, to his army of followers. What we need is to
become "virtuous," as per the founding fathers' clear instructions; for if we fail, "our entire culture may be lost." And from
the heights of Capitol Hill the great Brownback denounces
gangsta rap, inveighs against stem-cell research, and proposes
that the U.S. Senate hold hearings to investigate America's "cultural decline."[3]

The state's strategy for waging this war for America's soul
has been blunt and direct: Kansas has trawled its churches for
the most aggressively pious individuals it could find and has proceeded to elevate them to the most prominent positions of public
responsibility available, whence these saintly emissaries are then
expected to bark and howl and rebuke the world for its sins.
"I'm a Christian," the leader of the Wyandotte County GOP
once told a reporter by way of explaining his political plans.
"Primarily my goal is to build the Kingdom of God."[4]

And thus we have, as U.S. representative from central
Kansas, the legendary track star Jim Ryun, who says he ran for
office because God wanted him to and is glad to tell reporters the
exact date in 1972 when he "became a Christian." Ryun once
thrilled his followers at a campaign event by speaking in tongues,
and in 1995 he published an article describing the hyperprotec-
tive social order he imposes upon his female children:

> If a young man is interested in a young woman, he starts
> by praying about the relationship. With a go-ahead from
> the Lord and his parents, he then approaches the girl's
> parents. The parents pray and, if the young woman has a

reciprocal interest in the young man, her father talks through courtship and its expectations with the fellow.[5]

The young man has by now received two separate green lights from the Almighty, but it's still not enough for courtship to commence. Next he must demonstrate to Jim's satisfaction that he is "spiritually and financially prepared to marry"—evidently Ryun has to see the money up front!

From Wichita comes Todd Tiahrt, a man notable mainly for his perfectly swooping hair, who campaigns in the city's evangelical churches and peppers his conversation with biblical references. "What it's all about," the triumphant Tiahrt told the *Wichita Eagle* on the occasion of his upset victory over the district's long-standing Democratic Representative, is "bring[ing] America back to God."[6] Or, more accurately, scolding America for its insufficient godliness. On three separate occasions in 1998 Tiahrt admonished the nation from the floor of Congress for "losing its soul" by turning its back on God and family values.

Where Tiahrt is fiery, Sam Brownback is thoughtful and soft-spoken, the intellectual of the Kansas conservatives. If speaking in tongues is Ryun's trademark, Brownback's signature gesture was the time he washed the feet, in the manner of Jesus Christ, of an assistant who was leaving his service.* While the Kansas conservative style generally features loud, sweaty campaigning at the most energetic and antihierarchical sort of Protestant churches—charismatic, Pentecostal, Assemblies of God—Brownback favors the approach of the unhurried insider, the ultramontane, even. In 2002 he converted to Catholicism under the supervision of the Reverend John McCloskey, a leading light of Opus Dei, the

---

*One seasoned Kansas political hand I spoke to called this incident "religious harassment." When "your boss says, 'take your shoes off,' what can you do?"

ultraconservative prelature renowned for its role in the Franco regime in Spain. Nor is Opus Dei the only right-wing quasi cult with which Brownback has chosen to link himself. When in Washington, he lives in a town house operated by a Christian group known as the Family or the Fellowship, whose mission seems to be bringing together American lawmakers with capitalists and dictators from around the world. And studying the leadership secrets of Hitler.[7]

However bizarre such eruptions of zealotry might be, they are not enough by themselves to discredit these men. What makes the Kansas way so remarkable—and so dysfunctional—is that in each case the state's lawmakers combine this flamboyant public piety with a political agenda that only makes the state's material problems worse. Protestant fundamentalism, remember, is not necessarily friendly to big business; after all, it once gave the world William Jennings Bryan, who was widely regarded as being only a few steps shy of an anarchist. But even though Kansas is burning on a free-market pyre, each of the state leaders described here is as dedicated an apostle of the free-market doctrine as they are of the teachings of Jesus.

Each one, for example, receives high rankings from the U.S. Chamber of Commerce for his pro-business voting records. And each one has pledged himself to the sacred conservative causes of deregulating, dismantling government, and rolling back the welfare state. Jim Ryun, for example, may have built a wall around his daughters to protect them from our lascivious culture, but there is virtually no aspect of corporate orthodoxy that he has not internalized and endorsed. He has compared American economic policy of the pre-Reagan years to the Soviet Union and supported tax cuts for the rich on the grounds that the wealthy need incentives to keep on making their superhuman contributions to society. He supported the repeal of the estate tax on the delusional pretext that removing it would help family farms;* he expressed doubt about global warming; and he blamed the California electricity crisis not on deregulation but on "the state's political establishment," which "interfered with the free market."[9] You can go right down the list, checking off the items one after another: Ryun's earnest Christianity causes not a single deviation from the big-business agenda that I have been able to detect.

Todd Tiahrt was a manager at Boeing before going to Congress, and he may be even more ferociously committed than Ryun to the nation's corporate brass. In Washington he is known mainly for his single-minded hostility to the Department of Energy. According to Wichita's remaining Democrats, it is his hostility to organized labor that distinguishes him. In 1992 the *Wichita Eagle* dryly summarized his views on nonreligious matters: Tiahrt "dislikes government in general" despite Boeing's massive reliance on government defense spending; he calls for "privatization of prisons, says that some people are poor because they are determined to be poor and describes social-welfare programs as inefficient."[10] Four years later, the paper noted that this moral crusader had become the toast of corporate Wichita. When Koch Industries, a Wichita oil and gas concern that funds right-wing magazines and think tanks in addition to politicians,

---

*The Republican push to repeal the estate tax was often presented as a way to help small farmers in a difficult time. But by far the greatest beneficiaries of the tax's repeal have been the very rich. Only a tiny percentage of the assets taxed each year under the estate tax were farm properties, and one ag economist from Iowa State declared in 2001 that, even after studying the subject for thirty-five years, he had encountered not a single case in which a family had lost its farm due to the estate tax. "The problem is farm income and corporate concentration," wrote one Missouri farmer in an eloquent essay on the subject. "The estate tax isn't even on the radar screen of farm policy fixes that family farmers are fighting for."[8]

held a fund-raiser for Tiahrt, the newspaper seemed surprised at how far this young man with the common touch had come. "He's one of the new style of Republican conservatives," the paper pointed out. "His social views are what most people talk about. But his thinking on economics is what company officials are more interested in. Tiahrt is stridently pro-business, deeply suspicious of government, convinced Big Brother is lurking behind volumes and volumes of government regulations."[11]

Of the bunch, though, it is Sam Brownback, a member of one of the wealthiest families in the state, who has done the most distinguished service to God and mammon both. Admirers of Saint Sam will tell you about the much-publicized frugality of his D.C. lifestyle and refer you to his high-profile wars against human cloning and in support of persecuted Christians in third-world countries. They would also do well to examine the peculiar series of events that propelled Brownback into public life back in 1993. At the time Brownback was laboring in obscurity as Kansas secretary of agriculture, a position of little note but considerable power that he had held since 1986. Which is not to say that Brownback was elected ag secretary, or even appointed ag secretary by someone who was elected. At the time, the state's Department of Agriculture was a curious nineteenth-century throwback that did not answer to the people at all; Brownback had been chosen for the post by the state's largest agricultural interests—by the heads of the very industry he was charged with overseeing. For example, when he made limits on dangerous herbicides voluntary, Brownback was acting as a government regulator, but the kind of regulator conservatives approve of, the kind who answers to private industry instead of the public. Unfortunately, the cozy world of Kansas agriculture was turned on its head by a lawsuit pointing out the unconstitutionality of the whole arrangement, and Brownback was forced to make his way in the world by other means.[12]

As a leader of the "freshman class" of Republican congress-men elected in 1994, Brownback played the role of the princi-pled outsider, working out of a tiny office where he had scrawled the amount of the national debt on a whiteboard, and endlessly, tirelessly denouncing the role of big PAC money in politics. He even wrote a pious meditation distinguishing ambition of the spiritual variety from the sinful, worldly ambition that often tempted members of Congress.[13]

Before long, though, Brownback found that the two varieties of ambition could complement each other nicely. In his 1996 cam-paign for the U.S. Senate, he was materially assisted by a shadowy corporate front-group called Triad Management Services, which poured sufficient last-minute money into the race to drown out the messages of his foe. Brownback celebrated the resulting victory at a reception sponsored by the U.S. Telecom Association, a power-ful lobbying group for an industry whose deregulatory agenda the senator would advance diligently in the years to come. Along the way he learned to appreciate the virtue of big PAC money in poli-tics, even finding a reason to vote against the McCain-Feingold campaign finance reform measure.[14]

So it is with Sam Brownback right down the line: a man of sterling public principle, he seems to take the side of corporate interests almost regardless of the issues at hand. This is true even when the corporate interests in question are industries whose products Brownback considers the source of all evil. Such, at least, was the case in 2003, when one of Brownback's Senate commit-tees was called upon to consider the growing problem of monop-oly ownership in radio since the industry's deregulation seven years previously. Brownback, of course, has made a career out of denouncing the culture industry for its vulgarity, its bad values, presumably for the damage it has done to America's soul. Taking this opportunity to rein it in should have been a no-brainer. After all, as the industry critic Robert McChesney points out, the link between media ownership, the drive for profit, and the media's insulting content should be obvious to anyone with ears to hear. "Vulgarity is linked to corporate control and highly concentrated, only semi-competitive markets," McChesney says. And for many conservatives, "the radio fight was the moment of truth. If people are seriously concerned about vulgarity, this was their chance to prove it." For that reason, McChesney notes, certain right-wing culture warriors were happy to join the fight against further relaxation of radio ownership rules. But Brownback was not one of them. Faced with a choice between protecting corporate profits and actually doing something about the open cultural sewer he has spent his career deploring, Brownback chose the former. Deregulation is always for the better, he insisted, and he even proceeded to scold the witnesses *criticizing* the industry for acting out of—get this—*self-interest*.[15] The free-market system is inviolable, in other words, even when it's that branch of the system that you spend all your time campaigning against for coarsening our lives and leading us away from God.[16] In Kansas, mammon always comes first.

Mixing culture war and capitalism is not just a personal quirk shared by these three individuals; it is writ in the very manifesto of the Kansas conservative movement, the platform of the state Republican Party for 1998. Moaning that "the signs of a degenerating society are all around us," railing against abortion and homosexuality and gun control and evolution ("a theory, not a fact"), the document went on to propound a list of demands as friendly to plutocracy as anything ever dreamed up by Monsanto or Microsoft. The platform called for:

- A flat tax or national sales tax to replace the graduated income tax (in which the rich pay more than the poor).
- The abolition of taxes on capital gains (that is, on money you make when you sell stock).

- The abolition of the estate tax.
- No "governmental intervention in health care."
- The eventual privatization of Social Security.
- Privatization in general.
- Deregulation in general and "the operation of the free market system without government interference."
- The turning over of all federal lands to the states.
- A prohibition on "the use of taxpayer dollars to fund any election campaign."

Along the way the document specifically endorsed the disastrous Freedom to Farm Act, condemned agricultural price supports, and came out in favor of making soil conservation programs "voluntary," perhaps out of nostalgia for the Dust Bowl days, when Kansans learned a healthy fear of the Almighty.[17]

Let us pause for a moment to ponder this all-American dysfunction. A state is spectacularly ill served by the Reagan-Bush stampede of deregulation, privatization, and laissez-faire. It sees its countryside depopulated, its towns disintegrate, its cities stagnate—and its wealthy enclaves sparkle, behind their remote-controlled security gates. The state erupts in revolt, making headlines around the world with its bold defiance of convention. But what do its rebels demand? More of the very measures that have brought ruination on them and their neighbors in the first place.

This is not just the mystery of Kansas; this is the mystery of America, the historical shift that has made it all possible.

In Kansas the shift is more staggering than elsewhere, simply because it has been so decisive, so extreme. The people who were once radical are now reactionary. Though they speak today in the same aggrieved language of victimization, and though they face the same array of economic forces as their hard-bitten ancestors, today's populists make demands that are precisely the opposite. Tear down the federal farm programs, they cry. Privatize the utilities. Repeal the progressive taxes. All that Kansas asks today is a little help nailing itself to that cross of gold.

Chapter Four

Verns Then and Now

"It was his own fault, of course," wrote the historian Vernon L. Parrington of the midwestern farmer's predicament of the 1890s.

> Due to his own political slackness the farmer had allowed himself to become the common drudge of society. . . . While capitalism had been perfecting its machinery of exploitation he had remained indifferent to the fact that he himself was the fattest goose that capitalism was to pluck. He had helped indeed to provide the rope for his own hanging. He had voted away the public domain to railways that were now fleecing him; he took pride in the county-seat towns that lived off his earnings; he sent city lawyers to represent him in legislatures and in Congress; he read middle-class newspapers and listened to bankers and politicians and cast his votes for the policy of Whiggery that could have no other outcome than his own despoiling.

From his impoverished childhood on a farm outside of Emporia, Kansas, Parrington had gained an intimate familiarity with the politics of self-delusion. Out of an almost superstitious loyalty to free-market economics, the Kansas farmers of his boyhood had been accomplices in their own mulcting. The rise of Populism, though, was for Parrington a sort of political epiphany. The people had awakened to reality; the gaseous pieties of laissez-faire were dissipating; and rising to take their place was a newfound "critical realism" characterized by Mary Elizabeth Lease's famous advice to "raise less corn and more hell." The farmers had finally become "class-conscious," Parrington continued:

> They were enlisted in a class struggle. They used the vocabulary of realism, and the unctuous political platitudes and sophistries of county-seat politicians rolled off their minds like water from a duck's back. They were fighting a great battle—they believed—against Wall Street and the eastern money-power; they were bent on saving America from the plutocracy; and they swept over the county-seat towns, burying the old machine politicians under an avalanche of votes, capturing state legislatures, electing Congressmen and Senators, and looking forward to greater power.[1]

Parrington participated personally in the farmers' uprising, and when he wrote about it years later in *Main Currents in American Thought,* his famous history of American letters, he saw in Populism the first glimmerings of some of the great intellectual upheavals of the twentieth century—naturalism, muckraking, and hard-hitting social satire—which would eventually topple the genteel tradition of the nineteenth century. In a peculiar way,

Parrington seemed to think, Kansas was one of the birthplaces of literary modernism.

Vernon Parrington's book isn't widely read anymore, but it is worth remembering the man's confident progressivism today if only to give ourselves an idea of how much the Midwest and the country have changed in the seventy years since it was first published. The contrasts between his time and ours are stark and heavy enough to give one a headache for days. Today's Kansas has got the hell-raising farmers and the class-conscious workers, all right, but when they come sweeping through the state legislature, clearing out the old guard, what they are demanding is more power for Wall Street, more privatization, and the end of Progressive Era reforms like the estate tax. While they're at it, they rail against Parrington's beloved critical realism as nothing more than atheism and liberal bias.[2] Today Kansas longs to be the grave digger of modernism.

Parrington believed that the history of ideas moved majestically in a particular direction, away from superstition and the hollow pieties of the free market. Here, too, the contrast with today is remarkable. The laissez-faire religion of nineteenth-century economics is back; it is more firmly embraced than ever. To document the transition, we need look no farther than Kansas itself, and another one of its native sons, the economist Vernon L. Smith, winner of the 2002 Nobel Prize for economics.

Smith was raised a socialist in Wichita. His mother, he tells interviewers, cast her first ballot for Eugene Debs, and he himself once voted for the socialist bannerman Norman Thomas. Today, though, he is a minister of the market, a high priest of capitalism with an unshakable faith in his god's goodness and mercy. Like Kansas generally, Smith has changed sides. And his conversion serves a useful rhetorical purpose. Ordinarily when we come across someone who argues, as Smith does, that the national parks ought to be sold off to the highest bidder, that everything from electricity to water should be privatized, that government bungles whatever it touches, that federal poverty programs need to be abolished, that people have an innate "instinct for exchange" (Smith has conducted experiments in which people think about economics problems while he scans their head with an MRI machine), and that therefore markets are to some degree hardwired into the human brain,[3] we naturally assume that the person making such assertions is simply on the payroll of some unscrupulous oil and gas syndicate, promoting bad ideas so that their master can reap the rewards of lower taxes or lax environmental regulation.

But toss the man's former leftism into the mix—adding also the oft-remarked fact that Smith wears his hair in a ponytail—and we seem to have a genuine rebel on our hands, not some bought-and-paid-for shill. He cares about the little guy. He defies convention. When the *Wall Street Journal* slaps the headline "Power to the People" on a Smith essay shifting the blame for California's deregulated electricity disaster onto state regulators, we might well believe we're reading the words of an economist who cares.[4]

Or maybe our first impression was right. The Kansas sensibility with which Vernon Smith is most closely connected is not that of populism, but Koch Industries, the nation's second-largest privately held company. Based in Wichita, Koch's primary business is oil, but it is far better known for its owners' openhanded political activities than for its petroleum operations. The founder of the dynasty, Fred Koch, was a charter member of the John Birch Society. His billionaire son Charles founded the libertarian Cato Institute in 1977, and another billionaire son, David, ran for vice president on the Libertarian ticket in 1980. Koch money flowed through Triad Management Services, which delivered such crucial assistance to Sam Brownback's Senate campaign in 1996; and Koch money, mingled with the money of so many other oil interests, supported the presidential campaign of George W. Bush. Most important, though, Koch money subsidizes the mass production of bad ideas, zany free-market policy recommendations that usually aim to starve or otherwise disable government while making business ever more profitable. When I read that right-wing Kansas state legislators were proposing that the state sell off its highway system, for example, I knew instantly that Koch money was somehow involved in nurturing this daft notion.[5] Koch money props up such hothouses of the right as *Reason* magazine, the Manhattan Institute, the Heartland Institute, Citizens for a Sound Economy, and the Democratic Leadership Council. The Kochs' influence is so well-known in Washington that wags refer to their intellectual empire as "the Kochtopus." It is the Populists' "money power" in the flesh.

Koch money has also been instrumental in advancing the academic career of Vernon L. Smith. He was brought to George Mason University by a Koch Foundation grant; he is employed there by the Koch-funded Mercatus Center; his writing is published by the Koch-funded Cato Institute; and his market-worshiping ideas are praised to the skies by the Koch-funded Reason Institute, whose Web site includes an item referencing Smith's Nobel Prize as all-trumping evidence of his rightness. "Believe him," it commands.[6] A more straightforward take on Smith's Nobel and the credibility that it instantly generated for his bad ideas came from Charles Koch, who said, simply, "The Koch Foundation's gift was an excellent investment."[7]

The two Verns illustrate the changing views of my home state's intellectual class, but an even sharper contrast between the Kansas of old and the right-wing radicalism of today can be found in the state's folk art. Let me take you first to the tiny western Kansas town of Lucas, home to a remarkable sculpture garden illustrating that grandest of subjects, the condition of mankind. Constructed out of concrete in the early years of the twentieth century by an old fellow named J. P. Dinsmoor, the "The Garden of Eden" mixes biblical stories with the unmistakable political iconography of Populism: Here is Cain, having just slain Abel. There is "Labor Crucified" and surrounded by his tormenters—doctor, lawyer, preacher, and capitalist. Bigger animals eat smaller animals in an endless chain of exploitation and oppression.

The images are blunt, to be sure, but this has not saved them from our American forgetting disease. Visiting the place some years ago, I noticed a sculpture of an octopus grasping at a map of the Americas, with one tentacle reaching menacingly across Panama. For a viewer of the early twentieth century, such a tableau would have been easily recognizable as a left-wing denunciation of the imperial ambitions of the trusts, as obvious as a cartoon from the *Kansas Farmer*. But the way the caretaker explained it to me, what Dinsmoor had actually done was miraculously anticipate the treasons of the hated Jimmy Carter, who, according to backlash mythology, gave the canal away.

I don't blame the tour guide for this mistake. That a regular guy like J. P. Dinsmoor would have opposed U.S. imperialism, well, that's simply unthinkable out here; everyone knows that such views are the affectations of latte-drinking rich kids at fancy colleges, while the average working man stands tall for firearm and flag. After all, just look at the equally remarkable array of sculptures constructed by one M. T. Liggett over the last ten years outside the tiny western Kansas town of Mullinville. Liggett, like Dinsmoor, is a man in protest. His art shrieks at you for almost a mile as you drive by on U.S. Highway 400. It glitters with anger, its hundreds of arms whirling furiously in the unceasing Kansas wind. The sculptures themselves are ingenious grotesques of politicians, cleverly assembled from bits of discarded farm equipment, but there is nothing subtle or obscure about the message. This is the gospel according to Rush Limbaugh rendered in wood and steel, backed up with huge helpings of angry text when the sculptures themselves are insufficient to express the artist's disgust. There's a whirligig marked "Femi-Nazi" constructed from old car parts; there's a giant swastika with boots and a blond head captioned "Hillary Clinton / Sieg Heil / Our-Jack-Booted Eva Braun"; there's a hammer and sickle adorning a caricature of that favorite bogeyman of the Gingrich right, the Environmental Protection Agency; and for Limbaugh himself there's a valentine-shaped face sporting the wistful legend "Rush / President 1996 / Only 'Free' Men Speak." A giant screw turns in the breeze and mocks the Clinton health-care plan ("4012 Pages / Liberal Vomit"), while other installations mourn the Branch Davidians and assail James Carville ("You're a Pimp Stupid").

Kiowa County, where Liggett's sculpture farm is situated, is one of the poorer Kansas counties, with a median household income 22 percent below the state average. Like everywhere else in rural Kansas, it has been hit hard in recent years. It lost almost a quarter of its population between 1980 and 2002. Driving around there, I happened upon the world's largest hand-dug well and a church that had been converted into yet another thrift store, but I saw almost no people along the highways.

There are no caricatures of the economic forces that have done this to Kiowa County in the Liggett display, or, at least, none that I saw. No representations of Monsanto or Archer Daniels Midland with horns or gigantic teeth; no Kochtopus tightening its squishy grip around the nation's brainpan. What seems to enrage Kiowa County is the government power that has kept them afloat through their hardship. Nearly 29 percent of the county's total personal income comes in the form of government benefits and other transfer payments; in crop subsidies alone Kiowa County farmers have received $40 million since 1995.[8] And yet what Kiowa County wants—desperately, urgently, if the art of M. T. Liggett is any indication—is for the liberals to pack up their communist EPA and their fascist feminism and their "anti-Christian evolution" and leave them alone. Al Gore received only 18 percent of the vote out here, and in 1992 the county actually voted to secede from Kansas, to be done once and for all with the high-handed ways of those city slickers in Topeka.

Let me describe one final contrast between the spirit of the old Kansas and that of the new.

In 1888 the town of Ulysses, in far western Kansas, was engaged in a bitter contest with a nearby hamlet to become the seat of government for Grant County. In order to help secure this prize, believed in those days to guarantee eternal prosperity, Ulysses issued $36,000 in bonds. The official story was that the money would go for municipal improvements, but in fact it was used to prosecute the county-seat war, spent on "professional voters" and gunfighters (the town was founded by a cousin of Wyatt Earp) who would lend a hand in the great showdown. Naturally Ulysses prevailed, and after winning, it proceeded to erect a county courthouse—along with an opera house, four hotels, twelve restaurants, a host of saloons, and the rest of the *Gunsmoke* set—before collapsing swiftly into destitution. Drought, deflation, and the allure of new territory shrank its population from fifteen hundred down to forty.

In 1908 the bonds matured, to the tune of eighty-four grand. Not a lot of money these days, perhaps, but back then it was equivalent to one-third of the assessed value of the entire county. To pay off the bondholders in New York, the handful of citizens left in Ulysses would have had to shoulder an impossible burden.

What they did instead was toss the collections man in jail while they thought up a plan for moving the town. Impoverished but resourceful, the citizens of Ulysses cut the town's buildings into pieces and dragged them across the prairie to a new location, "leaving the bond-holders," as the 1939 WPA guide to the state puts it, "40 acres of bare ground on which to foreclose."[9]

The only social actor capable of that kind of defiance today is the corporation. Corporations are mobile; cities are not. They extract billions from us in bonds, tax abatements, water rights, and outright grants by threatening to pick themselves up and haul their machines and their buildings and their jobs to some sunnier clime. A state like Kansas that is watching its prime industries blow away in the hot summer wind is more vulnerable to this tactic than most. The meatpackers found it a prodigious help in dealing with Garden City. Sprint used it to great effect in Overland Park. Everyone doing business in Kansas City, Missouri, where the state line is never much more than a few blocks away, knows the power of the threat.

The firm with which the state will forever associate this particular species of extortion, though, is Boeing. As the largest employer in Wichita, Boeing has long been able to get that desperate city to a very expensive "yes." Then, in 2003, the corporation decided to fish in even deeper waters. It began taking applications from states to see which one would get to build its new 7E7 airliner. Ordinarily, of course, businesses are the ones that make bids for government contracts; in this case, though, it was Boeing that was reviewing the bids from governments, an innovation that unleashed a form of civic competition very much like the county-seat wars of the nineteenth century. The prospect of winning the 7E7 work triggered an immediate race to the bottom in Kansas and Washington, the states where the company's largest manufacturing facilities are located. Soon Michigan, Texas, and California had thrown their wallets into the ring as well. Anyone who wonders how, exactly, the corporate vision gets translated into the nuts and bolts of state law would do well to study the bidding war that followed.

The winning community, Boeing announced, would furnish the company with quality schools, low absentee rates among its labor force, good services, low taxes, cheap land, and "local community and governmental support for manufacturing businesses."[10] Got it? The competing states certainly did; they responded by generating statements of high romantic love for Boeing and obsequious promises of eternal meekness.[11] People in the Puget Sound area remembered how Boeing had once criticized the state for having high taxes and workers' comp costs;[12] now they declared themselves ready to change all that, with attractive tax incentives and a promise to make the state's troublesome environmental bureau into a "more business-friendly" outfit.

Plainspoken Kansas tried to compete in its direct, red-state way by heaping money at Boeing's feet. In April 2003, the company informed the state that it would need to cough up $500 million in order to stay in the running for the 7E7. The state legislature, meanwhile, was dealing with a damnably difficult budget shortfall, fighting over teachers' salaries and the penny-ante usual, but the assembled pols immediately dropped their cudgels and complied with Boeing's wishes. They voted a bond issue of the requested face value and added a special incentive, the sort of business-friendly innovation that Kansas wants to be known for: although Boeing would eventually have to reimburse the state for the principal, all interest on these bonds would come out of the state taxes of people working on the 7E7 project. These workers would not necessarily be new hires, remember, just existing Boeing employees who had been given a new task. The main change would be that their state taxes no longer went into the general revenue but into a special fund to pay back the debts of their employer.

Quite a deal for Boeing shareholders, and quite a curious move for a state government facing the worst budget shortfall in its history.[13] But can we blame Kansas, or any state, for reacting as it did? Every free-trade agreement we have signed in recent years has been designed to make cities vulnerable in precisely this way. If you're a medium-sized city like Wichita, hosting some giant multinational's plant is less of an achievement today than it is a gun pointed at your head, a constant reminder that some executive has the power to turn your town into an instant Flint, to destroy your citizens' lives, your property values, your merchants, and all the rest of it should the whim overtake him while he sits in the audience at some motivational seminar.

Boeing eventually decided to produce the 7E7 in pretty much the same manner as it produces its other jetliners: part of the work will be done in Wichita, and the final assembly will be done in the Puget Sound region. The bonds and tax breaks voted by the people of Kansas and Washington changed nothing but the company's bottom line. Still, Kansas leaders were proud of the "signal" they had sent. Everyone in the corporate-relocation community was "familiar with the Boeing legislation," boasted the state's lieu-tenant governor. "They know [Kansas is] pro-business and pro-jobs." A little more than a month later, however, Kansas would learn the true measure of the corporate world's respect, and the lesson would make the state's blood freeze: According to a memo leaked to a Seattle newspaper, Boeing was considering *selling* the huge plant on which Wichita's prosperity depended.[14] A decade's worth of legislative favors and florid pro-business declarations, it now appeared, were like so many valentines to a blackguard. Profit alone swelled Boeing's cold heart, and its fancy was now fixed on outsourcing. All that was left for Kansas to do was swoon in self-pity.

Chapter Five

Con Men and Mod Squad

The greatest and most consequential shift in Kansas has been within its Republican Party, where a civil war pitting moderates against conservatives has been raging for over a decade now. Republicanism has always been central to the state's identity: Kansas was founded by free-soil settlers who fought a running border war with slaveholding Missourians (that is, Democrats), and it has not sent a Democrat to the U.S. Senate since 1932. Republicanism here has not always been strictly conservative, however; those who represented the state on the national stage—William Allen White, Alf Landon, Dwight Eisenhower, even Bob Dole—were all from the party's "progressive" or "moderate" wing. And while the state was fiscally tight and banned what was quaintly called "liquor by the drink" until 1986, it also had some excellent public schools, some pretty good public services, and the slightly higher taxes that paid for them. It was much closer to Minnesota than it was to Alabama.

Most important, Kansas was traditionally ahead of the

crowd on women's rights. Women's suffrage was first proposed here in 1867 and achieved in full in 1912, and Kansas was one of the handful of states that had reformed its abortion laws even before the *Roe v. Wade* decision of 1973. In later years the state's largest city, Wichita, gained the dubious distinction of being the only place in the region where a woman could receive a late-term abortion, at a clinic operated by a doctor named George Tiller. As the *enragés* still like to say, Kansas was "the abortion capital of the nation."[1]

Kansas has always been a religious place, but when I was growing up there in the seventies and eighties there was not much of a religious right to speak of. There were the occasional nuts, of course—when I was young, a gang of right-wing ne'er-do-wells calling themselves the Capitalist Revolutionary Army robbed a Johnson County bank and shot several policemen—but by and large Kansas was as average and as ordinary in its politics as it was in every other regard. David Adkins, a state senator who was raised a fundamentalist Baptist in the plains city of Salina (today he is a moderate Republican), says, "I . . . can't recall a political issue—abortion, homosexuality, any of the issues of convenience that now dominate Republican dialogue—ever being mentioned in the course of my religious training, or in the course of my faith." When Dan Glickman, a former U.S. representative from Wichita (he is one of that rare breed, a Kansas Democrat), served on the city school board in the seventies, he says, "issues of ideology never came up." In the early eighties I myself attended a hearing called by an angry parent who wished to remove a number of books from our high school library; as she ran through her list of accusations—prefab stuff that she had probably procured from the John Birch Society—the presiding administrators had trouble restraining their laughter.

. . .

In the late eighties, Kansas was basking complacently in its traditional pragmatic centrism. Two of its U.S. representatives were Democrats; two others (one of them a woman) were moderate Republicans. Its famous U.S. senator, Bob Dole, had been labeled a conservative when he ran for the vice presidency in 1976; by the time he got his party's nomination for the top job in 1996, he was solidly in the moderate camp. Kansas's other senator, Nancy Kassebaum, the daughter of Alf Landon, could be called a liberal Republican.

All through the eighties, the state legislature was dominated by traditional moderate Republicans, passing legislation like a well-oiled machine. The state was still sufficiently unpolarized that in 1990 voters could elect, for only the second time since World War II, a Democratic majority in the Kansas house. More important for our purposes, however, was the small band of right-wing cranks who amused the citizenry by pulling an occasional filibuster on tax legislation, suspending the rules, and otherwise tossing wrenches into the workings of government whenever the opportunities presented. In the late eighties, there were maybe ten of these characters in the statehouse, one of them a pest of such damnable persistence that his colleagues nominated him for "state reptile" in 1986.[2]

In 1991, though, began an uprising that would propel those reptilian Republicans from a tiny splinter group into the state's dominant political faction, that would reduce Kansas Democrats to third-party status, and that would wreck what remained of the state's progressive legacy. We are accustomed to thinking of the backlash as a phenomenon of the seventies (the busing riots, the tax revolt) or the eighties (the Reagan revolution); in Kansas the great move to the right was a story of the nineties, a story of the present.

The push that started Kansas hurtling down the crevasse of reaction was provided by Operation Rescue, the national pro-life group famous for its aggressive tactics against abortion clinics. They called it the Summer of Mercy; the plan was to commit acts of civil disobedience all across the city of Wichita in July 1991, just as the organization's followers had done in Atlanta in 1988 and Los Angeles in 1990. Wichita was to be different, though. Here you had Tiller's clinic situated among a population that is world-famous for its spiritual enthusiasm. The protesters meant to make this contradiction manifest—to force one aspect of the Kansas identity to clash with another—to set up a conflict so unresolvable that everyone in the state would eventually have to choose up sides and join the fight.

What allowed Operation Rescue to succeed, and what made the summer of 1991 different from previous anti-abortion rallies, was the reaction of the city's clinics, which voluntarily closed up for a week when the protests began. Although this disastrous strategy had been undertaken on the advice of the Wichita police, to certain elements of the pro-life movement it represented a bona-fide miracle.[3] For once they had completely stopped what they called "the abortion industry" in its tracks. In July and August they descended on Wichita by the thousands, spreading out over the city, chaining themselves to fences, lying down beneath cars, filling the jails, and picketing the residences of abortion doctors and others they deemed complicit in the culture of death.

The summer's climactic event was a mass meeting in the football stadium at Wichita State University. At first organizers expected seven thousand people; they reserved only half of the stadium. More than twenty-five thousand showed up. They filled the entire complex; they spilled over onto the end zones. Pat Robertson took to the podium and declared, "We will not rest until every baby . . . is safe in his mother's womb"; the fundamentalist media critic Donald Wildmon lashed out against liberal bias in the news; the pro-life activist Joe Scheidler called for

Wichita-style protests across the country; and Operation Rescue leaders phoned in speeches from jail. In one *Spartacus*-like moment, an event organizer asked those from out of town to stand up; according to press accounts, two-thirds of the audience did so. Then she called on Wichitans to stand, and the whole crowd got to its feet.[4]

Lawrence Goodwyn, the historian of nineteenth-century Populism, proposes that "movement culture" is critical to mass protest: "The people need to 'see themselves' experimenting in democratic forms," he has written.[5] What Goodwyn no doubt had in mind were the Populists' huge "educational" gatherings and their day-long parades through tiny Kansas towns, but the observation applies just as accurately to that great inverted-populist frolic in Wichita one hundred years later.[6] This was where the Kansas conservative movement got an idea of its own strength; this was where it achieved critical mass. Other aspects of that summer may be hazy now, but every anti-abortion activist I talked to remembers this massive gathering with burning clarity. Mary Kay Culp, the Johnson County director of the anti-abortion group Kansans for Life (KFL), recalled how she and others from suburban Kansas City traveled by bus to the event. Bud Hentzen, a Wichita contractor who served at that time as a Sedgwick County commissioner, described the moment in the stadium as a kind of awakening. "My thought," he said, was "bring on the vote."

And bring it on they did. Tim Golba, a former president of Kansans for Life, recounted how KFL's mailing list grew by ten thousand names in the six weeks after the rally. At anti-abortion gatherings Wichita conservative leaders signed up candidates for Republican precinct positions. "These people were laying down their bodies on the highway," remembered Mark Gietzen, a Christian activist who was soon to become the chairman of the Sedgwick County GOP. "We said, 'We admire you for your courage, for your conviction, but we've got something a lot smarter for you to do than lying on the highway.'" By August 1992, Gietzen asserted, "we had 87 percent of our people in, identified, firm, Operation Rescue–type pro-lifers as precinct committeemen and women."[7]

Moderate Kansas was horrified. Newspaper accounts of the summer emphasized the hostility of native Wichitans to the deluge of outsiders. Legislation was prepared to slap the protesters back into place by mandating stiff penalties for clinic blockers and codifying the pro-choice position as Kansas law. (In case *Roe v. Wade* was ever overturned, the legislation would have ensured that abortions would still be readily available in Kansas.) In March 1992 the abortion bill cleared the state house of representatives by a towering margin, but came to grief in the Kansas senate a few weeks later, much to the irritation of the state's editorial writers.

The push to lock in *Roe v. Wade* as state law coincided, ironically, with another great journalistic theme of that year, the celebration of popular disgust with what was called "politics as usual." The *Wichita Eagle,* a leader in the "civic journalism" movement, ran endless stories marveling at the deteriorating popularity of the first president Bush, finding great significance in the defeat of various national politicians in primary elections, and conducting surveys and focus groups measuring the disaffection as Election Day drew near. Under the front-page headline "The People Are Fed Up," the paper mustered its best imitation of populist outrage and declared of "the people" that "they said they were fed up with the problems, the politicians and the system that produces both. They said that the voters' revolt is on, that they want to take back control of the system."[8] What the paper meant by all its calls to rebellion, of course, was merely that it would be nice if we all registered and voted. Preferably for nice moderate Republicans who would quit fooling around and pass the abortion bill.

The journalists were right about the coming "voters' revolt"; what they got wrong was the identity of the revolutionaries. This was no moderate affair. The ones who were actually poised to take back control of the system were the anti-abortion protesters. Theirs was a grassroots movement of the most genuine kind, born in protest, convinced of its righteousness, telling and retelling its stories of persecution at the hands of the cops, the judges, the state, and the comfortable classes. They had no newspaper they could call their own—the *Eagle*, for its part, ran story after story in which experts warned against the maniacal ambitions of the Bible-thumpers—but one of them did set up a "Godarchy hotline," a telephone number you could call to hear recorded suggestions for action.

These nascent Kansas conservatives were also willing to work far harder than ordinary folks to achieve their political vision. This was (and still is) critical to their success, and the conservatives knew it. "The other side doesn't have an agenda," said the Godarchy guy in 1992. "We have an agenda—the kingdom of God." They had lain beneath cars to stop abortion, and now they were putting their bodies on the line for the right wing of the Republican Party.[9] Most important of all, the conservative cadre were dedicated enough to show up in force for primary elections, which in Kansas are held in the distinctly unpleasant month of August. And in 1992 this populist conservative movement conquered the Kansas Republican Party from the ground up: in Johnson County, in Sedgwick County (Wichita), and in all the other heavily populated parts of the state, they swamped the GOP organizations with enthusiastic new activists and unceremoniously brushed the traditional Kansas moderates aside. In Sedgwick County, some 19 percent of the new precinct committee people responsible for throwing out the old guard actually had arrest records from the Summer of Mercy.[10] "I'm not here because I love politics," one of the activists declared on that momentous occasion. "I hate politics. I'm here because I love unborn babies. I've been to jail for the unborn."[11]

That fall Bill Clinton won the presidency, but in Kansas the reenergized Republican Party reconquered the legislature. One conservative novice—a carpetlayer in private life—even defeated the fourteen-year incumbent Democrat who was then Speaker of the Kansas house.

The pro-life origins of the Kansas conservative movement present us with a striking historical irony. Historians often attribute the withering and disappearance of the nineteenth-century Populist movement to its failure to achieve material, real-world goals. It never managed to nationalize the railroads, or set up an agricultural price-support system, or remonetize silver, the argument goes, and eventually voters just got sick of its endless calls to take a stand against the "money power." Yet with the pro-life movement, the material goal of stopping abortion is, almost by definition, beyond achieving. Ask even the hardest-core activists, and they will admit that there is little that can be done to halt the practice without a fundamental shift on the Supreme Court. Their movement, however, just seems to grow and grow. The material goal doesn't seem to matter.

On the losing side of all this energetic growth were Kansas's traditional rulers, its pro-choice Republican moderates. Although plenty conservative in the pro-business sense of the word, the Republican Mods were now finding themselves under deadly, unrelenting fire from their right. Now it was they who were tasting the backlash, who were being called "soft" on this or that, who were charged with enabling the secular-humanist disease, who were facilitating the cultural rot. Now the state's traditional leaders—people who fancied themselves the most Republican in

America—even found themselves taunted as "RINOs": Republicans in Name Only. And they were furious. Candidates who had patiently worked their way up the party hierarchy for years were seeing the positions they had coveted filled instead by some holy-rolling nobody screeching against big government and interested only in doing away with abortion and taxation. The Cons were organizing at their fundamentalist churches on the edges of town; they were turning out for primaries in numbers that casual Republicans could never hope to match; they were trouncing Mods in races for everything from precinct committeeman to sheriff. Kansas Republicans were reaping the whirlwind: the backlash mentality that their party had encouraged so sedulously since 1968 and that had won them the presidency so many times was now howling outside their own door.

The moderates deplored and denounced. A Republican Party without themselves as its leaders was not Republican at all, they said. Why didn't the malcontents simply start a third party, they demanded, instead of ruining theirs? Besides, they suggested, the religious conservatives secretly harbored all manner of vileness. These Cons were determined to bring "segregation of a different kind," one Johnson County Mod declared. "And they hate," wrote a columnist for the *Wichita Eagle*. "They want women to return to a time . . . when white gloves were required attire at afternoon teas, and when women were kept in their place by being taught that the men in their lives always knew best."[12]

In 1993 the Reverend Robert Meneilly blasted the Cons from the pulpit of Village Presbyterian, a fashionable church nestled on the Mission Hills border, warning that their efforts to baptize government would one day backfire, discrediting Christianity and setting back its larger spiritual mission. For this reason, Meneilly declared, the zealous cadres then taking over the local Republican Party represented "a threat far greater than the old threat of Communism." Meneilly was probably the most respected church leader in greater Kansas City at the time, and his sermon against the Cons catalyzed moderate dread through-out suburbia. It led to the founding of the Mainstream Coalition, a group established to fight the religious right, and the sermon was even reprinted in *The New York Times*. But for the Cons, being denounced by this Johnson County elder had a tonic effect, confirming to them their pet belief that society's real victims were evangelical Christians. Indeed, Meneilly's words can still be found reprinted today, uprooted from their context, in countless conservative publications as evidence of the persecution to which true believers are subject.

The prairie fire burned on. Nineteen ninety-four was a Republican year everywhere, and in Kansas the Cons managed to cleanse the state's congressional delegation of Democrats altogether, with Todd Tiahrt upsetting the pro-choice Democrat from Wichita, and Sam Brownback taking the seat of the state's other Democratic congressman, who left the U.S. House to run (unsuccessfully) for governor. Back in Topeka the Cons now made up the majority of the Republicans in the state legislature. They took all three leadership positions in the Kansas house and introduced what they called a "Contract with Kansas," a solemn pledge to send more convicts to the chair while defending the fetus.

The moment of outright triumph for the Cons came in 1996. When Bob Dole resigned his Senate seat in order to pursue the presidency, moderate Republican governor Bill Graves appointed Sheila Frahm, his own lieutenant governor, to the position. The Cons, though, had other ideas, and she was promptly clobbered in the GOP primary by the pious Brownback, who had by then become a celebrity of the conservative movement nationwide for his humble but uncompromising style. Brownback's congressional post, in turn, went to Jim Ryun, the praying track star. Later that year the two remaining women in the state's congressional delegation—both Mods, both pro-choice—also decided to call it quits. Abortion foes snapped up both positions, making the delegation 100 percent anti-abortion as well as 100 percent Republican. By the end of 1996, the conservatives had reason to celebrate: the state's pro-choice consensus, so haughty and cocksure back in 1991, had now been utterly routed.

The Cons partied jubilantly while Dole was crowned at the Republican convention in San Diego that year. They now controlled the state party apparatus so tightly that they kept Governor Graves out of the official Kansas delegation. The national media could not help but notice the revolution in the candidate's home state, and the Kansas Cons were the subjects of fawning write-ups in the *Weekly Standard* and the *American Spectator*. The admirable Brownback was profiled by George Will and Robert Novak. The Cons were the wave of the future.

By the late nineties, though, the Mods figured out how to push back, and the two sides settled in for years of electoral warfare, marked by constant escalations of verbal hostility. When the Mods took back the state party organization in 1999, the Cons simply set up their own parallel organization and pressed on.[13] At Republican gatherings such as the annual Kansas Day festivity the Cons now hold competing events. (Is there anywhere else where the state holiday is a partisan affair?)

The bitterness persists today, poisoning political activity right down to the roots of the grass. Republican precinct committee positions, the lowliest offices in the political hierarchy, are often hotly contested in Kansas.[14] Primary elections for state legislature seats and even school board positions often find the defeated Republican, whether Mod or Con, refusing to concede and instead battling on as a write-in candidate in the general election. There are squabbles over yard signs, and homemade slander campaigns startling in their barbarity: during the weeks leading up to the Republican primary of 2002, I saw hand-scrawled placards reading, "Help Homosexuals/Vote *Candidate X*" planted along a busy street in the outer-ring Kansas City suburb of Olathe. The candidate thus impugned, a man who would be considered a stalwart conservative anywhere else in the country, explained to me that he had alienated the suburb's leading Cons *ten years previously* by supporting the availability of AIDS literature in the public library. A short while later, he caught up with the gentleman planting the DIY signs and discussed the matter with him over fisticuffs.[15]

All the fratricide has had a predictable effect. With the more motivated Con faction dominating the primary elections, the Mods have found it expedient to do the unthinkable. In Johnson County, one of the most Republican areas in the nation, some moderate Republican leaders grew so disenchanted with the ultra-conservative, pro-life congressman who had been foisted on them in 1996 that two years later they helped jettison him in favor of—a Democrat! And when a Con took the Republican gubernatorial nomination in 2002, much of the state's Mod leadership conspicuously failed to get behind him, effectively throwing the election to the Democrat Kathleen Sebelius. This last result was so embarrassing to the national party—in a Republican year, here was ultra-Republican Kansas going to a Democrat!—that it prompted the Republican guerrilla Grover Norquist to calumniate the Mods as "quislings and collaborators" that he would "deal with" when the opportunity presented.[16]

It is true that total victory has so far eluded the state's conservatives, but Norquist has no reason to be so upset. The same conservative uprising that displaced the Mods also wore down the Kansas Democrats, Governor Sebelius notwithstanding, reducing their hold on the state legislature from an outright majority in 1990–92 to a mere 36 percent of the seats in the house and a feeble 25 percent in the state senate. In 2000, nine years after the Summer of Mercy, George W. Bush carried the state by a considerably greater margin than had his father in 1988 or even Bob Dole in 1996. The pro-choice bill that passed the state's lower house in 1992 would be unthinkable today. So utterly has the climate changed on this issue that the man who ran the Godarchy hotline back in 1992 is now—of all things—the head of the state's Consumer Protection Division.

The Cons have altered the state's political environment considerably, but their record as legislators is more mixed. Like their faction nationally, they have made virtually no headway in the culture wars. They have not halted abortion in Kansas or secured a voucher program or even managed to keep evolution out of the schools. Indeed, the issues the Cons emphasize seem all to have been chosen precisely because they are not capable of being resolved by the judicious application of state power. Senator Brownback, for example, is best known for stands that are purely symbolic: against cloning, against the persecution of Christians in distant lands, against sex slavery in the third world. Similarly, Phill Kline, the current attorney general of Kansas, has become famous in conservative Republican circles nationwide for intervening in cases having to do with the age of consent and homosexual rape. These are issues that touch the lives of almost nobody in Kansas; that function solely as rallying points for the Con followers. They stoke the anger, keep the pot simmering, but have little to do with the practical, day-to-day uses of government power. Thus they allow the politician in question to grandstand magnificently while avoiding any identification with the hated state.

In only one area have the Cons achieved a tangible, real-world victory. Their intractable hostility to taxes of all kinds has successfully brought disaster on the state government. After cutting taxes compulsively through the nineties—or by inducing frightened Mods to cut taxes in order to appease them—the Cons maneuvered the state into a position where any economic downturn would have catastrophic effects on revenues. The train wreck has happened as scheduled: today Kansas, like many other states, is struggling with the worst fiscal crisis in recent history. Nor will the Cons allow taxes to be increased to get the state out of its hole. The only route remaining is the one conservatives have insisted we take all along, on the state as well as the national level: government, that hated entity, will simply have to wither away.[17] For most people this may seem bad enough, but as hard times propel the state into the ditch, the fun for conservatives is only just beginning.

When national correspondents come to cover the Kansas revolution, they scratch their heads, mystified. They watch one group of Republican Kansans bombard another group of Republican Kansans, and they marvel at the strangeness and sadness of the spectacle. If pressed for a sociological explanation, they will attribute the conflict that roils the state to a squabble between fundamentalists and mainline Protestants, or a fight between the ignorant and the educated, or even to the Cons' relative newness to modern, big-city ways.[18] But above all it is a class war.

Class animus has been a persistent theme in the Great Backlash since the beginning, when George Wallace railed against liberalism on behalf of the "average man on the street, this man in the textile mill, this man in the steel mill, this barber, the beautician, the policeman on the beat."[19] Class animus has just as persistently been ignored by mainstream observers of the evergrowing conservative movement. The subject of social class is always a disconcerting one for Americans, and most journalists find it simpler to blame the backlash on racism, sexism, or some unfathomable religious conviction than to broach this troubling topic.

The Mods are the worst offenders in this regard. As a rule, they do not admit the possibility that what separates them from the Cons is social class. They will acknowledge a geographic divide, however, separating the older, inner suburbs of Johnson County, where the Mods tend to live, from the newer, outer suburbs, where everyone seems to be pro-life, pro-gun, and anti-evolution. The line between these two suburbias is so stark and so broad that Steve Rose, editor of the *Johnson County Sun* and a de facto leader of the Mods, laments that there are today "two Johnson Counties."[20] One of them is the old familiar sprawl of my childhood, the one with the shady lawns and purring Porsches and schools with high test scores. This is the land of sensible, moderate Republicanism.

Ah, but the other Johnson County, personified by the outer, newer suburb of Olathe, perplexes Rose. This Johnson County is cantankerous and troublesome. It insists on being what he calls "a bastion of right-wing conservatism," and it consistently takes the most outrageous positions on the issues of the day. Rose is unable to use the standard blue-state/red-state narrative to describe the difference between the two Johnson Counties because, of course, both of them voted for Bush. So the source of the split remains a mystery.[21]

When you examine the two Johnson Counties with your own eyes, though, the mystery evaporates instantly. One Johnson County lives in landscaped cul-de-sac communities with statuary in the traffic islands and a swimming pool behind each house and a neighborhood golf course that you occasionally glimpse from between the three-car garages. In this Johnson County, all you see in election years are yard signs cheering for Team Mod. The other Johnson County is a place of peeling paint and cheap plywood construction and knee-high crabgrass and shrubbery dying in the intense heat and expired cars rotting by the curb.

Drive through this Johnson County, and you read nothing but the battle cries of the Cons. The difference between the two Johnson Counties is a class difference.

I mean this in the material, economic sense, not in the tastes-and-values way our punditry defines class. On demographic maps of Johnson County, the hard-core right-wing parts of Olathe and Shawnee stand out for their slightly lower real estate values and lower per capita incomes. Generally speaking, people who live in these neighborhoods are probably more likely to have blue-collar jobs; they are probably less likely to have college degrees; and they probably experience the ups and downs of the business cycle with a greater sense of dread and insecurity than do the lawyers and executives of Mission Hills. Whether people in Olathe and Shawnee have more of a taste for country music or snowmobiles or NASCAR than do the moderate Republicans of the more affluent suburbs, I cannot say.

This much is clear, though, from the elections of the last ten years: those parts of Johnson County with the lowest per capita income and lowest median housing values consistently generated the strongest support for the conservative faction. The areas with the highest income and highest real-estate values—Mission Hills and Leawood—were just as reliably loyal to the moderate machine.[22] The more working-class an area is, the more likely it is to be conservative.

This situation is the opposite of what it was thirty years ago. And it is the complete and utter negation of the Kansas of a hundred years ago, when those in the hardest-hit areas were the most desperate—and the most radical. In Kansas, the political geography of social class has been turned upside down.

When I was a kid and politics was still partially concerned with material issues, Mission Hills was a solid redoubt of conservatism, whereas Shawnee and Olathe were the parts of Johnson County most likely to vote Democratic (admittedly, a rare occurrence under any circumstances).[23] Our neighbors in the seventies liked Ronald Reagan long before Reagan was cool. They were the kind of men who would ax half their workforce before lunch without a second thought. And they still are. If anything, they now preside over a system in which workers have even less power, in which corporate crime is even more brazen.

But the context of politics has changed. So far rightward has the spectrum moved that the people who live in the great mansions around the Frank teardown now find themselves closer to the center. Today they are the financial muscle behind the state's moderate Republican faction. They are not liberals, by any means; they are still far to the right on any issue having to do with taxation or the economy, and they still rally to the national Republican ticket regardless of who is at its head.* They are also the ones who stand to benefit the most when the Cons slash state taxes and agitate for the dismantling of federal regulatory agencies. But by and large the people of Mission Hills support gay rights; they are pro-choice; they accept the separation of church and state.

Moderate Republicanism has a distinct upper-class flavor to it. Mod candidates invariably raise far more in campaign contributions than their conservative rivals. The advisory board of the Mainstream Coalition, the region's foremost Mod organization, is thick with CEOs and other pillars of the community. Its offices are even located next to a golf course, and when I visited them one time, I kept looking up to see people cruising by in golf carts. So upscale is Mainstream's appeal that it once sent out a

---

*The people of Mission Hills chose Bush over Gore by a towering 71 percent to 25 percent. This, despite the fact that many of them drive Volvos and enjoy an occasional latte.

mailing encouraging Mods to "reach out to less-educated and lower-income voters."[24] As it happens, the board of directors of the Community Foundation of Johnson County, the area's leading charitable organization, is packed with prominent Mods. The two groups—Mod and millionaire—interlock on so many levels that for many Kansans they are indistinguishable. When my dad's neighbor has returned from his weekly spin in the Ferrari, he will no doubt be happy to give you a lecture about the virtues of diversity.

The class divide manifests itself in hundreds of ways. Consider the following vignette, described in 1998 for readers of the *Washington Post* by the journalist Thomas Edsall. Bill Graves, the moderate Republican governor of Kansas, heir to a trucking fortune and a resident of Mission Hills, was facing a primary challenge from the leader of the party's conservative faction. Graves was campaigning, if you can call it that, in the comfortable Johnson County offices of Lathrop & Gage, a well-connected Kansas City law firm. Satisfied Republican bonhomie was in the air as the partners gathered in a tenth-floor conference room of one of suburban Overland Park's glass office towers. Then came the buzzkill. A woman stepped forward and announced, to Graves's face, that she wanted him to know she would *not* be voting for him come Election Day. The brave individual who dared harsh the governor's mellow: a secretary, one of the lowly worker-bees in the Johnson County hive. The reason for her decision: abortion. Graves was pro-choice and hence too liberal for her tastes.[25] And that is Kansas for you: a state where the working-class heroes are even more Republican than their bosses.

Dwight Sutherland, Jr., a deeply conservative Mission Hills lawyer and onetime member of the Republican National Committee, is refreshingly direct about all this. "It is a class struggle," he tells me. "The roles have been slightly reversed." Sutherland is a caustic critic of the moderate Republicans. The way he tells the story, the Mods look out at a state where working-class people are flocking to the Republican banner, swarming out of low-caste churches and lying down under cars in front of abortion clinics, and they have reacted with pure shocked snobbishness. "We are the better people," the Mods supposedly think, "and we are entitled to lead this community, and we don't want uppity sorts getting in the way and interfering in the process to ratify our anointed guardians of the public." Sutherland even relates to me several anecdotes of outrageous anti-Con prejudice he has encountered at the Kansas City Country Club, a notorious bastion of privilege.[26] His point is hard to miss: the halls of even the most rarefied enclaves of the plutocracy ring today with the sanctimonious bushwah of political correctness. The primary targets of upper-class bigotry are now blue-collar people, with their funny religions and conservative politics.

This is true across the country, Sutherland says. He gives me photocopies of several pages from one of those coffee-table books depicting the lives and possessions of very rich people in some posh corner of the world. This one is called *Brandywine*, and its object is to adulate the fox-hunting folks of "du Pont–Wyeth Country," the region between Philadelphia and Wilmington, Delaware. The text oozes with a form of upper-class pretentiousness it would be impossible to invent: It introduces a couple who have known each other since childhood, when "they whipped in for the same pack of beagles." Recently the wife became alarmed by some local Christian Coalition activism and decided to get into politics. Surprise: she is "a moderate Republican" who believes in gun control, "women's rights," and "the separation of church and state." Her bland politics, as well as the euphemisms with which they are described,

Sutherland suggests, are as much a product of the family's social position as is their taste for riding to hounds.

The Kansas conservatives like to refer to moderate Republicans as "liberals," and in their struggle with the Mods for control of the Republican Party the Cons imagine that they are confronting a local arm of the fabled "establishment." For them the war is a set piece right out of the works of Ann Coulter or the monologues of Rush Limbaugh: the common people versus a haughty, know-it-all liberal power structure.

The Mods are plenty conservative in their economic views, as noted previously. But they also fulfill the liberal-elite stereotype, if all you consider are the cultural attributes of liberaldom made famous by the good-natured loathing of commentators like David Brooks. There are moderate Kansas Republicans who drink chardonnay and who put Martha's Vineyard stickers on their Saabs. There are Mods who insist on European-style coffee and whole-grain breads and high-end chocolates. There are Mods who shop at Restoration Hardware and Whole Foods and who look down on those who shop at Wal-Mart. There are Mods who listen to NPR and who insist on speaking French to the waitress when at a French restaurant. There are Mods who go to gay-friendly, super-Waspy Episcopal churches and who disapprove of the Patriot Act and who rally in support of immigrant rights. And there are Mods who assume that all working-class whites are racist.

But such people aren't liberal. What they are is corporate. Their habits and opinions owe far more to the standards of courtesy and taste that prevail within the white-collar world than they do to Franklin Roosevelt and the United Mine Workers. We live in a time, after all, when hard-nosed bosses compose awestruck disquisitions on the nature of "change," punk rockers dispense leadership secrets, shallow profundities about authenticity sell luxury cars, tech billionaires build rock 'n' roll museums, management theorists ponder the nature of coolness, and a former lyricist for the Grateful Dead hails the dawn of New Economy capitalism from the heights of Davos. Conservatives may not understand why, but business culture had melded with counterculture for reasons having a geat deal to do with business culture's usual priority—profit.

And as corporate types, these Mods are the primary beneficiaries of the class war that rages against them. Although the Cons vituperate against the high and the mighty, the policies they help enact—deregulating, privatizing—only serve to make the Mods higher and mightier still. And while it may hurt the Mods' feelings to overhear their secretaries referring to them as RINOs, the many rounds of tax cuts the Cons have accomplished have surely made the sting subside. The Mods win even when they lose.

This situation may be paradoxical, but it is also universal. For decades Americans have experienced a populist uprising that only benefits the people it is supposed to be targeting. In Kansas we merely see an extreme version of this mysterious situation. The angry workers, mighty in their numbers, are marching irresistibly against the arrogant. They are shaking their fists at the sons of privilege. They are laughing at the dainty affectations of the Leawood toffs. They are massing at the gates of Mission Hills, hoisting the black flag, and while the millionaires tremble in their mansions, they are bellowing out their terrifying demands. "We are here," they scream, "to cut your taxes."

PART II:

The Fury Which Passeth All Understanding

Chapter Six

Persecuted, Powerless, and Blind

How are we to square all these circles? How is it that the Kansas conservative rebels profess to hate elites but somehow excuse from their fury the corporate world, even when it has so manifestly screwed them? How do they find recruits for an uprising of the common people that only makes the upper crust even crustier than ever? How do they decide that one man is a snob for being rich but that the riches of another show him to be a regular fellow?

At the center of it all is a way of thinking about class that both encourages class hostility of the kind we see in Kansas and simultaneously denies the economic basis of the grievance. Class, conservatives insist, is not really about money or birth or even occupation. It is primarily a matter of *authenticity*, that most valuable cultural commodity. Class is about what one drives and where one shops and how one prays, and only secondarily about the work one does or the income one makes. What makes one a member of the noble proletariat is not work per se, but unpretentiousness, humility, and the rest of the qualities that our punditry claims to spy in the red states that voted for George W. Bush. The nation's producers don't care about unemployment or a dead-end life or a boss who makes five hundred times as much as they do. No. In red land both workers and their bosses are supposed to be united in disgust with those affected college boys at the next table, prattling on about French cheese and villas in Tuscany and the big ideas for running things that they read in books.

This sounds like a complicated maneuver, but it should be quite familiar after all these years. We see it in its most ordinary, run-of-the-mill variety every time we hear a conservative pundit or politician deplore "class warfare"—meaning any talk about the failures of free-market capitalism—and then, seconds later, hear them rail against the "media elite" or the haughty, Volvo-driving "eastern establishment."

We have already caught a whiff of this peculiar way of thinking from the red-state/blue-state literature. The great divide between those parts of the country that voted Republican in 2000 and those bits that voted Democratic, as we have seen, is supposed to have something to do with social class: the producers versus the parasites, the hardworking versus the comfortable, the common people versus the snobs, and so on. The conservative commentator Andrew Sullivan even uses the straightforward term *class war* to describe the face-off between rich liberals and more humble Republicans. But it is a class war in which, as David Brooks puts it, there is "no class resentment or class consciousness." The paradox—a class divide in which class doesn't matter—is repeated virtually without fail through the "two Americas" literature, often only a few sentences after the pundit has finished mocking blue-staters for their fancy cars, or their snob coffee, or their expensive nannies, or their taste in wine.[1]

The key element of this repackaging of class is the notion of a "liberal elite." The idea has taken many forms over the years—

Spiro Agnew called them "nattering nabobs of negativism," the neocons dubbed them "the new class," while others simply refer to them as "intellectuals"—but in its basic outlines the grievance has remained the same. Our culture and our schools and our government, backlashers insist, are controlled by an overeducated ruling class that is contemptuous of the beliefs and practices of the masses of ordinary people. Those who run America, the theory holds, are despicable, self-important show-offs. They are effete, to use a favorite backlash term. They are arrogant.[2] They are snobs. They are liberals.

The idea of a liberal elite is not intellectually robust. It's never been enunciated with anything approaching scholarly rigor, it has been refuted countless times, and it falls apart under any sort of systematic scrutiny.[3]

Yet the idea persists. It did not die with Richard Nixon or peter out with the busing controversy or depart the national scene with the wily Bill Clinton. Indeed, it has greater currency on the street today than do twenty years' worth of blue-ribbon studies and a lifetime of responsible sociology.

Here is G. Gordon Liddy, the celebrated Watergate felon, telling us how it all works in his best-selling 2002 backlash book, *When I Was a Kid, This Was a Free Country*.

> There exists in this country an elite that believes itself entitled to tell the rest of us what we may and may not do—for our own good, of course. These left-of-center, Ivy-educated molders of public opinion are concentrated in the mass news media, the entertainment business, academia, the pundit corps, and the legislative, judicial, and administrative government bureaucracies. Call it the divine right of policy wonks. These people feed on the great American middle class, who do the actual work of this country and make it all happen. They bleed us with

an income tax rate not seen since we were fighting for our lives in the middle of World War II; they charge us top dollar at the box office for movies that assail and undermine the values we are attempting to inculcate in our children.[4]

The same bunch of sneaking intellectuals are responsible for the content of Hollywood movies and for the income tax, by which they steal from the rest of us. They do no useful work, producing nothing but movies and newspaper columns while they free-load on the labor of others. Liberals, in other words, are parasites.

From the mild-mannered David Brooks to the ever-wrathful Ann Coulter, attacks on the personal tastes and pretensions of this stratum of society are the stock-in-trade of conservative writers. They, the conservatives, are the real outsiders, they tell us, gazing with disgust upon the ludicrous manners of the high and the mighty. Or, they tell us, they are rough-and-ready proles, laughing along with us at the efforts of our social "betters" to reform and improve us. That they are often, in fact, people of privilege doing their utmost to boost the fortunes of a political party that is the traditional tool of the privileged is a contradiction that does not trouble them.

The conservatives cast their acid gaze upon college towns in New England, where self-righteous young students flirt intensely with some species of lifestyle experimentation, party away the nights, and consume their special, special lattes. The conservatives laugh derisively at the earnest young vegans of Washington, D.C., two years out of Brown and already lording it over the hardworking people of the vast interior from a desk at the EPA. The conservatives sneer at the child-rearing habits of the hippie set; they quote incredulously from the frothy statements of fashion designers; they rage righteously against the carnival of Ivy

League treason at this year's conclave of the Modern Language Association, always taking the pseudo-radical claims of those Ivy Leaguers—along with the pseudo-radical pronouncements of those fashion designers and those hippies—at face value.

Whatever the target, the conservative social critique always boils down to the same, simple message: liberalism—meaning everything from racy TV to deconstructionists in the Yale French Department—is an affectation of the loathsome rich, as bizarre as their taste for Corgi dogs and extra-virgin olive oil. "That's the whole point of being a liberal: to feel superior to people with less money," seethes the inimitable Coulter.

> Only when you appreciate the powerful driving force of snobbery in the liberals' worldview do all their preposterous counterintuitive arguments make sense. They promote immoral destructive behavior because they are snobs, they embrace criminals because they are snobs, they oppose tax cuts because they are snobs, they adore the environment because they are snobs. Every pernicious idea to come down the pike is instantly embraced by liberals to show how powerful they are. Liberals hate society and want to bring it down to reinforce their sense of invincibility. Secure in the knowledge that their beachfront haciendas will still be standing when the smoke clears, they giddily fiddle with the little people's rules and morals.[5]

Coulter instantiates this thesis about the rich not by opening a copy of *Fortune* or *Cigar Aficionado* but by turning to what's on TV. See, there's all sorts of filth, put there by liberals. We know the liberal elite hate the common people because of what we see on TV, what we read in highbrow modern fiction, all of which can be laid at the doorstep of liberalism. On the other hand, we know that the GOP is the true party of the workers, since the hard-guy Republican Tom DeLay is "more likely to have a beer with a trucker" than the wealthy senator Barbara Boxer of California. We know it because the two social possibilities of American life are mimicking the liberal "beautiful people" of Hollywood or embracing "the working-class hillbillies who go to NASCAR races," that favorite litmus test of the populist right.

Apparently, there is no bad economic turn a conservative cannot do unto his buddy in the working class, as long as cultural solidarity has been cemented over a beer. Ann Coulter's case is instructive. A daughter of the creamy suburb of New Canaan, Connecticut, she grew up in what she describes as a happy right-wing family headed by a corporate lawyer who, in 1985, helped engineer a landmark union decertification (that is, the total destruction of a bargaining unit) for the greater glory of the Phelps Dodge mining interests. This coup was one of the earliest fruits of the anti-union policies of the Reagan administration, which over the years have done so much to shrink the power of organized labor and to rain down blessings on the inhabitants of New Canaan and their upper-bracket brethren across the nation.

Coulter was there at the union-busting creation—"for the union to be going on strike at that point was just absurd," she says[6]—but she insists nonetheless that discussions of *that* aspect of social class are simply a figment of liberal propaganda. To believe that "Democrats are the Party of the People and Republicans the Party of the Powerful" is to embrace a "preposterous conceit," a historical fiction that Coulter simply cannot begin to fathom. In saying this, Coulter is not referring to the cold shoulder that Bill Clinton's New Democrats have turned to the labor movement; like most conservatives, she believes that Clinton was in fact a man of the radical left. Rather, she is trying to construct an entire system of class relations on the observation that the haughty hedonists of Hollywood are largely Democrats. Republicans, on the other hand, drink beer, go to church, and own guns; they are, ipso facto, the true representatives of the common man. Economics simply do not count in her world.

Thanks to its chokehold on the nation's culture, liberalism is thus in power whether its politicians are elected or not; it rules over us even though Republicans have prevailed in six out of the nine presidential elections since 1968; even though Republicans presently control all three branches of government; even though the last of the big-name, forthright liberals of the old school (Humphrey, McGovern, Church, Bayh, Culver, et cetera) either died or went down to defeat in the seventies; and even though no Democratic presidential nominee has called himself a "liberal" since Walter Mondale. Liberalism is beyond politics, a tyrant that dominates our lives in countless ways great and small, and which is virtually incapable of being overthrown.

Conservatism, on the other hand, is the doctrine of the oppressed majority. Conservatism does not defend some established order of things: It accuses; it rants; it points out hypocrisies and gleefully pounces on contradictions. While liberals use their control of the airwaves, newspapers, and schools to persecute average Americans—to ridicule the pious, flatter the shiftless, and indoctrinate the kids with all sorts of permissive nonsense—the Republicans are the party of the disrespected, the downtrodden, the forgotten. They are always the underdog, always in rebellion against a haughty establishment, always rising up from below.

All claims on the right, in other words, advance from victimhood. This is another trick the backlash has picked up from the left. Even though Republicans legislate in the interests of society's most powerful, and even though conservative social critics typically enjoy cushy sinecures at places like the American Enterprise

Institute and the *Wall Street Journal,* they rarely claim to speak on behalf of the wealthy or the winners in the social Darwinist struggle. Just like the leftists of the early twentieth century, they see themselves in revolt against a genteel tradition, rising up against a bankrupt establishment that will tolerate no backtalk.

Conservatism, on the other hand, can *never* be powerful or successful, and backlashers revel in fantasies of their own marginality and persecution. On their Listservs it is not uncommon to read missives in which conservatives greet fellow conservatives with phrases like "fellow rubes of the flyover" or equate themselves with the most hideously victimized people of them all: "Into the ghettos, kids, we're not wanted in polite society." "I'm stupid," writes Blake Hurst in one of his dispatches from Red America to the readers of *The American Enterprise,* "and if you're reading this, you probably are too." An advertisement promotes a recent right-wing best seller with the line "Are You Stupid? The elites think so." And Ann Coulter's *Slander* is, in its essentials, nothing more than a compilation of the many ways over the years that those conceited liberals have sought to insult the people they clearly regard as their mental inferiors.

On the flip side is that all-too-common spectacle of conservatives boasting of their own subversiveness. *Politically Incorrect* is the title of a book by the Christian Coalition leader Ralph Reed; *How to Beat the Democrats and Other Subversive Ideas* is the title of one tossed off by David Horowitz. Conservative columnist John Leo gave his 1994 book the title *Two Steps Ahead of the Thought Police.* Sometimes this straining for insurrectionary language puts the backlashers in some pretty curious company: *Incorrect Thoughts* is both the title of Leo's 2001 book and the title of a 1981 album by the leftist hard-core punk band the Subhumans.

The object of all this breast-beating underdoggery is not to unvictimize the average Americans for whom conservatism claims to speak. While most of us think of politics as a Machi-avellian drama in which actors make alliances and take practical steps to advance their material interests, the backlash is some-thing very different: a crusade in which one's material interests are suspended in favor of vague cultural grievances that are all-important and yet incapable of ever being assuaged.

Even when it is judged on its own terms—as a struggle over values, patriotism, national honor, and the correct way to wor-ship the Almighty—the backlash has pretty much been a com-plete bust.[7] Culturally, it has achieved almost nothing in the past three decades. TV and movies are many times coarser than they were in 1968. Traditional gender roles continue to crumble. Homosexuality is more visible and more accepted than ever. Counterculture has been taken up by Madison Avenue and is today the advertising industry's stock-in-trade, the nonstop revo-lution that moves cereal and cigarettes by the carload.

Nevertheless, the leaders of the backlash—the same canny people, remember, who are responsible for such masterpieces of political strategy as the Florida 2000 election result and the campaign for Social Security privatization—have chosen to wage cultural battles where victory is impossible, where their followers' feelings of powerlessness will be dramatized and their alienation aggravated. Take, for example, the backlash fury-object *du jour* as I write this, the Alabama Ten Command-ments monument, which was erected deliberately to provoke an ACLU lawsuit and which could come to no other possible end than being pried loose and carted away. Or even the great abortion controversy, which mobilizes millions but which can-not be put to rest without a Supreme Court decision overturn-ing *Roe v. Wade*.

As culture war, the backlash was born to lose. Its goal is not to win cultural battles but to take offense, conspicuously, vocally, even flamboyantly. Indignation is the great aesthetic principle of backlash culture; voicing the fury of the imposed-upon is to the backlash what the guitar solo is to heavy metal. Indignation is the privileged emotion, the magic moment that brings a consciousness of rightness and a determination to per-sist. Conservatives often speak of their first bout of indignation as a sort of conversion experience, a quasi-religious revelation. The radio and TV personality Sean Hannity tells readers of his best seller, *Let Freedom Ring: Winning the War of Liberty over Liberalism*, how he first saw the light during the 1986 Iran-Contra hearings, a landmark event in the history of the backlash.

> These hearings had a profound effect on my life. I found myself getting furious at the sight of congressmen and senators excoriating a dedicated patriot like Ollie [North]. I was so riveted by the Iran-Contra hearings that I wouldn't go to work. I'd stay home and watch the hearings all day. I even taped them so I could watch them over again. . . . The more I watched and listened, the angrier I got. And in my search to express my views—to hear a different viewpoint on the subject from what was available on TV—I began calling in to radio talk shows to defend Ollie and beat up on the sanctimonious con-gressmen and senators. . . . And somewhere along the way, I found my calling in life.

The virtuous are persecuted by the "sanctimonious," by the arrogant, by the falsely pious, by the corrupt; for Hannity, it is an epiphany, a revelation of the Christlike nature of the right. Liberals are relativists to whom nothing is sacred and yet, at the same time, omnipotent inquisitors able to call down instant cen-sure on the heads of innocent Americans.[8]

Televised Senate hearings are just the start. *Everything* seems to piss conservatives off, and they react by documenting and cataloging their disgust. The result is what we will call the *plen-T-plaint,* a curious amassing of petty, unrelated beefs with the world. Its purpose is not really to evaluate the hated liberal culture that surrounds us; the plen-T-plaint is a horizontal rather than a vertical mode of criticism, aiming instead to infuriate us with dozens, hundreds, thousands of stories of the many tiny ways the world around us assaults family values, uses obscenities, disrespects parents, foments revolution, and so on. The plen-T-plaint winds us up. It offers no resolution, simply reminding us that we can never win. The plen-T-plaint is the rhetorical device that makes Bill O'Reilly's TV show a hit, as he gets indignant one day about the Insane Clown Posse and gets indignant the next about the Man-Boy Love Association. The plen-T-plaint is the modus operandi for that cyberspace favorite, the political-correctness scoreboard, in which ridiculous examples of liberal intolerance (hypersensitive minorities, discrimination against Christians, silly mascot issues) are heaped up by the thousands.[9]

You see the plen-T-plaint in the author Bernard Goldberg's careful recounting of every personal slight he endured after he commenced his career as a spotter of liberal bias in the news. You see it in the many writers who attempt to tally the exact extent to which TV disrespects the average American, obsessively piling up long lists of fussy objections to nightly newscasts or taking different degrees of offense at petty insults perceived amid the wash of forgotten sitcoms. You see it in the conservative editor R. Emmett Tyrrell's solemn accusation of liberalness against *Bartlett's Familiar Quotations,* a reference volume that, he glowers, has only three entries from Milton Friedman and yet eleven from John Kenneth Galbraith.[10]

The plen-T-plaint achieved a sort of transcendent state of indignation in a 1996 book called *Unlimited Access,* an early anti-Clinton best seller written by a former FBI agent named Gary Aldrich. The book's most spectacular claim—that President Clinton was sneaking out of the White House for nightly trysts in the Washington Marriott—was discredited soon after publication, but this has not dimmed Aldrich's popularity among the backlash rank and file.[11]

The source of Aldrich's continuing appeal to the angry man on the street, I believe, is his hair-trigger irritability with the everyday world. *Unlimited Access* is essentially a long list of minor protocol infractions observed by its impossibly straight-arrow author while he worked in the Clinton White House. Aldrich ticks off the bad manners he notices among the Democrats in the White House cafeteria, taking umbrage at the guy he once saw eating yogurt prior to weighing it on the cafeteria scale. He clucks primly at George Stephanopoulos's messy office and boils at the memory of the Clinton staffers who didn't return his phone calls. He suspects that people are hiding something when they're happy to meet him; he suspects that people are hiding something when they're *un*happy to meet him. Aldrich even passes on a complaint from a fellow officer that Hillary Clinton *looked at him wrong.*

Although it typically describes only the most superficial aspects of American life, the obvious implication of the plen-T-plaint is that liberalism can be held responsible for the world around us, that each of these objections to the way people drive, the way they cut in line, the way they talk with their mouths full, is somehow an indictment of the left. It doesn't matter that liberals have long since lost their power over government; in the backlash mind liberalism is still what changes our mores, what determines what's on TV and in the magazines, what makes (or, rather, interprets) the laws. There is nothing— not the Constitution, not guns, not electoral victories—that can protect us from it or slow it down. It is an alien, conspiratorial force that cannot be held accountable and that does not care when its projects go awry.

Viewed through the eyes of the backlash, liberalism's impositions are so intolerable and so bizarre and taken with so little regard for the sensibilities of the regulated that it will stop at nothing. Who knows what "precedent" the Supreme Court will pull out of its ass next? Or which figure of everyday speech—the word *pet,* the word *wife,* any reference to Christmas—the commissars of political correctness will criminalize, even as they enlarge the list of swear words permissible for broadcast on TV? Backlash culture abounds with tall tales of liberals out of control, with hippies spitting on veterans, with Jane Fonda narking on American POWs to their Vietnamese captors, with OSHA forcing farmers to haul portable outhouses around their acreage for the use of their field hands, with plans for depopulating the Great Plains so that it can be turned into a gigantic national park. Conservative Listservs abound with bizarre speculation about what atrocity the liberals will inflict on us tomorrow, each wild suggestion made and received with complete seriousness. The liberal elite is going to outlaw major league sports. Forbid red meat. Mandate special holidays for transgendered war veterans. Hand our neighborhood over to an Indian tribe. Decree that only gay couples can adopt children. Ban the Bible.

Of course, to believe that liberalism is all-powerful gets conservative lawmakers off the hook for their flagrant failure to make headway in the culture wars, but it also makes for a singularly negative and depressing movement culture. To be a populist conservative is to be a fatalist; to believe in a world where your side will never win; indeed, where your side almost by definition *cannot* win. Where even the most shattering electoral victories turn out to be hollow, and the liberal stranglehold on life can never be broken.[12]

This is a curious set of beliefs for a coalition that quite literally rules American politics. And it only gets worse. Not only do conservatives often lament that their side never wins; according to backlash mythology, even if by some luck they manage to prevail on some question, their victory will quickly be nullified by shadowy liberal machinations.[13] Conservatives are without agency, they imagine, hapless victims adrift in a fatalistic universe where only liberals may act—and where every act undertaken by those liberals is an imposition on the good people of Middle America.[14]

Liberals, for example, are thought by backlashers to enjoy a near-total monopoly over moral condemnation, dropping their H-bomb charges of *racism* and *sexism* on people incapable of responding in kind. Thus, George Gurley, a columnist for the *New York Observer* (and a former columnist for the *Kansas City Star*), recounts the insult he once endured when he revealed his conservatism at a party. He remembers a "hippie girl" who "berated" him for saying he admired Margaret Thatcher: " 'She's a capitalist pig!' she screamed at me. I stammered. Then one of my best friends defended her, saying, 'George, sorry, you got no leg to stand on, man.' I had left the party ashamed, powerless."

Powerless is a curious choice of words here since power is, in reality, what genuine liberals lack and what the Republican Party represents. Yet one cannot deny the feeling: Whereas liberals are thought to erupt self-righteously whenever they feel like it, conservatives believe that they themselves are never permitted to say what they really think. "Tongue Tied" is the name of the online PC scoreboard mentioned above, its hundreds of examples of liberal excess illustrated with a drawing of a gagged face. *None Dare Call It Treason,* screamed the title of an early backlash text. Hell, none dare call it *anything*. No one dares speak the truth, for fear of the awesome retaliatory capacity of liberaldom. The University of Chicago professor Mark

Lilla evokes the feeling well in a sympathetic 1998 summary of conservative thinking.

> It is not that anyone thinks that incivility, promiscuity, drug use, and irresponsibility are good things. But *we have become embarrassed to criticize them* unless we can couch our objections in the legalistic terms of rights, the therapeutic language of self-realization, or the economic jargon of efficiency. The moral condition of the urban poor, romanticized in pop music and advertising, shames us but *we dare not say a word.* Our new explicitness about sex in television and film, and growing indifference to what we euphemistically call "sexual preference," scares the wits out of responsible parents, who see sexual confusion and fear in their children's eyes. But ever since the sixties *they risk ridicule for raising objections* that earlier would have seemed perfectly obvious to everyone. [emphasis added][15]

None of what I have described here would make sense were it not for a critical rhetorical move: the systematic erasure of the economic. Some species of conservative are happy to discuss economics, of course; you can find them any day of the week in the country's management schools or its business magazines, prattling on about the mystical inerrancy of the free market or the benevolence of global capitalism. But most of the conservatives I've been discussing don't say much about the business world at all. With limited exceptions, Hannity, O'Reilly, Coulter, Limbaugh, and Aldrich just don't go there. Liddy pauses briefly to assert that the California electricity disaster of 2001 can be entirely laid at the doorstep of idiotic politicians and then just goes back to griping about crazy environmentalists and the "hysteria" over global warming.

To backlash writers, the operations of business are simply not a legitimate subject of social criticism. In the backlash mind business is natural; it is normal; it is beyond politics. Take the Enron case, for example, the subject of so many rich tales of corporate malfeasance. When Ann Coulter, whirling furiously through her 2002 book about media distortions, momentarily encounters the Enron affair, one of the biggest news items of the year, she simply dismisses the journalism on the subject as obvious evidence of liberal bias, mendacity, corruption, and so on.[16] Enron's bankruptcy was, you will recall, then the largest in history; it brought profound consequences to all corners of the economy; and yet Coulter implies that one would have to be a scheming, lying liberal even to be interested in it.

This makes sense when we recall that the great goal of the backlash is to nurture a cultural class war, and the first step in doing so, as we have seen, is to deny the economic basis of social class. After all, you can hardly deride liberals as society's "elite" or present the GOP as the party of the common man if you acknowledge the existence of the corporate world—the power that creates the nation's real elite, that dominates its real class system, and that wields the Republican Party as its personal political sidearm.

The erasure of the economic is a necessary precondition for most of the basic backlash ideas. It is only possible to think that the news is slanted to the left, for example, if you don't take into account who owns the news organizations and if you never turn your critical powers on that section of the media devoted to business news. The university campus can only be imagined as a place dominated by leftists if you never consider economics departments or business schools. You can believe that conservatives are powerless victims only if you exclude conservatism's basic historical constituency, the business community, from your analysis. Likewise, you can only believe that George W. Bush is a man of the people if you have screened out his family's economic status. Most important, it is possible to understand popular culture as the product of liberalism only if you have blinded yourself to the most fundamental of economic realities, namely, that the networks and movie studios and advertising agencies and publishing houses and record labels are, in fact, commercial enterprises.

Indeed, the economic blindness of backlash conservatism is also a *product*, in large part, of those same commercial cultural enterprises. Conservatives are only able to ignore economics the way they do because they live in a civilization whose highest cultural expressions—movies, advertisements, and sitcoms—have for decades insisted on downplaying the world of work. Conservatives are only able to compartmentalize business as a realm totally separate from politics because the same news media whose "liberal bias" they love to deride has long accepted just such compartmentalization as a basic element of professional journalistic practice.[17]

In some ways, the backlash vision of life is nothing more than an old-fashioned leftist vision of the world with the economics drained out. Where the muckrakers of old faulted *capitalism* for botching this institution and that, the backlash thinkers simply change the script to blame *liberalism*. Until the late sixties, for example, the standard criticism of the press that one heard in America was that newspapers tilted to the right, serving the interests of the capitalists who published them and the capitalists who advertised in them. Today, as everyone knows, it is liberal reporters and liberal editors who are supposed to twist the news to suit their elitist personal preferences. The same treatment has been administered to old critiques of higher education. Where Thorstein Veblen and Upton Sinclair once assailed universities as nothing but upper-class finishing schools, Roger Kimball and

Dinesh D'Souza now damn them for their "tenured radicals" and compulsive anti-Americanism. Old leftist analyses of the legal establishment, the foreign policy establishment, the world of architecture, and the government itself are also stood neatly on their heads, with each institution now said to be a slavish servant—not of The Interests but of liberalism.

Even the rhetoric of the backlash, with all its regular-guy flourishes, sometimes appears to have been lifted whole cloth from the proletarian thirties. The idea that average people are helpless pawns caught in a machine run by the elite comes straight from the vulgar-Marxist copybook, which taught generations of party members that they inhabited a deterministic world where agency was reserved for capitalists—or, more precisely, for capital itself. Or consider the set of accusations against the liberal elite having to do with their unmanliness, their effeteness, their love of things French—all of which we heard so much about during the run-up to the recent war with Iraq.[18] The old-left lineage of this particular backlash stereotype is undeniable. Here is Mike Gold, the two-fisted literary critic for the *Daily Worker,* waging old-school culture war on the religious pretenses of the novelist Thornton Wilder:

> It is that newly fashionable literary religion that centers around Jesus Christ, the First British Gentleman. It is a pastel, pastiche, dilettante religion, without the true neurotic blood and fire, a daydream of homosexual figures in graceful gowns moving archaically among the lilies. It is Anglo-Catholicism, that last refuge of the American literary snob.[19]

Toss in references to the novelist's "devitalized air," his "rootless cosmopolitanism," his familiarity with a "discreet French drawing room," and presto: you've got the latte libel. The Bobos. The establishment. The blue-state elite. The difference, of course, is that Gold attributed these characteristics to the lazy, denatured rich. Aldrich, Brooks, Coulter, Limbaugh, and the rest simply turn the stereotype on liberals.

One problem the old left didn't have was explaining how the world worked: class struggles, they thought, could pretty much account for everything. But drain economics out of the world, and you're left with few tools for explaining anything. Why is our culture the way it is? Why does TV get coarser with each passing year? What makes certain styles or words or ideas suddenly so visible while others disappear? These are matters of dark, bitter obsession among backlash conservatives; they have all been the subject of fairly sophisticated academic inquiry in recent years, and yet the only answer that the backlash can offer is to blame liberalism. Our culture is the way it is because manipulative liberals have decided to make it so.

Backlash books abound with inventive ways of presenting this essentially conspiratorial understanding of culture. R. Emmett Tyrrell, one of the premier intellectuals of the right, chooses literally to becloud the issue. Culture, he says, can be understood as a kind of air pollution, a swirling, shapeless, impenetrable fog of "progressive ideas, noble values, momentous events, and baseless fears that floats over America." Only one thing is certain about this "Kultursmog": liberalism "is the main perpetrator." Liberalism causes culture, and culture, in turn, politicizes every aspect of life.[20] A more sinister formulation is offered by Ayn Rand lieutenant Leonard Peikoff (in a book comparing pre-Reagan America to Nazi Germany that garnered fulsome praise from none other than Alan Greenspan): all the great cultural developments of the early twentieth century, he insists, whether in literature, art, education, philosophy, or journalism, were elements in a political project to remake American life along "progressive," that is, German, lines.[21]

Ann Coulter is, naturally, the worst offender of them all. Her theory of the operations of the media has a bluntness and mechanical determinism about it that would make the *Daily Worker* look subtle. Other conservatives like to talk about "bias" in the news; Coulter prefers sterner phrases like "the opinion cartel" or "the monopoly media." The media isn't just slanted to the left; it's a propaganda tool pure and simple. "Liberals explicitly view the dissemination of news in America," she tells us, "as a vehicle for left-wing indoctrination." And also for left-wing political operations. According to Coulter, the culture industry doesn't just misjudge the outside political world; it is a liberal tool for *controlling* the outside political world, for picking off Republican politicians whenever the opportunity presents. "The media will tolerate any disreputable behavior in order to win," Coulter says. "Principle is nothing to liberals. Winning is everything."

But winning what? What do the liberals want so badly to win? In the old-fashioned critique of the media, of course, the answer was always *money*. What twisted the news was always the power of advertisers, the profit-seeking publishers, the obscene demands of Wall Street.

Such an explanation is unthinkable for Coulter. No. Liberals tell the news and interpret the laws and publish the books and make the movies the way they do not because it sells ads or it pleases the boss or it's cheaper that way; they do it simply because they are liberals, because it helps other liberals, because it promises to convert the world to liberalism.

The truth is that the culture that surrounds us—and that persistently triggers new explosions of backlash outrage—is largely the product of business rationality. It is made by writers and actors, who answer to editors and directors and producers, who answer to senior vice presidents and chief executive officers, who answer to Wall Street bankers, who demand profits above all else. From the megamergers of the media giants to the commercial time-outs during the football game to the plots of the Hollywood movies and to the cyberfantasies of *Wired* and *Fast Company* and *Fortune,* we live in a free-market world.

The Supreme Court doesn't make American culture; neither does Planned Parenthood nor the ACLU. It is business that speaks to us over the TV set, always in the throbbing tones of cultural insurgency, forever shocking the squares, humiliating the pious, queering tradition, and crushing patriarchy. It is because of the market that our TV is such a sharp-tongued insulter of "family values" and such a zealous promoter of every species of social deviance. It is thanks to New Economy capitalism and its cult of novelty and creativity that our bankers glory in referring to themselves as "revolutionaries" and our discount brokerages tell us that owning stock will smash conformity and usher in the rock 'n' roll millennium. We are encouraged to consume Dr Pepper because it will make us more of an individual; to consume Starbucks because it is somehow more authentic; to pierce our navels and ride souped-up Jet Skis and eat Jell-O because these are such "extreme" experiences. Indeed, counterculture is so commercial and so business-friendly today that a school of urban theorists thrives by instructing municipal authorities on the fine points of luring artists, hipsters, gays, and rock bands to their cities on the ground that where these groups go, corporate offices will follow.

Ordinary working-class people are right to hate the culture we live in. They are right to feel that they have no power over it, and to notice that it makes them feel inadequate and stupid. The "Middle Americans," after all, are the people the ads and the sitcoms and the movies warn us against. They are the prudish preacher who forbids dancing, the dullard husband who foolishly consumes Brand X, the racist dad who beats his kids, the square cowboy who is gunned down by the alternative cowboy, the stifling family life we are supposed to want to escape, the hardhat who just doesn't get it.

Conservatives are good at pinpointing and magnifying these small but legitimate cultural grievances. What they are wrong about are the forces that create the problem. Take, for example, the backlash hero Gary Aldrich, who complains in *Unlimited Access* about liberals thinking "it was oppressive to have to wear a tie." Aldrich is correct in noticing that in the nineties there was a movement against formal dress in the white-collar workplace; where he goes wrong is in attributing this change to leftist traitors boring from within. As those who worked in the corporate world remember, the ones pushing this change along were not communists but the hypercapitalist heroes of the New Economy: the "business revolutionaries" who benefited most handsomely from the votes of Aldrich's angry conservative fans. It's not because radicals have secretly taken over the world that people like the intensely anal Aldrich feel so uncomfortable; it's because the new, turbocharged capitalism has no place for hyperorderly, gray-flannel people like him, and it informs him of this every chance it gets. It tweaks a nation of Gary Aldriches in all its signature cultural outlets—in management books, TV commercials, and Tom Peters PowerPoint presentations. Consumer capitalism's only use for such ramrod-straight men is in showing them to be visibly upset by the liberating potential of some Internet portal or corn chip, filming them as they inveigh against some soda pop because it breaks the rules or lets the consumer be an individual or tastes too outrageous or whatever.

But the backlash can never see it that way. Our culture is the way it is simply because liberals have made it so. And this is the logical terminus of backlash reasoning. When you have rejected all the accepted social science methods for understanding the way things work, when you can't talk straight about social class, when you can't acknowledge that free-market forces mightn't always be for the best, when you can't admit the validity of even the most basic historical truths, all you're left with are these blunt tools: journalists and sociologists and historians and musicians and photographers do what they do because they are liberals. And liberals lie. Liberals cheat. Liberals do anything, in fact, that promises to advance their larger partisan project, to create more liberals, and thus to "win." Liberalism is not a *product* of social forces, backlashers believe, it *is* a social force, a juggernaut moving according to a logic all its own, as rigid and mechanical as anything dreamed up by the Stalinists of yesterday.

When the populist right was young and frisky in the late sixties, it developed this understanding of the mechanics of culture as just one among many fronts in the political war. The bias complaint was always factually tenuous, however, and responsible Republicans of the old school never dared to put too much weight on it. Talking about the "liberal media" was safe only as long as it was reserved for filigree around the edges of an occasional campaign speech. To take it more seriously would be to sail off into a world of paranoia and conspiracy theory.

Today conservatism has arrived in that dark place. Even as American journalism lurches palpably to the right, the best-selling right-wing media critics go from shrill to shriller, from charges of "bias" to Coulteresque accusations of outright "left-wing indoctrination." The backlash worldview is less true than ever, and yet conservatives rely on it more and more. It has migrated from the periphery to the very center of the backlash worldview. It is the assertion on which all else rests.

Conservatives have been forced into this position partially by their own success. Clinton is out of the picture, as are labor unions and other troublesome grassroots movements. Right-wingers can hardly blame things on Communists anymore. Business is back in the saddle, taxes are falling, regulations are crumbling, and the very wealthy are enjoying the best years for being very wealthy since the twenties. But the right can't simply declare victory and get out. It must have a haughty and despicable adversary so that its battle on behalf of the humble and victimized can continue. And culture—that infinitely malleable malefactor, upon which any evil design can be projected—is the only plausible oppressor left.

Not only plausible. The existence of profound, all-corrupting liberal cultural influence is an absolute ontological necessity if conservatism is to make any sense.

The Great Backlash began with the coming together of two very different political factions: traditional business Republicans like the Kansas Mods, with their faith in the free market; and working-class "Middle Americans" like the Kansas Cons, who signed on to preserve family values. For the former group, the conservative revival that resulted has been fantastically rewarding, despite the occasional bits of silliness (such as crusades against evolution) that they've had to endure. After all, they are wealthier as a class today than ever before in their lifetimes.

But for the latter group, the aggrieved "Middle Americans," the experience has been a bummer all around. All they have to show for their Republican loyalty are lower wages, more dangerous jobs, dirtier air, a new overlord class that comports itself like King Farouk—and, of course, a crap culture whose moral free fall continues without significant interference from the grandstanding Christers whom they send triumphantly back to Washington every couple of years. By all rights the charm of Republicanism should have worn off for this part of the conservative coalition long ago. After all, how can you lament the shabby state of American life while absolving business of any responsibility for it? How can you complain so bitterly about culture and yet neglect to mention the main factor making culture what it is? How can you reconcile the two clashing halves of the conservative mind?

By believing in bias, that's how. Alone among the many, many businesses of the world, the backlash thinkers insist, the culture industry does not respond to market forces. It does the ugly things that it does because it is honeycombed with robotic, alien liberals, trying to drip their corrosive liberalism into our ears. Liberal bias exists because it *must* exist in order for the rest of contemporary conservatism to be true. As in Saint Anselm's proof of the existence of God, which flummoxed generations of our ancestors, it simply cannot be any other way. Bias has to be; therefore it is.

Few of the writers I have described in this chapter are meticulous or systematic thinkers. Their theories don't hold water; their books are jam-packed with errors and omissions and preposterous interpretations. But backlash readers don't mind; theirs is an intensely personal politics, concerned far more with the frustrations and indignities of everyday life than with scholarly rigor or objective material interests. Backlash thinkers understand this, and they have developed an elaborate theoretical system for generating the politicized anger that is so much in evidence these days and for diverting this resentment from its natural course. By separating class from economics, they have built a Republican-friendly alternative for the disgruntled blue-collar American. Nor is this system really as laughable as I have made it seem. While its proponents might get the facts wrong, they get the subjective experience right. And it is to this subjective experience that we now turn, by examining one person's backlash days in detail: my own.

Chapter Seven

Russia Iran Disco Suck

I have never met Mr. G. Gordon Liddy, the Watergate felon and best-selling author. I am not sure that I would like to. His radio show, to judge by the three or four times I have accidentally tuned it in or been forced to listen by some cabdriver's angry fancy, seethes with bullying bluster of a distinctly paranoid variety. In the mid-nineties, during the brief surge of interest in the far right that followed the Oklahoma City bombing, Liddy became notorious for broadcasting advice on killing federal agents—a line in which, coincidentally, he once found employment himself. Then there is the man's insufferable boasting. In his 2002 book we read about his souped-up cars, the civic awards he has won, the many books he read as a child, the fine schools he attended, the high marks he received, the powerful guns it has been his privilege to fire, and the many remarkable ways in which he has bested other people, both in prison and out. On his book's cover he appears in a civilian sport coat that he has decorated with his paratroopers' wings, presumably so that—in contrast to the unpretentious war heroes whose quiet modesty he likes to celebrate—all who encounter him might know his martial achievements.

I am not a fan. And yet I feel like I know this G. Gordon Liddy. So do you, if you grew up in just about any midwestern city in the seventies or eighties. I recognized him immediately when I saw the cranky refrain that is both the title and the recurring catchphrase of his 2002 book: *When I Was a Kid, This Was a Free Country*. Its theme is simple: Liddy looks around him as he ages and finds that this country is free no longer. This tragic loss of freedom might be invisible to you, but Liddy knows it has happened because he is "a member of the last generation to remember what this country was like when it was free."

What are Liddy's criteria? What distinguishes a free country from an unfree one? Well, in a free country, which was what America was back in the forties when Liddy was little and all was right with the world, a guy could burn leaves if he felt like it. Or he could cut down a tree whenever the urge took him. Or he could shoot birds with his gun, which he could also carry about however he chose. Or he could buy fireworks and dangerous chemicals and blow things up at his leisure. Alas, "these freedoms and more are gone now," victims of a grasping federal government that has smothered the schoolboy paradise of Liddy's childhood.[1]

When *I* was a kid, on the other hand, this was a backlash country. I do not remember the golden age of Liddy's memories, nor do I remember the brief time when America was ruled by honest-to-god liberals. If I went in for Liddy-style self-dramatization, I suppose I could declare that this makes me a member of the first generation not to remember what liberalism really was. Richard Nixon's election, the first great blow to the liberal coalition, took place in 1968, when I was three years old; the book that predicted what would happen for the next thirty-odd years, *The Emerging Republican Majority,* was published when I was four.

In my school days I didn't shoot birds, but I did know adults who thought about the world the way Liddy does. They saw decline and downfall wherever they looked, they expected everything to work out for the worst, and they saw creeping totalitarianism in the most piddling things. They objected to zoning laws. They objected to water fluoridation. They thought the world was ending when the United States left the gold standard for good in 1971. And their anger was endless, implacable, spectacular.

There weren't a lot of these angry men back then, but they made themselves noticed. A suburb a few miles west of Mission Hills actually boasted several landmarks testifying to their particular brand of stubborn bitterness. When this unfortunate town wanted to widen a right-of-way where a guy's garage stood, the fellow adamantly refused to play ball. Eventually, the town just condemned the land and physically sawed his garage in half—after which the guy continued to use the still-standing part, hanging his tools up on the exposed wall of his martyred garage-remnant where everyone could see them as they drove by on the new road. When the same suburb refused to zone another guy's property precisely the way he wanted, he retaliated by filling the lot with the ugliest house he could imagine, a perfectly square plywood box, conspicuously accessorized with tall weeds and a mansard roof apparently made of tarpaper.

The angry men that I knew personally were not aggrieved blue-collar folks, by any means. They were all fairly successful people, self-made men who had done quite well in their fields of accounting or construction or sales—the sort of folks who are supposed to regard American life with a certain satisfaction, not infinite bitterness. And yet something had gone so wildly wrong for them in the sixties—and had stayed so steadfastly wrong ever since—that life had permanently lost its luster. It's not that they had any real material beef with the world. These guys were comfortable and prosperous. But the culture—the everyday environment they lived in—rankled them the way pollen affects someone with hay fever. Their favorite magazines, movie heroes, and politicians would never let them forget it, either, parading before them an ever-swelling cavalcade of grievances: tales of foulmouthed kids, crime in the streets, rabid feminists, out-of-control government agencies, crazy civil rights leaders, obscene art, welfare cheats, foolish professors, and sitcom provocations, each one sending them deeper into the fever swamps of bitterness.

For the politicians who wound them up, all this anger paid off. Over the years they fashioned the never-ebbing mad-as-hellness of a small knot of bitter self-made men into an unstoppable electoral coalition. They rolled from triumph to triumph. And still nothing assuaged the fury of the bitter self-made men. However righteously Reagan might drone, however boldly Bush Senior might pose with the flag or Gingrich snarl at those elitist "McGoverniks," the culture wars they enlisted in were always lost, and the age of polite consensus and public decency that they thought they remembered from their youth slipped ever farther out of reach. "America is back, standing tall," proclaimed the TV commercials for Ronald Reagan in 1984. But for the true Reaganite, America was *never* back; it was *always* betrayed, *every time* those sixties people sneaked in the back door and ruined everything. It never mattered how wealthy the bitter self-made men became or how many times their candidates won; their side always lost in the end. Their way of life was always under siege.

The bitter self-made men thought of themselves as relics of a nobler time. Like Liddy, they believed they were the last people who remembered what America was like before everything went to hell. They were an endangered species, doomed by the passage of time itself. America was in decline; they themselves were getting older; and soon there would be nobody around, they thought, who could recall that robust country of their youth.

What they really were was a vanguard, reaching out to one another across the country. Today bitter self-made men—and their doppelgängers, the bitter but not quite as well-to-do men— are all over the place. They have their own cable news network and their own TV personalities. They can turn to nearly any station on the AM dial to hear their views confirmed. They have their own e-mail bulletin boards, on which you can find hundreds of thousands of them plen-T-plaining about this outrage and that, from the national to the local. And although they like to fancy themselves rugged individualists (better yet, *the last* of the rugged individualists), what they really are is a personality type that our society generates so predictably and in such great numbers that they almost constitute a viable market segment all on their own.

One more thing about the backlash personality type: every single one of the bitter self-made men of my youth was a believer in the power of positive thinking. If you just had a sunny disposish and kept everlastingly at it, they thought, you were bound to succeed. The contradiction between their professed positiveness and their actual negativity about nearly everything never seemed to occur to them. On the contrary; they would oscillate from the one to the other as though the two naturally complemented each other, giving me advice on keeping a positive mental outlook even while raging against the environmentalist bumper stickers on other people's cars or scoffing at Kansas City's latest plan for improving its schools. The world's failure to live up to the impossible promises of the positive-thinking credo did not convince these men of the credo's impracticality, but rather that the world was in a sad state of decline, that it had forsaken the true and correct path.[2] It was as though the fair-play lessons of Jack Armstrong, Frank Merriwell, and the other heroes of their pre-

war boyhood had congealed quite naturally into the world bitterness of their present-day heroes, Charles Bronson, Dirty
Harry, Gordon Liddy, and the tax rebel Howard Jarvis.

For me this connection between the backlash and the idealistic
culture of childhood seems obvious and natural, because for me
backlash *was* the idealistic culture of childhood. Looking at it
today, the backlash sometimes seems like an old man's disorder,
a frustration with adult life compounded by the knowledge that
one's best days are long past—a simple projection of life's
inevitable disappointments on the political culture. For me,
though, backlash was a way of expressing teenage anomie. Like
every middle-class schoolboy, I was earnest and idealistic, but the
objects of my idealism were lost forever in the pre-sixties past. I
believed in national decline and the persecution of the virtuous
and the inevitability of failure the way others believe in progress
or providence: the good were forever under siege by the bad; the
labors of the righteous always went unrewarded; the hardworking were ripped off by the lazy.

For you it may have been the groovy seventies, with bell-
bottoms and Deep Purple and all the dope you could smoke, but
for me it was a time of national shame and honor betrayed; a
fallen decade, a faint shadow of the World War II era, when
(I believed, Liddylike) it had been a truly great time to be a kid. I
listened to the bitter self-made men, and I absorbed it all dutifully. I missed out on *The X-Men,* but I read and reread the more
martial titles in Random House's "Landmark" series, *The Flying
Tigers,* say, or *The Story of the Naval Academy,* books whose
jaunty militarism was only slightly more realistic than such clas-
sics of martial juvenility as *The Boy Allies on the Somme.* I whis-
tled Sousa marches walking down the street. I wrote odes to the
flag and paid special, reverent visits to a park in Olathe, where

retired navy jets sat on pedestals like sculptures. I knew the names of all the ships sunk at Pearl Harbor, and I could identify by silhouette the fighting planes one was likely to see overhead in Britain or Guadalcanal in the early forties.

I pored over books of the racing planes and the skyscrapers and the very rich men of the twenties. I thrilled to the romantic competition between Harvard and Yale at the turn of the century. I marveled at the gigantic houses of the Kansas City gentry, solidly built in the prewar era and utterly beyond the construction skills of the shoddy nineteen seventies.

I was also vexed by the decade's Fonzified entertainment, with its moronic message that life is but a contest between pleasure-denying authority figures and subversive individualists in the John Travolta/Burt Reynolds mold. I firmly believed that our culture could only get progressively trashier; I thought we suffered from vague spiritual disorders like a shortage of heroes; and I was not surprised when the United States was humiliated by Iran. *Of course* the rescue effort failed. America couldn't do anything right anymore.

A fifteen-year-old subscriber to the Boy Scout idealism of fifty years previous, I may have been out of step with my peers, but I was the perfect target audience for Ronald Reagan. Adults, I now believe, should have known better, but to me Reagan made complete sense. Events, for Reagan, arranged themselves unproblematically according to his heroic myths of American life. From his fixed ideas about rugged individualism and the venality of government no amount of fact or history could budge him. "Just as Reagan seems incapable of believing anything good about 'govment,'" wrote Garry Wills in 1987, "he is literally blind to the possibility that businessmen may be anything but high-minded when they lend their services to government," a faith in which Reagan persisted even as one after another of his corporate associates went down for conflicts of interest.[3]

I was the same way. What mattered were the ideals; everyday reality was too degraded to count. For other kids in Kansas this adolescent longing for certainty manifested itself in periodic bursts of piety: One of my friends would go off to summer camp a foulmouthed porn-monger and then come back two weeks later all solemn and confiding and anxious to know whether I'd accepted Christ as my personal savior. I even knew one guy who managed to reconcile his Holy Spiritedness with the traditional vice of high school. When I asked him what he was doing on his summer vacation, he said, "Drinkin' beer. Thinkin 'bout Jesus."

For me the longing, whether beer-fueled or not, was all political. Like the Jesus-questers, I craved the solid rock of certainty, and, also like them, I set about finding it without benefit of history, sociology, theory, or philosophy. I did, however, have what I considered to be the handbook: the U.S. Constitution, which I regarded as being so rich in wisdom that all philosophical conclusions could be drawn from its pages. You still hear every now and then about a group or movement that sincerely believes the Constitution to have been handed down by the Almighty, and I understand the error. As an adolescent, I thought the connection between Constitution and Bible was self-evident: these were the shop manuals to the human condition. They were all you needed to know, the original texts from which everything else could be deduced. While I knew the Constitution to have been the work of man, I also believed that it was a document beyond questioning, somehow above the decade's sneers. Like a baby Bircher, I carried a copy of the thing around with me and remember being honestly troubled for a week or so by the thought that when the earth is consumed by the sun millions of years from now, the original of that sacred document would be destroyed.

While the Constitution was writ in stone, it occurred to me that what had brought on the problems of the seventies—by which I mean our much-discussed cultural "malaise" as well as the taxes and regulation of which the bitter men always complained—were artifice and meddling and human error. Our politics, I figured, had become as inauthentic as our culture, with its plastic and its refined sugar and its shoddy suburban buildings. The nation had departed from the course clearly indicated by God and nature, otherwise known as free-market capitalism. We had gotten above ourselves. We were prideful. We were playing God.

Amping up all this adolescent political conviction was my feeling that we in the late seventies were living in some political equivalent of biblical end times. There was more to this presentiment than the millenarian religious stew in which Kansas City always simmers. Recall for a moment the distinct sense of terminal crisis, of things coming apart, in the culture of those years: the endless hostage situation, the powerless president with his somber pessimism, the gasoline shortage, the crumbling cities, and, of course, the deliberately apocalyptic imagery of punk rock, which we in KC only knew from scaremongering news items. In 1979 the bitter self-made men were hoarding gold and reading *How to Prosper During the Coming Bad Years,* a personal-finance best seller as recklessly gloomy as the best sellers of the nineties were senselessly optimistic. For a kid who had been raised on tales of the GI generation's heroic accomplishments, it was obvious that our civilization was in decay, that we had gotten too far away from the natural order of things. As anyone could see from the movies, America was rotten with sycophants and dope and processed foods and entire classes of public hangers-on. The tyranny of fashion required the city's entire population of fifteen-year-old boys to dress like sexually troubled middle-aged swingers, carefully shaping the feathered hairdos that made 90 percent of us look like fools. We were clearly approaching the end.

In this climate I undertook my first literary effort. It was 1980, my first year at Shawnee Mission East high school and my first year on the debate team, and I wrote what was called in debate circles a "dis-ad"—a "disadvantage" broad enough that, with a little ingenuity, you could tie it onto any proposal you were charged with refuting. On a beautiful late-summer day, I sat me down in the placid, wooded Mission Hills yard of the house not yet known as the teardown and pieced together quotes from *Reader's Digest* and *Vital Speeches of the Day* into a thundering denunciation of "creeping government regulation." In the heat of the debate rounds themselves I would read this mini-oration to "prove" that whether it was a stronger FTC our opponents were calling for or a ban on beer commercials, they were advancing an agenda that would eventually result in the destruction of freedom itself.

I didn't know much about the writing of dis-ads then. Later in my debate career I learned that any argument worth its salt had to end with the other team's plan somehow precipitating a nuclear war, or "nukewar" as we casually referred to it. I had also padded the regulation dis-ad with lots of Buckleyesque rhetorical turns, when all anyone cared about was the number of quotes you marshaled, not how elegantly you evoked the sentiments of 1776. Still, I delivered this early effort with the conviction of the true believer, imagining myself traveling the trail blazed by my hero Ronald Reagan, who had spent years giving a single speech that made the same antigovernment point. Even though debaters are required to take both sides of every issue, I fancied myself an ideological warrior. My debate partner and I would stand in front of a wall-sized mirror in the dining room of my dad's house, tying and retying our ties to more closely resemble the one worn by Herbert Hoover in a picture that we fancied, then heading off in the family Oldsmobile, Led Zeppelin blaring, to tear the liberal world apart.

Here is the oddest part of this story of adolescent conservatism. Had you asked me or any of the bitter self-made men what manner of political movement it was that we were part of, we would have replied, without hesitation, that it was a movement of "average Americans" or even the "working class." Not that I knew anything about the working class per se in those days—at Shawnee Mission East high school, a well-funded suburban institution famous locally for producing large numbers of National Merit Scholars, finding out about the labor movement was simply not on the agenda. The bitter self-made men hated unions, considered them criminal organizations, and that was good enough for me.

Like everything else I believed in those days, this fantasy of working-classness was strictly theoretical. I had arrived at it by deduction. Businessmen were the working class, I reasoned, because they worked to earn their living. They were the producers. They paid the taxes; they built the buildings; they bought the cars. Businessmen were average, authentic people by definition, since they accounted for all the adults I knew. Government, on the other hand, lived by imposing taxation. It produced nothing; it interfered with real people's business and then arrogantly handed out their hard-earned money to a population of parasites. This, then, was the conflict: Workers versus government. Producers versus parasites. Nature versus artifice. Humility versus pride. The swaggering personal habits of the bitter self-made men only confirmed my adolescent understanding of the social order. Riding a BMW motorcycle without a helmet, taking no shit from the police, drinking Wild Turkey at all hours of the day, carrying a .45 automatic tucked into their waistband—if that wasn't working class, what was?

I knew of no actual blue-collar types who agreed with my take on the world, but like some present-day pundit pondering the majesty of the red states, I could deduce their existence as well. For example, there was a viaduct in a poor neighborhood of Kansas City, Kansas, on which someone had spray-painted

"Russia Iran Disco Suck." Driving underneath it on my way to and from a debate tournament one day, I gloried in the succinct eloquence of this bit of proletarian wisdom. The logic was flawless. As sucked disco, so sucked communism. So sucked Iran. Even more inspiring was the unspoken corollary: as rocked Van Halen, so rocked Ronald Reagan.

Similarly, I thought of western Kansas, a place I then knew only as a landscape seen from a car going seventy, as a sort of Holy Land of working-class naturalness and authenticity. In my imagination I peopled it with all sorts of righteous Jeffersonian yeomen, and I wrote stories for school in which self-reliant farmers on the High Plains were the last holdouts against the whining, welfare-addicted culture of the big cities. I developed elaborate mental pictures of towns I had never visited, imagining places like Great Bend to be filled with tidy, prosperous shops and quiet, rustic Hemingway types, stoically enduring their round of toil on the banks of the romantic Arkansas so that all of the undeserving city people could freeload through life.

At some point in my high school days, one of my debate colleagues, a kid from a less exalted part of Johnson County, told me he planned to be a Democrat in his upcoming political career (all debaters imagine themselves as future politicians) because that was the party of the working class, and there would always be more workers than there were rich people. After all these years I remember the moment he said this with the perfect, frozen clarity that the brain reserves for great shocks: Pearl Harbor, 9/11. The idea stunned me. Class conflict between workers and businessmen? Could this be true? The thought had simply never occurred to me before.

Many years after he made his name fighting Populism and writing his pro-business editorials for small-town Kansas newspapers,

William Allen White looked back and saw in his earlier, conservative self "a young fool," a cocksure lad who never suspected that his political ideas were derived more from his fortunate social position than from reason and learning. While the world of the 1890s burned, he clucked primly and corrected readers with wisdom he had picked up from his college economics textbook. "Being what I was, a child of the governing classes," he wrote in his *Autobiography,* "I was blinded by my birthright!"

An even more telling side of that blindness was the way White spent his leisure time in those days. When not writing his editorials, designed either to puff Kansas business or elect the Republican ticket, he would pass the time composing "dialect verse,"

> trying to portray the heart of a sturdy peasantry, though I did not recognize it as peasantry. My dialect verse was supposed to reflect the colloquial idiom of midwestern middle-class people, presumably well-to-do and substantial farmers, out of New England by the Ohio Valley. In my rhymes was no touch of the wide sense of rancor in the hearts of those people which was . . . manifesting itself in the elections of the day. One would have thought, from reading that verse, that the Kansas people were all prosperous, contented, emotional, smug, and fundamentally happy. As a poet, I was deaf to the cries of a bewildered people as I was blind in politics.[4]

Scion of the state's ruling class, the young Will White wrote dreamy pastoral poems extolling the cultural authenticity of an imaginary Kansas peasantry even as actual Kansas farmers went to the wall all around him—even as White himself scolded those actual Kansans for not playing by the economic rules he had just learned in college!

My own authenticity-rich daydreams about the sturdy peasants of western Kansas never moved me to write sonnets, thank goodness. Otherwise, however, it was as though I was following White's script to the letter. The theories of the universe that I developed so painstakingly in the seventies and eighties were but fantasies that arose directly from my peculiar perch in life. Here was I, a Mission Hills lad, growing up in one of the perfect regional arcadias of American capitalism, a place more like the grounds of Versailles than the average postwar suburb, and what I had managed to do was invent a romantic justification for precisely the system of social arrangements that had made Mission Hills possible. I had laboriously reinvented the wheel of laissez-faire thought, deciphered it painstakingly from the world around me, re-created the first principles of capitalist society by close observation of capitalist institutions, and had all the while imagined that what I was actually doing was discovering the timeless laws of nature and all human society.

A humble mid-American yeomanry, pure of heart and free of class resentment, giving the existing social order their plebeian imprimatur; it is an endlessly recurring dream of the ruling class. From Marie Antoinette to today's panegyrists of the red states, conservatives love populism in theory, always imagining super-authentic working people as witnesses to nature's endorsement of their privileges. Our intellectual universe is crowded today with unreconstructed Will Whites. From Fox News and the Hoover Institute and every newspaper in the land they sing the praises of the working man's red-state virtues even while they pummel the working man's economic chances with outsourcing, new overtime rules, lousy health insurance, and coercive new management techniques.

William Allen White eventually yielded to the great wave of history that Populism anticipated, doing an about-face and becoming a prominent progressive, as well as one of the most honored journalists of the twentieth century. But hardly anybody moves from right to left today. The volcanic social forces that so altered White's world are spent now, and for a rising journalist or protopundit to choose to side with the left for reasons of conscience would be to choose to step off a career cliff.

Besides, who needs to? Today Will White's pastoral fantasies are reality. Today there is no shame in writing conservative editorials by day and pseudoproletarian authenticity-elegies by night, because today so many of the proletarian bearers of authenticity are, in fact, allies of the onrushing conservative juggernaut. There is no contradiction to embarrass one. No radical farmers or hardened kids from blue-collar homes are likely to shatter the illusion with a brusque word. The sturdy yeomen really *are* providing their imprimatur to the existing social order. And our entire punditry is writing those poems.

It is not my intention to dismiss all the conservatism of my adolescence as a juvenile mania or to brush these ideas aside as though they were transparently preposterous, determined by my privileged place in the world. On the contrary; these were strong ideas, a compelling way of looking at the world. They have many millions of adherents, drawn from all different walks of life.

Consider the father of a friend of mine. He wasn't nearly as successful as the rest of the bitter self-made men, but from tax revolt to gold standard he shared their views nonetheless. In fact, he believed in the social arrangements of capitalism regardless of what capitalism did to him. Naturally, he was a positive thinker, and in his ability to overlook the world's cruelty and focus exclusively on reforming himself he embodied what the historian

Donald Meyer has called the "social anesthetic" side of positive thinking.[5]

His family had come through the Great Depression in Kansas City, Missouri, scraping along in the kind of poverty that middle-class people can't really envision anymore. This required pluck and heroism, no doubt, but the thirties aren't a time that many people remember through Horatio Alger lenses. Except for him. In a city that was then turning out 75 percent majorities for Democratic candidates, his family remained steadfastly Republican, voting like the people they wanted to be rather than the people they were. He had the campaign pins to prove it, too: "Landon" in the center of a cheerful Kansas sunflower, emblem of the idealist's ability to paper over economic hardship in even the worst of times. Once he avowed, in response to some leftism that had come up, that the captains of American industry were "Christian gentlemen" (a phrase typical of positive thinking)[6] who would never commit the sort of crimes that had been suggested.

In his student days at the University of Kansas, my friend's dad wasn't in a fraternity. The fraternities held immense social power in those days at KU—one of my friends used to refer to them as a "sex cartel"—and they acted the part. Not only were their members selected from the uppermost strata of the state's elite—you know the routine: the rich kids, the athletes, the politicians' sons, the fellows with clear blue eyes and square jaws—but average students weren't even given the opportunity to compete with them. Pledges were chosen while they were still in high school; once the college year started, the frats didn't bother hosting open functions to meet anyone else. In the frat boys' view of the universe, a gawky, religious street kid from Kansas City like my friend's dad was nothing more than an irritant, one of those air-breathing obstacles who clogged the sidewalks but who otherwise did not exist in their unfolding adventure of conquest and connections. They had nothing but contempt for *him,* but my friend's dad believed in *them* nonetheless. In his eyes they represented the dazzling pinnacle of youth's possibilities, and he urged my friend and me to be *like* the frat boys, even if we couldn't actually arrange to join their ranks.

These are not peculiar views, by any means. The peculiar thing was me. When I finally did go off to college, my reaction was precisely the opposite.

I finally learned about social class. Growing up in the Edenic preserves the local elite had fashioned for themselves had anesthetized me to the system that made them an elite in the first place. I honestly thought that Mission Hills, with its castellated palazzi, was normal and that other places were the aberration. I played with the tots of millionaires and convinced myself that America was a classless society, where all that mattered was ability and one's willingness to work.

The summer after high school I was not offered a cushy summer job at a downtown law firm or a prestigious local bank, as were other boys I knew. The world showed no interest in my skills, such as they were, or in my idealistic faith in the fairness of capitalism. Instead I did temp work in offices around Kansas City, often assigned to tasks that seemed designed to show me the round of boredom and frustration that is most people's lot in life. At one firm where I worked, the only person who understood computers (this was 1983) was on vacation; they actually hired me to duplicate a computer printout on a typewriter, hammering out slightly changing five-digit numbers all day long for weeks.

To make it worse, I did not win a spot at some highly selective eastern college, as many of the other kids from Mission Hills did. I did not understand what had caused me to be sifted one way and them the other; I just took myself dutifully off to KU, which had open admissions for all.

At KU my former friends were channeled by some unseen

hand into the various fraternities. I was not. The frats' differing levels of exclusivity meant that some of my friends would still talk to me when I caught sight of them on campus. The ones who had landed a berth in the upper reaches of the sex cartel would not. They were too dedicated to their new project of mimicking the precise habits of the state's political and financial masters. Which is not to say that KU frat boys were Christian gentlemen or superclean, buttoned-down WASPs. On the contrary. They saw their beau ideal in *Animal House:* they were the dominant class, but a dominant class with its middle finger in the air to the world, brawling, cheating, getting down to wretched eighties rock, drinking, and puking.

Meetings of the College Republicans, which I attended for a short while, only reinforced the impression of cliquishness. The leadership had all been chosen, it seemed, by some mysterious process to which the rank and file was not privy. Maybe I just missed the election; I don't remember. At any rate, the leaders all knew one another, they were all such great friends, and they made no effort to disguise their oozing insincerity. They revolted me. The sole purpose of the organization, I quickly understood, was to groom likely prospects for positions in Kansas's Republican machine. There was about as much idealism among these governors- and congressmen-to-be as there was on the slick-tongued high school debate teams that I had recently been accustomed to demolishing.

These complaints are of course small beer by the usual standards of oppression and unfairness. I was never beaten for trying to vote or shot at for walking off the job. But these developments were nonetheless sufficient to awaken me to the existence of class, of the elite. Also to the startling fact that I was not part of it. The Franks may have lived near them, but I could no more choose to join them at their well-appointed table (to return to David Brooks's cafeteria metaphor) than I could flap my arms and fly to the moon. I had about as much of a stake in the order that propped up Mission Hills, I now realized, as did the Section Eight residents in decrepit midtown Kansas City, shuffling along the street muttering curses to themselves.

So I did a very un-Kansan thing: I started voting Democratic. And then I did something that, I have since found, was utterly typical of my generation of college-educated Kansans: I left.

Chapter Eight

Happy Captives

I am not the only one to be repulsed by Kansas City's "close-knit business community" or to penetrate the sweet pink lies that cover Cupcake Land. But I may well be the only one among my peers who turned to the *left* out of disgust with the place. Out here, remember, the gravity of discontent pulls to the right, to the right, farther to the right. The standard reaction in Kansas to the vulgar machinations of the state's self-perpetuating ruling class, to its cronyism and its brazen flaunting of its wealth, to its business scandals and the grinding destruction of the farm communities, is to push ever deeper into the alienated right-wing world of the culture wars.

This happens, I believe, because the conservative movement, while saying little about the material problems that plague us, nevertheless presents Kansans with an attractive and even a seductive way of dealing with an unfair universe. The backlash is a theory of how the political world works, but it also provides a ready-made identity in which the glamor of authenticity, combined with the narcisissm of victimhood, is available to almost anyone. *You're the salt of the earth, the beating heart of America,* the backlash tells all those cranky suburbanites who tune in to Fox News; *and yet you are unfairly and outrageously persecuted.* But now they, too, can enjoy the instant righteousness that is flaunted by every other aggrieved group.

The backlash is about individual identity, and so it is to individuals that we now turn, to the people who traffic in the curious cultural goods that make up the Kansas conservative mind-set. By this I mean both the people who generate the backlash fantasies and the people who consume them, who find this ready-made identity so compelling that they have internalized it, made it their own, shaped themselves according to its attractive and uniquely American understanding of authenticity and victimhood.

John D. Altevogt, a former county GOP chairman who achieved local notoriety when he was given a column in the *Kansas City Star,* is a one-man symphony of indignation, a composer of rhapsodic rages as well as dark dirges of self-pity, all of them orchestrated around a single, favorite note that he pounds again and again. Religious conservatives, he argues, asserts, hollers, and wails, are the victims of unspeakable persecution by the ruling class, that is, by liberals.

The key word in Altevogt's vocabulary of victimology is *hate:* the moderate Mainstream Coalition, he absurdly insists, is in fact a "hate group" that is "refocusing the area's previous . . . hatred of Jews and blacks onto the growing evangelical Christian political movement." Mainstream's founder, the Reverend Robert Meneilly, he mocks as Kansas City's "Ian Paisley," the notorious Ulster Protestant leader who has, as Altevogt puts it, "fomented religious strife to keep working class folks from focusing their angst on their real oppressors." Which is to say, on liberals.[1] The news media, though, is Altevogt's favorite target, and he has singled out a Topeka-based reporter (as it happens, a particularly good reporter) as "the most biased and hateful reporter in the state of Kansas" and ridiculed the *Topeka Capital-Journal* as "The *Klan Journal*," "one of Kansas' most bigoted and unprofessional newspapers" because "its writers routinely referred to people of faith as 'wingnuts.'" And when a series of embarrassing news stories and legal setbacks befall one of his favorite Kansas Cons, Altevogt declares that it all reminds him of "the lynch mobs we used to see back when black folks were accused of being too uppity."[2]

This is preposterous stuff, and by all rights it should be an embarrassment to the conservative cause. Yet Kansas Cons I talked to regard Altevogt as an inspiration. By spinning his lurid fantasies of victimhood, he makes a valuable contribution to the movement, providing its followers with a basic therapeutic good. Understanding themselves as victims besieged by a hateful world absolves conservatives of responsibility for what goes on around them. It excuses them for their failures; it justifies the most irresponsible rages; and it allows them, both in politics and in private life, to resolve disputes by pointing their fingers at the outside world and blaming it all on a depraved liberal elite.

In setting up this vision of a hostile world, Altevogt draws heavily on the language of the other side. Once upon a time, protecting the victims of bigotry and directing the anger of the working class onto their real oppressors were qualities associated with the left. They were what gave the left its purpose, its righteousness, its sense of juggernaut inevitability. And that is why backlash leaders work so hard to claim these qualities for themselves, swiping leftist ideas and phrases wherever they can. Altevogt himself does this quite consciously. Commenting on a news story about the squabble in the Anglican Church over homosexual marriages, he writes: "All of the rhetoric of the sixties comes alive describing our totalitarian liberal establishment. Fascist pig, baby killers, sick society, it's all applicable. What we need to do now is change it by any means necessary. Power to the people."[3]

Dwight Sutherland, Jr., the Kansas City brahmin mentioned previously, also uses the analytical framework of the left, but in a far more measured and thoughtful way, employing it to decipher the denatured cupcake Republicanism of his wealthy neighbors in Mission Hills. When I talk to him, he inveighs against "wedge issues," deploring the way abortion, gun control, and evolution have been used to manipulate voters. But he means this in precisely the opposite of the usual way. For Sutherland "wedge issues" aren't a Republican strategy to split off parts of the New Deal coalition, but a moderate and maybe even a Democratic strategy to keep conservatives in check, to split working-class conservatives from the upper-middle-class conservatives who ought to be their allies. "They cynically play these social issues to scare the soccer mommies with guns," Sutherland tells me, "scare the Jewish community with the bugaboo of the religious right, scare the suburban ladies that Planned Parenthood is going to be shut down, when there's no chance that any of these [conservative] people, even if it was their fondest desire, could overturn *Roe v. Wade*."

It's all sham battles and empty culture-war issues, distracting the rich from their real concerns. It is even "false consciousness." In using this Marxist term, the archconservative Sutherland is not referring to workers being tricked by some misguided fear of black people into ignoring their interests and voting Republican, but to wealthy people being tricked by some misguided fear of the religious right into ignoring their interests and voting Democratic. "A friend of mine who's a multimillionaire," he says, "told me in all seriousness that he couldn't vote for [George H. W.] Bush's reelection because Bush was less than committed to a woman's right to choose. Of course in '93 this guy's taxes go up, hundreds and hundreds of thousands of dollars, and he's screaming and yelling about Clinton and the Democrats, and I said, 'Yeah, but you made the symbolic choice and repudiated those nasty pro-lifers, and that's worth it in psychic income alone.' "

All the contradictions come together in the person of Jack Cashill, a Kansas City media figure possessed of a felicitous prose style and an astonishing array of political interests. Anyone trying to understand the Kansas mind-set comes across the man repeatedly. I have sat in the audience while Cashill gave a rousing lecture to an anti-evolution conference. I have seen him propose a grandiose anti-abortion scheme at a Republican gathering. I have watched funny TV commercials made by him for a Kansas conservative candidate. I have listened to his talk show on a Kansas City radio station. I have followed his sleuthing through the mystery surrounding the 1996 crash of TWA Flight 800. I have even read a dystopian novel he wrote about armed rebellion against the creeping liberal tyranny.

But above all else, Cashill is a class warrior, fond of telling stories from his own working-class childhood and heaping scorn on the precious affectations of Kansas City's Johnson County overlords. He derides Cupcake Land's cars and its clothes and its shrubbery and the names of its subdivisions and its compulsive fear of East Coast disapproval and its lemminglike tastes in consumer goods. And he does it well.

What's peculiar is that he does most of this bourgeoisie-baiting from his perch as the executive editor of *Ingram's,* the local business magazine. Does this mean that *Ingram's* is a crusading business magazine, like Dwight Macdonald's *Fortune,* sniffing out local Enrons before they explode? On the contrary; it is in fact a run-of-the-mill booster sheet, offering "Forty Under Forty" lists and plans for how KC can position itself for this or that future windfall. Its most notable innovation is the aforementioned annual feature, "The Power Elite," which is startling in its forthright sycophancy. The same Jack Cashill who loves to mock upper-middle-class etiquette usually writes it.

So how does one go from criticizing privilege to fawning over a region's business leaders? How do you square your concern for the downtrodden with a drooling admiration for the very rich?

Cashill makes it look easy. He gives us beaten-down workers, sweating their hopeless lives away, and caricatures of the effete, dandified rich worthy of the *New Masses*. Then comes the sleight of hand: the exploiting parties who eventually suffer the well-deserved payback are not capitalists; they are liberals.

Cashill's great ability, I think, is as a builder of theoretical systems. One source of conservatism's considerable power, as noted, is its airtight explanation of reality, its ability to make sense of the average person's disgruntlement while exempting laissez-faire capitalism from any culpability. The backlash narrative lets us feel brave when we grumble about offensive TV and patriotic when we complain about liberals ruining this aspect of life or that. It brings us together—management and labor, Protestant and Catholic, black and white—in mutual outrage against a common enemy. Not only does Jack Cashill apply this framework skillfully to local circumstances; he also develops schemes for taking the offensive, plans whereby people from every walk of life can play a valiant and fulfilling part in the backlash drama.[4]

In one of his better essays Cashill proposes that the real divide in America is between "the Consensus," the polite, superior people from Mission Hills to the Ivy League; and the "Snake-handlers," the abortion-protesting fundies who "wonder why tax dollars cannot be used for a nativity scene, but can be used to underwrite works like *Piss Christ.*" Although fewer in numbers, the Consensus is the ruling class; it always thinks it knows better; it shakes its head disapprovingly at the God-happy hillbillies of the hinterland and does its best to instruct them in proper, sensitive behavior. The Snake-handlers—a.k.a. Red America, Middle America, et cetera—are we the governed.[5]

Push the analogy just a little further, and we are *all* despised Snake-handlers, rich and poor alike under the thumb of liberal know-it-alls from the East Coast. Here is Cashill summing up "federal power" over Kansas City in an installment of "the Power Elite":

> Not since the reconstruction has one area seen so much of it. The federal government is the area's largest employer. It runs the area's biggest school district and its biggest housing authority and regulates everything else. Federal power destroyed the mercantile empire of arguably the city's foremost power broker . . . , and sent the man who would be governor . . . to jail. Scarier still, its force is almost entirely beyond citizen control, and its enforcers beyond recall.[6]

That was in 1994, after only two years of Democratic administration in Washington. We here in the Midwest were said to be living under an imposed federal regime that we were unable to question and powerless to control. Like the vanquished Confederacy under Reconstruction, we were a conquered people.

After six more years of Clinton and company, Cashill was ready to go much, much further. Now he looked into his crystal ball and produced *2006*, a novel in which America is enduring the second term of the Al Gore presidency and the common people lie prostrate beneath the iron heel of liberalism. The old-school Populists were fond of a novel called *Caesar's Column*, a vision of a hideous future in which nineteenth-century capitalism had expanded without restriction. And Cashill gives us the contemporary equivalent: a vision of a hideous future in which all the elements of the conservative persecution fantasy have flowered just as grotesquely. The government has forced Rush Limbaugh off the airwaves, Supreme Court justice Antonin Scalia has been assassinated,* and SUVs are no longer being manufactured. Runaway trial lawyers have destroyed the tobacco industry, and the wineries are next. Laws against "hate crimes" are being used to punish ordinary speech, motorcycle riders have to wear helmets, as do Amish factory workers, and jack-booted federal thugs dispense stiff jail sentences to patriotic Americans. It's what the world would look like if some evil sorcerer made reality conform to the op-ed page of the *Wall Street Journal*.

So anyhow, Cashill's protagonists—a bunch of Latin-mass Catholics, Indians, and gun fanciers, all led by a sportswriter—form a militia, stage a heroic rebellion, and capture several of the nation's most ee-vill liberals. One of these soulless creatures has to be shot, and a special South African gun for which considerable admiration has been expressed gets to do the honors. Before its steely Boer chastisement, this liberal scoundrel, his body as hollow and corrupt as his politics, simply flies to pieces.

In Cashill's world the plen-T-plaint is fully elaborated, taken to grand conclusions and literary heights. The tyrannical impulses Aldrich suspected liberals of harboring when he saw them wolfing yogurt in the White House cafeteria blossom here into a full-blown system. Even the tiniest things *do* have great political significance, and everything you thought *might* be true

---

*This element of the conservative victim-fantasy is particularly ironic given that the only Supreme Court justice to have been the target of what may or may not have been an assassination attempt in recent years was Harry Blackmun, the author of *Roe v. Wade*, in 1985.[7]

actually is. Everything fits the pattern. And everything has a lesson to teach us about the perfidy of the state and those who believe in it. The crash of TWA Flight 800 couldn't simply be an unsolved mystery; the Clinton administration must have ordered a "politically motivated" cover-up, which the media then dutifully accepted because of their loathing of the right.[8] And the Republicans of Johnson County couldn't have any good reason to disdain the conservative faction. No, they must have been manipulated by a secretive former communist.[9]

Even the most ordinary events now have an explanation. When Cashill finds that his daughter's friends don't know who Benedict Arnold is, he erupts about the "betrayal" of American students, insisting that "the question we have to ask ourselves is whether the betrayal is by accident . . . or by design." Since it's obviously the latter, "we need to identify these Benedict Arnolds in our midst and, at a minimum, reeducate them." And when Cashill gets two traffic tickets in a single day, the conspiracy has come dangerously close to exposing itself. "This was beginning to seem like a pattern," he writes. He graciously declines to blame the ticket-writing officer himself, as his own dad had been a cop once. "But if this wasn't his idea, just whose was it?"[10]

After which, it's back to the usual fare for a regional business magazine: marveling at the "power" possessed by some suburban developer or the ingenuity of some local entrepreneur. When markets flex their muscles, it is productive, organic, democratic; when government know-it-alls take the wheel, power becomes destructive, top-down, arbitrary, and tyrannical.

I caught my own first whiff of the weird class animus that drives Kansas politics as I sat down one brilliant summer morning at the breakfast table of the teardown and commenced reading the *Johnson County Sun*. Steve Rose, the Mod chieftain, had devoted his usual page-one editorial to denouncing some character named Tim Golba, who was evidently causing inexcusable problems for the moderate faction of the local Republican Party. Now, Steve Rose is a well-known character in these parts. He inhabits one of the stateliest Mission Hills homes of them all, an Italianate palazzo with a clay-tiled roof. But who was Tim Golba? Then I read the rest of the story. This monster Golba, whom Rose described as "brilliant" and "cunning" and leaving his "imprint . . . all over Kansas," was in fact "a worker at the Pepsi bottling plant in Olathe"—Olathe being the suburb Rose had identified previously as the *other* Johnson County, the fever-swamp of the conservative revolt.[11] I called Golba up; he answered his own phone. What kind of work did he do at the bottling plant? Just regular line work, he told me. A curious day job, I thought, for a man who bosses the entire state.

The block Tim Golba lives on is a tidy row of simple suburban homes built in the seventies, hardly what you would expect for a man who bears as much responsibility as anyone for the conservative revolution in Kansas. It's the sort of neighborhood that hasn't aged too well: The houses all hew to the same general design, with only a few cheap ornamental features—fake balconies, plywood fleurs-de-lis—to dress up the box and distinguish one from another. There are few trees, and on summer days like the one when I paid my visit, the sun pounds the wood-shingled roofs relentlessly. Without intensive irrigation the grass and shrubbery would quickly die; much of it was getting ready to do just that. There were no people to be seen on foot anywhere; the distances are too great and the temperatures far too high for that.

The day I visited, Golba's house was spotlessly tidy and almost ornament-free, with the exception of a clock and a familiar portrait of Jesus laminated onto a piece of wood. A single magazine sat neatly on the coffee table. Golba himself looked the part of the dedicated Spartan: well-scrubbed, in neatly trimmed hair, a polo shirt emblazoned with the name of his employer and tucked neatly into a pair of clean, new jeans. He never missed a day of school from kindergarten through high school graduation, his mom once told the *Kansas City Star,* and I believe it. But don't be misled. Golba is also known for fierce political combat: noting in late 2003 that the hated Mainstream Coalition had neglected to reregister its name with the state, Golba snapped it up for himself.[12] I found his reputation for fierceness difficult to square with my impression of the man himself. He speaks with a slight lisp in an unvarying monotone, and in an accent I have always associated with the hardworking and the laconic, not the fiery hurler of political invective. Everything Golba said was matter-of-fact, with no boasting and no histrionics.

Yet this "little old blue-collar worker," as he describes himself, has helped make possible Kansas's conservative movement. With only a high school diploma and little resources to speak of, Golba built his organization, Kansans for Life, into one of the most powerful political groups in the state. Traveling the state in the eighties and nineties, Golba recruited hard-line antiabortion conservatives to stand for election and, more important, recruited a base to make sure his candidates won. Here in Johnson County it was Golba who signed up all those precinct committee people back in 1992, eventually conquering the local Republican Party.

He did it all in his spare time. After all these years Golba remains a line worker at a soda pop bottling plant. For him there has been no cushy sinecure, no patronage job in Topeka. He will never be named "Johnson Countian of the Year" or sit on the board of a charitable Kansas City foundation. For him it is all about principle, and principle is precisely the thing the bland, comfortable Mods do not have. "They're all these businesspeople, they have a ton of money, some of the wealthiest people in the country," Golba says, "but we've been able to beat them because they have no base." He tells me story after story about the high and the mighty laid low by working-class people: the carpetlayer who beat the Speaker of the Kansas house; the wealthy Mod who outspent one of Golba's candidates by a factor of ten, but who still lost "big-time."

The other team also fails because what principles they *do* have don't resonate for voters. Sam Brownback says Kansans don't care about economic issues, that they're all on fire for culture war, and Tim Golba seems to agree. "You can't stir the general public up to get out to work for a candidate on taxes or the economy. People today are busy," he tells me. "But you can get people who are concerned about the moral decline in our nation. Upset enough to where you can motivate them on the abortion issue, those type of things."

In his absolute dedication to principle Golba personifies one of backlash conservatism's greatest strengths. Ignoring one's economic self-interest may seem like a suicidal move to you and me, but viewed a different way it is an act of noble self-denial; a sacrifice for a holier cause. Golba's monastic lifestyle reaffirms the impression: this is a man who has turned his back on the comforts of our civilization, who has transcended the material. From this barren suburb on the edge of town he rebukes the haughty and the worldly. He defies the men in the great palaces. He smites their candidates; he wastes their money; he ends their careers. "If you're like me, consider yourself to be a born-again, Bible-believing Christian, then the issues are black and white," Golba says. "There's not much room for gray area. You've got to take a stand." When he tells me that his movement would be the rightful contemporary home of the Kansas hero John Brown, an ascetic Christian who died trying to awaken the world to the evil of slavery, I momentarily think Golba might be on to something.

Although Golba resists any comparison between his movement and organized labor, I can't help but think of him as sort of an upside-down Cesar Chavez. Like that legendary union organizer, Golba is deeply religious, utterly dedicated to his task, toiling selflessly every day of the year—all to make the powerful even more powerful. He travels about the state, agitating, educating, organizing, without any hope of material recompense. Working ceaselessly but without worldly ambition, he summons the upper class back to the paths of righteousness from which they have strayed. And he teaches though the people hear not. He denies himself so that others might luxuriate in fine mansions; he labors night and day so that others might enjoy their capital gains and never have to work at all. Humility in the service of its exact opposite; is there not something Christlike about it all?

Kay O'Connor, a conservative state senator from Olathe, would probably agree that there is. She has been fighting the Mods for twelve years now—she knocked off one of their most prominent leaders in the Republican primary of 2000—and she has, like certain other Cons, noticed the gaping class divide between the two sides. When I ask her if she has an explanation for it, she thinks for a minute and then tells me that the class thing reflects the same essential "personality difference" that people's politics do: folks who live in the marbled mansions of Mission Hills "are probably demonstrating that they have higher ambitions for monetary gains as opposed to, shall we say, spiritual gains."

> The one who is more materialistic or more interested in building résumés, and running for office, and being the CEO, or owning a big company, and having the material things . . . that is the person who is more moderate, and they understand what it takes to get to the top of

the mountain, to get to the top of the heap. You gotta
work hard, and sometimes you stomp on people. The
conservative, on the other hand, he just wants to go to
church on Sunday, or he wants to go fishing on Sunday,
and he just kind of wants to be left alone.

Yet Kay O'Connor hardly "wants to be left alone." She
courts controversy almost every time she opens her mouth. She
is, for one thing, a tireless proponent of school vouchers in a
region of the country that adores its public schools; for another
thing, she is the one who famously identified women's suffrage
as a symptom of America's moral decline. For the latter remark
she was mocked from coast to coast. Newspaper editorials
laughed at loopy Kansas, and Jay Leno called her "Taliban
woman of the year." State officials called for her resignation, and
some of her constituents got a recall petition going.[13]

It's a funny thing, though; I find this same wacky Kay
O'Connor genuinely charming. The first time I met her was at an
unhappy Republican campaign party in the fall of 2002. The
candidate whose prospects we were supposed to be celebrating
was way behind in the polls. Some anonymous band played
anonymous Republican rock while everyone drank watery three-
two beer[14] and tried to avoid talking about the looming election.
But there was Kay O'Connor, irrepressibly jolly, wearing one of
those satin jackets favored by union guys, standing right in front
of the amplifiers, shaking her sixty-year-old locks, and getting
down to Big Joe Turner's blues classic, "Kansas City." "That was
my song," she said joyfully, a favorite from the days when she
and her husband moved here from Iowa.

Kay is a mother of six and grandmother of many. She wears
thick-lensed plastic glasses that give her a strangely innocent
appearance, magnifying her big blue eyes and making it seem

that she is always on the verge of tears. The office in her white vinyl–sided Olathe house is massively cluttered, with patriotic wallpaper and photos of conservative heroes peeking through the riot of paper and books and computer equipment. Naturally there is a Bible (she is a Latin-mass Catholic, she says), and on the wall she displays a poster graphically attributing all the ills of the present day to the halting of school prayer back in 1962: SAT scores down 10 percent! "Illegal drugs" up 6,000 percent!

O'Connor seems peculiarly given to dizzy ideas such as this one.[15] Like many of the Cons, she gives the impression of intelligence, choosing and enunciating each word carefully, but she also seems oddly naive, like a person who has sat down and worked out the world's problems all on her own. She tells me, for example, that one of the reasons the older parts of Johnson County are less conservative than Olathe is that they are more densely populated, which always eventually makes people into Democrats. She goes on to explain how big-city blight is caused by state tax abatements.

O'Connor may be naive, but she is remarkably consistent. Government and unions, especially the teachers' union, cause the problems; tax cuts and free enterprise fix them. She is one of the many Kansas politicians who have sworn to vote against "any and all efforts to increase taxes," and she is also one of a handful who lobbied to allow corporate evildoer Wittig to go through with the devious Westar spin-off plan described in chapter 2. When I ask what she thinks about progressive taxation, she tells me first that it's impossible to raise taxes on the wealthy, because they just pass the increased costs on to the rest of us, and then declares that progressive taxation is theft, plain and simple. "Why should we be penalizing people for being financially successful?" she asks. "When you take from the rich and give to the poor, that really is Robin Hood, and that's just theft. Robin Hood was a thief."

The O'Connors are not wealthy people, by any standard. Her husband works as a monitor technician at a nearby hospital, and she went out of her way to impress upon me their lack of means. But her thoughts on the issues seem all to have been drawn from the playbook of the nineteenth-century Vanderbilts and Fricks. O'Connor's solution to urban decline, for example, is school vouchers and the low-wage economy. First we unleash market forces to improve the schools, then "these better schools will produce good workers, that will become attractive to more businesses, that will move in to get these good workers, who will work for lower wages, because [they're] from poverty families. They aren't expecting eighty thousand a year. They're content to work for six, eight, ten dollars an hour." And then someday these obedient paupers will be granted the same shot at the good life as everybody else. At least, I hope that's the plan.

O'Connor so believes the promise of this low-wage utopia that she sank her own money into the voucher effort, founding an organization to promote grassroots action on the issue.[16] She even took out loans and refinanced her house in order to get the voucher group off the ground.

What's in it for Kay O'Connor? Why would a person of limited means make such great sacrifices for a politics that can only leave people like her worse off? What makes a person who is just scraping by want to help the CEO of Westar pile up the pelf? The answer seems to lie at least partially in the breathtaking beauty of the conservative worldview itself. Everything fits together here; everything has its place; everyone ought to be happy in their station. The god of the market may not have much to offer you personally, but that doesn't change its divinity or blur the awesome clarity of the conservative vision. Besides, there are different ways to serve. The O'Connors themselves may not stand to gain much from, say, a cut in top marginal income tax rates, but there is still joy in doing what is right, in being part of a movement that is advancing so robustly toward its goals.

The same is true on women's issues, where strong, resourceful Kansas females like Kay O'Connor work tirelessly to turn back the clock on their own kind. Although O'Connor says she does not oppose a woman's right to vote (obviously she votes all the time), she freely admits to holding old-fashioned views of relations between the sexes. "I'm a happy captive of forty-three years," she tells me, "and I am obedient to my husband in all things moral. And the other half of it, for a Christian, is my husband has to love and care for me as Jesus loved and cared for the church. And Jesus died for his church, so my husband has to be willing to die for me. And if he's willing to die for me, the least I can do is be obedient in moral things, right?"

O'Connor ran through this chain of reasoning, which she clearly found very convincing, sitting in the office from which she manages her political career and from which she plans her next move in the vouchers campaign. When the subject came up, she had been pronouncing on all manner of controversial topics with a great deal of authority for more than an hour. Her husband did come in the room once, but he quickly and politely took his leave when he saw we were doing an interview. Nor is O'Connor alone in this curious political place. From the Summer of Mercy to the crusade against evolution, authoritative females have been prominent in every act of the Kansas conservative drama. They are no-nonsense types who are every bit the equal of the menfolk in the war to restore the mythic social order of a distant past.

About ten minutes after relating her "happy captive" theory, O'Connor and I had to drive to a meeting of a Republican women's group that she leads. She was anxious to get there on time, she said, and she sent the family Chevrolet barreling down College Boulevard, the main drag of outer suburbia, at fifty miles an hour. I was supposed to follow along in my own car, but, wary of running red lights or getting stopped for speeding, I fell farther and farther behind, until all I could see were the taillights of her car, roaring obliviously down the empty street between the darkened glass towers and the acres and acres of carefully cultivated corporate lawn.

Prior to meeting Mark Gietzen, I knew him only by reputation—a reputation acquired during the early days of the conservative revolt, when the Wichita newspaper reeled in horror at the prospect of "theocracy" right here in the Air Capital. Gietzen, the director of a Wichita Christian singles network, served as chairman of the local Republican Party through much of the nineties, and the paper had not treated him kindly. The photo that always ran in the paper showed some small-town Lothario, a man in a pencil mustache and the half-tinted aviator-style glasses of the disco era. The way they described his election as county chairman, it sounded like a coup d'état; once they ran a cartoon that seemed to falsely suggest that he was a wife beater.

The man I sat down with bore no resemblance to any of these personas. Gietzen is tall and physically imposing, a former marine. And like nearly everyone you meet in Wichita, he is an airplane enthusiast. In his garage is a Piper Tri-Pacer, the classic civilian aircraft of the fifties, which he is restoring piece by piece. And on the left lens of those aviator glasses is a tiny drawing of the same plane. Gietzen is also as friendly and enthusiastic as anyone I've ever met. Indeed, he talked nearly nonstop for a solid two hours, barely pausing between anecdotes.

Thanks to all its union members, Wichita was once one of

the state's few Democratic areas. It went gradually Republican through the eighties, Gietzen tells me, but it was the 1991 Summer of Mercy that definitively shifted the city to the right and brought Gietzen thousands of conservative recruits who were enthusiastic about campaigning door to door.[17] In the years before then, he recalls, a very different breed filled the party's precinct positions; the sort of folks who "would donate a thousand-dollar check to the Republican Party, and do not a darn thing."

After 1991, Gietzen's conservative recruits had little money, but they were enthusiastic about working for pro-life candidates. "If you have somebody willing to . . . meet the voter face-to-face and one-on-one, not only does it not cost any money in terms of postage, . . . you can hand them the material and you can give them that personal touch." He recalls working on campaigns until 2 a.m. on numerous occasions, giving his spiel in countless churches, and carrying voter registration materials with him wherever he went, always ready to switch someone from Democratic to Republican.

Gietzen was building a social movement, one convert at a time. On the left it is common to hear descriptions of the backlash as a strictly top-down affair in which Republican spellbinders rally a demographically shrinking sector of the population for one last, tired drive. What the Wichita Republicans have accomplished, though, should dispel this myth forever. They shouted their fighting creed to every resident of the city, sharpening the differences, polarizing the electorate, letting everyone know the stakes. Gietzen and company wanted not only Wichita's votes but its participation. They were going to change the world.

While the Wichita Cons worked hard to build their movement, they would not have succeeded so extravagantly had it not been for the simultaneous suicide of the rival movement, the one that traditionally spoke for working-class people. I am referring, of course, to the Clinton administration's famous policy of "tri-angulation," its grand effort to minimize the differences between Democrats and Republicans on economic issues. Among the nation's pundit corps "triangulation" has always been considered a stroke of genius, signaling the end of liberalism's old-fashioned "class warfare" and also of the Democrats' faith in "big govern-ment." Clinton's New Democrats, it was thought, had brought the dawn of an era in which all parties agreed on the sanctity of the free market. As political strategy, though, Clinton's move to accommodate the right was the purest folly. It simply pulled the rug out from under any possible organizing effort on the left. While the Cons were busily polarizing the electorate, the Dems were meekly seeking the center. In Wichita Republicanism appeared dynamic and confident; the Democrats looked dispir-ited, weak, spent.

However well it was received on Wall Street, Clinton's strat-egy played right into the hands of Mark Gietzen and hundreds of other Christian conservative organizers like him around the coun-try. If basic economic issues are removed from the table, Gietzen has written, only the social issues remain to distinguish the par-ties. And in such a climate, Democratic appeals to people of ordi-nary means can be easily neutralized. "Years ago, it was assumed that the Republican Party was *'the party of the rich,'* and that the Democrats stood for working people," Gietzen writes.

Not anymore!

Today a working family with children is far more likely to be a Republican family, than a Democrat family.

Democrat leaders themselves have discarded the old notion of their party being a party for the poor.

Today, Democrat Party fund-raising events are more likely to cost $1000 per person, than a similar Republi-can Party event. . . .

> Recently, a member of the Clinton administration [evidently a reference to James Carville] referred to poor people as "trailer-trash" and his comment was greeted with a yawn from the media.[18]

The title of the pamphlet in which these thoughts appear: *Is It a Sin for a Christian to Be a Registered Democrat Voter in America Today?*

Plenty of Wichitans clearly came to believe that it was. In the election of 1994 they took their frustrations out on Democratic representative Dan Glickman, a staunch Clinton loyalist who supported NAFTA—a free-trade agreement originally drafted by Republicans—even though the labor unions back in Wichita that made up his electoral base adamantly opposed the trade accord. Says Dale Swenson, a union painter at Boeing (and a Republican state legislator): "When [Glickman] voted for NAFTA, I couldn't any longer vote for him. I know a lot of union members were really mad at Glickman when he voted for NAFTA." With Democrats and Republicans having merged on free trade, the issues that remained were abortion and guns. And, of course, government itself. Glickman was solidly pro-choice, and he had supported the administration's measures to restrict assault weapons; he had also been involved in the House check-bouncing scandal, which seemed to confirm people's worst suspicions about career politicians. On all three issues he ran headlong into the city's growing populist backlash.

On election night 1994, the blue-collar districts of south Wichita went for the conservative Republican Todd Tiahrt. Remembering it today, Glickman speaks with the same ironic perspective as Dwight Sutherland. While losing his base, he says, he managed to win what he calls "the elitist vote"—"the high-income, east-side Wichita Republican precincts." The inversion was complete: the Democrat could only count on support from the professional people who felt embarrassed by the Summer of Mercy and its aftermath.

That 1994 campaign had an air of genuine populism about it: Tiahrt did it all without much of a TV presence or significant financial help from the city's moneyed class. Before too long, though, the rift healed between Tiahrt and his "high income" constituents, and today the congressman is capable of airing as many TV commercials as he wishes. The corporate powers-that-be in Wichita, it seems, don't really mind a politician's God-talk or his Operation Rescue sensibilities if he will help them fight their great enemy, government. After all, as Kay O'Connor put it so well, the people on top know what they have to do to stay there, and in a pinch they can easily overlook the sweaty piety of the new Republican masses, the social conservatives who raise their voices in praise of Jesus but cast their votes to exalt Caesar. Dwight Sutherland, for his part, knows the gulf can someday be bridged—just look at how Mission Hills turns out for the born-again George W. Bush—and Jack Cashill's day-to-day fieldwork among the "power elite" suggests he knows it as well. The Mods, for their part, will probably never give Tim Golba the keys to Leawood, and they will surely never toast John Altevogt, the raging Marat of the Kansas revolution, at the finest restaurant in Corporate Woods. But somehow, I think, they'll find it in their hearts to take the tax cuts, thank you, and the deregulation and the helping hand in dealing with those troublesome labor unions.

Chapter Nine

Kansas Bleeds for
Your Sins

Ask a liberal pundit what ails the red states, what has induced them to work so strenuously against their own economic interests, to vote Republican when Republicans simply wreck the arrangements that benefit them—ask a liberal pundit to explain this, and he will probably tell you it's all because of racism. Republicans have perfected the coded racial appeal, and they rally white voters to their cause by subtly appealing to their hatred of blacks.

There are undeniably a great number of places where this analysis holds true, but today's Kansas is not one of them. The state may be 88 percent white, but it cannot be easily dismissed as a nest of bigots. Kansas does not have Trent Lott's disease. It is not Alabama in the sixties. It was not tempted to go for George Wallace in 1968. Few here get sentimental about the Confederate flag. Kansas may burn to restore the gold standard; it may shriek for concealed carry and gasp at imagined liberal conspiracies; but one thing it doesn't do is racism.

I do not mean this as any sort of rebuttal to the considerable historical work done on the racial elements of modern conservatism. Obviously white fears played an enormous role in building the backlash in the sixties, seventies, and eighties, when the centers of right-wing populist sentiment were the South and the urban North, and when the hot-button issues were busing, welfare, and integration.[1] None of those is an important factor in the Kansas story, however. What we see here is something very different, and equally disturbing: the backlash in full cry without the familiar formula of racial conflict to serve as an interpretative guide. People here are moving to the right—as they are in many places—with only the most cursory references to the traditional racial divisions. Those who believe that conservatism will wither away as racism becomes less and less acceptable should take note: the backlash here owes little to prejudice of that kind. In Kansas, right-wing partisanship is an equal-opportunity affair, with a ready-made complaint for every demographic and a grievance for every occasion.

Race just doesn't seem to be what triggers indignation here. In the aftermath of the Supreme Court's June 2003 decision upholding universities' right to consider race in admissions, the Kansas Conservative Listserv had little to say. When the Court struck down state sodomy laws a few days later, however, the list erupted in indignation. This was a "Sodomite Pearl Harbor," one participant raged. A short while later, he called his correspondents' attention to an unmistakable sign of God's displeasure with the sinful United States: a "plague of locusts" that had been sighted out West.

If anything, the conservative movement in Kansas is conspicuous for its tolerance on racial issues. I learned this firsthand while attending services at the Full Faith Church of Love, a charismatic church in a down-market Kansas City suburb. The church is famous for having produced a number of lesser Con politicos, but on the morning I sat in its vast, ramshackle auditorium, the preacher leading the all-white congregation through the service was black. John Altevogt, the onetime *Star* columnist who has described himself as "the Jackie Robinson of Kansas journalism" (because he's the only Con), has written at some length about his efforts to make a place for blacks in the backlash victim-world. He has even bragged about his role in designing radio ads targeted at blacks that blasted Social Security, which, he claims, helped to elect a right-wing Republican to a Virginia district that is 39 percent black.[2]

As we have already learned, what Kansas conservatives do with the language of prejudice is apply it to their moderate foes, mocking them as "bigots" or members of a "hate group" for supposedly disliking evangelicals in the same way that actual bigots dislike minorities. And certain conservatives go much further. The Kansas uprising's great hero, Senator Sam Brownback, may be as far to the right as they come on most issues, but when it comes to courting minority voters he is a man of almost Clintonesque ability. He has befriended the black caucus, mainly by supporting the construction of a national museum of African-American history, and he has also been honored by the National Council of La Raza for his staunch support of open immigration policies. Stories about the senator's racial tolerance sometimes point out that he has adopted children from Guatemala and China, and I have even heard admirers describe his conversion to Catholicism as a gesture toward the growing Latino population of southwestern Kansas.[3] (I have yet to hear anyone describe his association with prominent Opus Dei leaders as a sign of his respect for the culture of Spain, but it is not beyond the possible.)

As Brownback likes to point out, this tolerance is very much in keeping with Kansas's mythic identity. The state's founders were northerners who settled here at least in part to prevent slavery

from moving west. Free-soilers in Kansas fought a running guerrilla war with slave owners from Missouri for five years before
the start of the Civil War, and the spectacle of "Bleeding
Kansas" energized the brand-new national Republican Party and
mobilized free-soil voters across the (north of the) country. John
Brown, who went on a murderous rampage against pro-slavery
men near Osawatomie in 1856, is revered in Kansas as though he
were the state's founder. The destruction of Lawrence by
William Quantrill's bloodthirsty Confederate irregulars in 1863
cemented the state's eternal hostility to the "slave power." Even
the cute li'l jayhawk, lovable mascot of the University of Kansas,
has a violent abolitionist past: "Jayhawkers" were members of
free-soil militias, terrorizing slaveholders along the Missouri
border. So familiar were these facts at one time that NAACP
lawyers deliberately chose Topeka as the target of their landmark
desegregation case, *Brown v. Board of Education,* in order to
remind the country of its commitment to civil rights.[4]

The rest of us may have forgotten the days when Kansas bled
for the nation's racial sins, but for the local backlash crowd it's
as if it all happened yesterday. The Kansas Cons jealously defend
the state's free-soil honor against all nitpicking historians who
might express doubt.[5] They glory in speaking of themselves as a
new breed of abolitionists, a perfect parallel of the heroic original. Brownback, for instance, makes much of his opposition to
slavery in the third world; he's even been awarded the William
Wilberforce Prize (named for the nineteenth-century British abolitionist but bestowed by a right-wing fundamentalist group)[6]
for ingeniously extending the pro-life offensive to such issues as
stem-cell research and human cloning.

When I first noticed how frequently pro-lifers compare themselves to abolitionists, I assumed that this was just the flip side of
comparing their liberal enemies to Nazis: in each case they were
just reaching for the ultimate in obvious metaphors—we're

good, they're bad. But there is a logic to the comparison: after all, both abolitionism and the pro-life movement revolve around controversial definitions of human life ("Am I Not a Man and a Brother?" was the slogan of abolitionism); both are based on powerful religious conviction and take an uncompromising stand against what they perceive as an absolute evil; both have violent partisans on the fringes; and both are, of course, loyal to the Republican Party.

Then there is the abolitionist imagery of Bibles and guns. The original free-soil settlers dispatched to Kansas brought with them what were called "Beecher's Bibles": rifles that had been donated by the celebrity preacher Henry Ward Beecher. Near the town of Manhattan, Kansas, these settlers built what they called a "Beecher Bible & Rifle Church"; in the statehouse in Topeka a famous mural depicts John Brown, in the grip of otherworldly outrage, clutching a Bible in one hand and a rifle in the other as he leads the nation into civil war. For the Cons this makes it a no-brainer: God, guts, and guns, now as then, are the combo that makes America great.

Comparisons to the heroes of old come easily to conservative lips. When a minor fiscal dispute with Missouri arose in the winter of 2003, the hard-right attorney general of Kansas, Phill Kline, called the attorney general of the neighboring state a latter-day Quantrill: "It's time for Jayhawkers to get up and ride again." "If John Brown lived today, he'd be considered a right-wing religious fanatic," Tim Golba told me. "He'd be considered one of us today."* Pro-life activists compare *Roe v. Wade* to the *Dred Scott* decision of 1857, which struck down state laws banning slavery within their boundaries. They marked the

---

*A more sinister invocation of John Brown came from Timothy McVeigh, the Oklahoma City bomber, who justified his slaughter of innocent people as a Brownian effort to provoke a righteous civil war.

tenth anniversary of the Summer of Mercy by walking defiantly into the Wichita city manager's office and reading an "Emancipation Proclamation for Unborn Children." Even the vile Fred Phelps, a figure scorned by Mod and Con alike, tries to grab legitimacy for his "God Hates Fags" campaign by comparing it to the civil rights movement. Pointing out that he arrived in Topeka on the very same day that the Supreme Court handed down the *Brown* judgment on that wicked city, Phelps insists that "the same establishment power-mongers who opposed the simple request by black people to be treated equally in education oppose us today. There's something about power and elitism that corrupts a man, and we've seen it time and again. But there is no kingdom on this earth that can defeat the will of God."[7]

To be sure, this way of seeing things may be unusually pronounced here because of the state's peculiar history, but it is not unique to Kansas or even to conservatives. Anti-abortion leaders everywhere are fond of comparing themselves to abolitionists and to civil rights leaders of the past—much to the irritation of civil rights leaders of the present. Mainstream historians of the movement also repeat the analogy, comparing the struggle over abortion to the controversy of the pre–Civil War years, with, presumably, the anti-abortion crusaders taking the role of the abolitionists.[8]

It is no doubt comforting to imagine oneself a latter-day partisan of such a Christlike movement. Abolitionists were despised and persecuted for their views—views that nearly everyone agrees with today. Perseverance, unwavering dedication to the cause, ultimate victory—these are the things that political parables are made of.

But there is another way of looking at the parallels between "Bleeding Kansas" and the present situation. Then as now, one heard ferocious denunciations of snobbish, lily-livered, interfering intellectuals from the East; charges of media bias; hearty affirmation of that rough-and-ready species of man who knew the value of concealed carry; and expressions of partisanship so blind as to overlook virtually any election irregularity.

But one did not hear any of this overheated rhetoric from the Free-Soil Party in Kansas. These were the trademark attitudes of the other side, of the pro-slavery "border ruffians" and their supporters in Congress. And it is in their thoughts and deeds that we can make out the true ancestors of today's backlash conservatives.

The Free-Soilers called them "pukes," no doubt out of arrogant liberal contempt for their backwoods ways. The pukes' signal accomplishment was the organized invasion of Kansas and the election—at gunpoint in many places—of what was known as the "bogus legislature." Like Ann Coulter, who wants so badly to live in a land that is completely liberal-free, these pukes had a distinct allergy not just to reform but to reformers. They wanted unanimity; they wanted no troublesome questions about their "peculiar institution"; and their legislature's first act in 1855 was to expel the handful of Free-Soil delegates who had somehow survived the electoral deluge. Their second important act was to move the capital from Fort Riley in the state's interior to a site conveniently located on the Missouri border so that in the future the members of the government wouldn't actually have to travel among those they governed. For a set of state laws, they merely copied out the statute book of their home state, crossing out *Missouri* and substituting *Kansas* wherever required—except with regard to slavery, where they proceeded to get just a wee bit Xtreme. Not only was slavery to be legal in the new territory, but it was to be protected by law from *criticism*. Holding anti-slavery views was to be a felony in Kansas; transporting into the territory any publication that might cause slaves to feel they oughtn't be slaves (such as the greatest best seller of the day, *Uncle Tom's Cabin*) was a capital crime. And, naturally, those who held doubts about the institution were deprived of the right to vote.[9]

Supported from without by the official recognition of the U.S. government and the zealous partisanship of southern senators,[10] and from within by armed force and the most inventive franchise-restricting stratagems to come to light before Florida 2000,[11] the bogus legislature managed to ride the bucking bronco of popular hatred for several years without being thrown. Supervising Kansas in those days was nearly impossible; territorial governors resigned one after the other, often under threat of murder on account of some slight or rebuke or doubt they had directed at the super-touchy pro-slavery party. Living under the legitimate (that is, pro-slavery) government was equally unacceptable for the conscientious; the free-state settlers, who outnumbered the pukes by a considerable margin, elected their own legislature, chose a governor, and set up their own capital in Topeka (which were all duly ignored by the pro-slavery administration in Washington).

Despite it all, the pukes saw themselves as victims, unassuming grassroots people who were defying imperious, arrogant Yankee designs on their humble regional ways and their sacred rights of property. Not that they possessed any said "property" themselves; as in the South generally, few white people in these parts owned any slaves. Like the backlashers of our own time, the pukes fought for a system that offered them only the most illusory sort of economic chances. Their struggle was ultimately that of the South's wealthy planter class, just as today's backlasher embraces a politics that will only make his boss richer. Yet the pukes clung stubbornly to their red-state self-image: humility, ordinariness, anti-eastern, and anti-elite. In 1856 the British journalist Thomas Gladstone spent a night on a riverboat in the company of a group of well-armed border ruffians, fresh from some depredation on the hated free-soilers of Lawrence, Kansas, and recorded the following monologue, delivered by one of them at the ship's bar.

> Here, you sir; don't be askeard. One of our boys, I reckon? All right on the goose, eh? [i.e., on the southern side of the slavery issue.] No highfalutin' airs here, you know. Keep that for them Yankee Blue-bellies down East. If there's any of that sort here, I reckon they'd better make tracks, mighty quick. . . . We ain't agoin' to stand them coming here, we ain't. Isn't their own place down East big enough for them, I should like to know? We ain't agoin' to stand their comin' and dictatin' to us with their — nigger-worshipping, we ain't. I reckon we'll make the place hot enough for them soon, that's a fact.[12]

During the journey Gladstone learned to keep his mouth shut; his British accent, it seemed, was enough to trigger puke rage all by itself. This was before the term *populist* had been launched on its long history of misuse, or else some sympathetic newspaper columnist would no doubt have described the pukes as such.

The abolitionists, on the other hand, were the kind of folks who, were they alive today, would set the *Wall Street Journal* to howling about political correctness, threats to the Constitution, and elitist, know-it-all meddling in the affairs of others. In fact, in the happy times before the sixties came and ruined everything, abolitionists were generally presented in school textbooks in just this way: as intolerant moralists, screeching proponents of a dictatorship of virtue who, through their self-righteous intolerance, did no less than cause the Civil War. Identifying oneself with them was a tactic of far-left groups such as the Weathermen and the Communist Party. Abolitionism only became respectable—and suitable for purposes of conservative legitimacy-building—thanks to the efforts of radical and, yes, revisionist historians of the sixties and seventies.[13]

And the abolitionists themselves? Strictly blue-state: effete, Anglo-Saxon, tea-sipping, college-educated—the sort of people that David Brooks would mock for turning up their noses at NASCAR and whom Bill O'Reilly would razz for not understanding real life as it's lived by tough mugs on the street.[14] Indeed, they were strongest in those states—Massachusetts, Connecticut, New York—and on those liberal college campuses—Oberlin, Grinnell, Amherst—that are routinely reviled by conservatives today for their speech codes and third-world sympathies. And while they were indeed religious people, the denominations to which abolitionists belonged were the mainline Protestant churches now pilloried by the right for not spreading the damnation around sufficiently: Unitarians, Congregationalists, Presbyterians, Quakers.

Once upon a time, that was the Kansas identity, too. The Beecher Bible & Rifle Church may seem to some like evidence of protosurvivalism, but the man for whom it was named, Henry Ward Beecher, was in fact one of the day's leading theological liberals, a long-haired favorite of New York society. Similarly, the state of Kansas was to some degree an outpost of New England. The town of Lawrence, a free-soil stronghold, was populated with families whose passage was paid by the New England Emigrant Aid Society, a group established to block slavery's path west. Free-soilers called the town "the Boston of the prairies": it was named for a Boston Brahmin, and its main street is Massachusetts Avenue. As its future residents came west, they sang

"The Kanzas Emigrants," a once-famous lyric written by John Greenleaf Whittier.

> *We go to rear a wall of men*
> *On Freedom's southern line,*
> *And plant beside the cotton-tree*
> *The rugged Northern pine!*

"Yankeetown" was what pro-slavery types called Lawrence. With Coulteresque passion they longed for its complete erasure from the earth: they marched against it repeatedly, successfully sacking it twice.[15]

Kansas looked east, but the pukes looked south, burning and pillaging their way through Lawrence under a flag that bore the inspiring legend "Southern Rights." And Lawrence, at least, continued to look east, becoming the seat of the University of Kansas. Today, as the state's politics shift farther and farther to the right, it remains one of the only truly liberal places in Kansas. For my generation, growing up in the churchified suburbs of Kansas City, Lawrence meant bohemian paradise: cheap rent in ramshackle Victorian houses, cheap beer in rickety jerry-built bars, secondhand record stores, a place where everyone was in a band. It was on Lawrence station KJHK that I first heard the Sex Pistols, then an unthinkable perversion for the classic rock stations of Kansas City, with their interminable Styx and REO Speedwagon.

Lawrence's enemies are different today, but when they rail against the liberal professors at the University of Kansas, or when they purge the punk rockers at KJHK, or when they deplore the addled denizens of the "roach-clip district," or when they gerrymander the city in order to minimize its poisonous electoral effects, their eyes are fixed on a sentimental vision of order that was pioneered in the Alabama, Georgia, and Texas of Wallace, Gingrich, and Bush. It may please the Kansas Cons to think of themselves as born-again John Browns when they holler for low taxes and concealed carry, but one suspects they would find themselves far more comfortable in the company of Quantrill and the pukes.

Consider the enlightened Sam Brownback. He may be against slavery—and what a bold stand that is 140 years after the Civil War!—but when faced with a tough challenge in 1996 from Democrat Jill Docking of Wichita, his campaign inundated the state with TV commercials that sought to tarnish her by pointing out that she was raised in the now-hated state of Massachusetts and that before she was married her name wasn't Docking at all (the Dockings are a famous Kansas family) but *Sadowsky*. Get it? As though to drive the point home, voters across the state received mysterious phone calls in the week before Election Day reminding them that "Docking is a Jew."[16]

Whoever made the phone calls knew what they were about. "I don't worry too much about who's in control because I think God is in control," one Wichita voter told the Associated Press a few weeks before Election Day. "But I'd rather have a Christian in there."[17]

Chapter Ten

Inherit the Whirlwind

An observer could decide to brush off that outburst of anti-Semitism as a brief, inconsequential bit of ugliness and decline to give it a second thought. But one could also read it as a clue to the malaise that lies at the heart of everything we have been discussing throughout this book. In the cosmology of bigotry Jews are not just another despised minority. The stereotype with which they are always smeared is a very particular one: they are held to be affluent, alien, cosmopolitan, liberal, and above all, intellectual.

Anti-intellectualism is one of the grand unifying themes of the backlash, the mutant strain of class war that underpins so many of Kansas's otherwise random-seeming grievances. Contemporary conservatism holds as a key article of faith that it is fruitless to scrutinize the business pages for clues about the way the world works. We do not labor under the yoke of some abstraction like market forces, or even flesh-and-blood figures like executives or owners. No, it is *intellectuals* who call the shots, people with graduate degrees and careers in government, academia, law, and the professions.

David Brooks calls them the "Résumé Gods." He charts their comings and goings by following what he considers the ultimate guide to the ruling class: the weddings page of *The New York Times* (ironically, the publication that now employs him), where "you can almost feel the force of the mingling SAT scores." Brooks has a high old time lampooning the fashions and fantasies of this class of righteous strivers, but the tone usually taken by his colleagues on the right when discussing the professional classes is one of darkest suspicion. The way Rush Limbaugh tells it (in a book edited by Brooks), he himself is a symbol of "middle America's growing rejection of the elites," by which he means " 'professionals' " and " 'experts' " including "the medical elites, the sociology elites, the education elites, the legal elites, the science elites . . . and the ideas this bunch promotes through the media." The enemy of the plain people, of good ol' red-state America, is intellectuals. They are the haughty liberal elite under whose tyranny "Middle America" suffers.[1]

Brooks believes that the rise of intellectuals is a recent development, that only in the last handful of decades—that is, since the sixties—have we come under the thumb of the professional class. And that may be true, depending on how you define the terms. But the *resentment* of intellectuals as a dominant class is a tradition of long standing on the right. The origin of this ill will lies not so much in some ancient culture war but in a defensive maneuver taken long ago by a business class that felt itself to be under attack. Anti-intellectualism in its present form can be dated back to the thirties, when President Roosevelt turned a flock of college professors loose on the economic structure of the nation. Intellectuals designed the New Deal's regulatory apparatus, they set up Social Security, they did studies and wrote reports, all of which was regarded by the business community of the time as inexcusable and arrogant meddling with the rights of private property.

A second anti-intellectual efflorescence came in the fifties, when U.S. senator Joe McCarthy led his Republican rebels in unearthing a leftist conspiracy that involved not some radicalized proletariat but instead an assortment of spoiled ingrates born to the highest-ranking families and educated at the finest universities: condescending intellectuals like Alger Hiss, the upper-class, Harvard-educated New Dealer who may well have been a Soviet spy. Whittaker Chambers wrote that when he made his famous accusation against Hiss, he exposed a "jagged fissure" running "between the plain men and women of the nation, and those who affected to act, think, and speak for them. It was, not invariably, but in general, the 'best people' who were for Alger Hiss and who were prepared to go to almost any length to protect and defend him. It was the enlightened and the powerful, the clamorous proponents of the open mind."[2]

This was a fairly novel suggestion at the time. The intellectuals were the ones betraying capitalism, while the working class— once the object of conservative dread—was standing tall for the American way. Thanks to endless repetition in the decades since then, however, this vision has become common sense, something we all know instinctively.

Today this kind of anti-intellectualism is a central component of conservative doctrine, expressing in glorious brevity the unifying theme of nature beset by overweening artifice. The corporate world, for its part, uses anti-intellectualism to depict any suggestion that humanity might be better served by some order other than the free-market system as nothing but arrogance, an implied desire to redesign life itself. The social conservatives, on the other hand, use anti-intellectualism to assail any deviation from a system of values that they alternately identify with God and the earth-people of Red America. Just who the hell do these conceited eggheads think they are?

In rallying average people against those infernal PhDs with their blue-ribbon studies and their government agencies,

Republicans have hijacked several legitimate, even honorable, anti-intellectual traditions. The first of these is Protestant evangelicalism, which values the individual's direct emotional contact with God while rejecting the need for a church hierarchy made up of professional clergymen. Critical thinking merely gets in the way of holiness, this tradition holds, and evangelicals have consistently favored charismatic individual preachers over any form of learned organization.[3]

Another tradition the backlash swipes is the powerful suspicion of professional expertise associated with the historical left. This attitude originally arose, of course, in *opposition* to the impositions of the business world, not as a way to get corporations off the hook. As Barbara Ehrenreich has pointed out, "nonviolent social control" was the founding rationale for many of the American professions. The professional middle class sold itself as the group that would keep the workers in line, whether with efficiency studies, with public relations experts, or with the pseudoscience of corporate management. And workers responded to its claims, naturally, with skepticism and derision. "For working-class people, relations with the middle class are usually a one-way dialogue," Ehrenreich continues. "From above come commands, diagnoses, instructions, judgments, definitions—even, through the media, suggestions as to how to think, feel, spend money, and relax. Ideas seldom flow 'upward' to the middle class, because there are simply no structures to channel the upward flow of thought from class to class."[4]

Today, both of these traditions have been folded into the inverted class war of the backlash. Republicans today rail against obnoxious Ivy League stuffed shirts even when they themselves graduated from those same institutions. Republicans grumble about interfering professionals when they are themselves lawyers or doctors or MBAs. And as they rail and grumble they align themselves with the common people, rising up righteously against the puffed-up know-it-all who wants to reorganize and reform every aspect of private life. In every social issue Republicans perceive the same pattern: a conflict of the authentic and the natural and the democratic with the arrogant and the meddling and the foolish. This is the thread that unites each of the issues that I've mentioned in this book, from rails-to-trails to the metric system to farm subsidies to zoning laws; in every twentieth-century reform effort conservatives can see nothing but imposition, the fanciful designs of man pressed down on the immutable way of God, a.k.a. the free market.

The Republicans today are the party of anti-intellectualism, of rough frontier contempt for sophisticated ideas and pantywaist book-learning. *Harvard Hates America,* screamed an early backlash classic, and today's GOP hates Harvard right back. Today's Republicans are doing what the Whigs did in the 1840s: putting on backwoods accents, telling the world about their log-cabin upbringings, and raging against the over-educated elites. (Even George W. Bush, Yale '68, has complained about how Easterners regard his Texas cronies "with just the utmost disdain.") The symbols of aristocracy have to be trashed so that the real lives of the aristocracy might be made ever more comfortable.

Much has been invested in this war against intellectuals: in addition to all the familiar best-selling denunciations of life on campus, conservatives have built counterinstitutions and alternative professional associations from which they denounce the claims of traditional academia; they have set up think tanks that support writers strictly for partisan reasons; they publish pseudoscholarly magazines that openly do away with the tradition of peer review.

All this has not come without a certain amount of pain for old-fashioned Republicans who, like so many of our Kansas Mods, are often highly educated suburban professionals and no strangers to intellectual achievement. Expertise is something such people deplore only when it is wielded by government bureau-crats or interfering liberals. But having spent decades unleashing the ferocious language of anti-intellectualism on federal commis-sions that, say, want to study the effects of their businesses on the groundwater, these Republicans are now chagrined to find the same language turned on them for, say, believing in the theory of evolution. Here, too, the old-fashioned Republicans are reaping the whirlwind, trapped by the success of their own strategies.

Hence the situation in Kansas, where the most prominent conservatives, themselves an assortment of millionaires and lawyers and Harvard grads, lead a proletarian uprising against the millionaires, lawyers, and Harvard grads—and also against the doctors, architects, newspaper owners, suburban developers, and the corporate types who make up the moderate faction.

As it happens, there is considerable precedent for a pseudo-populist war against the professions in Kansas. In the twenties and thirties the state was home to a quack doctor of national celebrity, Dr. John Brinkley of Milford, who claimed to cure impotence by surgically transplanting bits of goat testicle to humans. Brinkley was also a pioneer in radio, obtaining a license in 1923 for a clear-channel station on which he broadcast word of his miraculous cure across the entire country. (The station was voted the most popular in America in 1929.) His hospital in Milford had long waiting lists, and Brinkley himself prospered spectacularly from his practice, sporting large diamond rings on both hands and driving a magnif-icent Cadillac that bore his monogram in gold in thirteen places.

Brinkley's goat operation was a fraud, though, and his med-ical credentials were questionable,* and since he was the most

---

*Brinkley's medical degree was from an "eclectic" institution, one of the philosophies of medicine, such as osteopathy and homeopathy, that stood apart from "regular" AMA practice, or "allopathy." At that time, Kansas was one of the few remaining states where "irregular" medical degrees were offi-

prominent quack in the country the American Medical Association (AMA) was determined to make an example of him. In this effort they were joined by the Federal Radio Commission, which revoked his broadcasting license, and the *Kansas City Star,* the owner of a rival radio station, which ran a serious of articles exposing Brinkley's medical failures. Instead of destroying Brinkley, however, this awesome combination of the professions, the government, and the media only served to make him a martyr.[5]

So in the Depression years of 1930 and 1932 Brinkley ran for governor, always seeking to identify his victimization with the victimization of ordinary Kansans at the hands of the bankers and the big landowners. Brinkley fever swept the state as the doctor barnstormed with a country music band and a series of local preachers, often arriving at campaign events in his private plane. Old-timers compared the feeling in the state to the mood during the Populist days of the 1890s. The doctor was only beaten through prodigious underhanded efforts on the part of the state's traditional rulers—the responsible fathers of today's responsible Moderate Republicans.

Political Brinkleyism was just as strange as Brinkley himself. The doctor was a fervent fundamentalist and an enemy of Darwinian evolution, and yet the politics he espoused were standard-issue thirties radicalism. *Leftist* radicalism, that is to say: pro-labor, anti-corporate, and in favor of state-subsidized health care and old-age retirement schemes. (Brinkley also had a plan for increasing rainfall in Kansas.)

Brinkley was a charlatan and an opportunist, but in those days when an opportunist wanted to take up the politics of anti-professionalism, he turned naturally to the left. This made sense

---

cially considered to be on an equal footing with mainstream degrees. Stamping out the legitimacy of these irregular disciplines was, in addition to exposing quackery, one of the cardinal objectives of the AMA.

in the larger context as well; the AMA, remember, was for decades the power that blocked any effort to set up a national health program. It was no friend of the working class. Today, however, the obvious political home for a man with Brinkley's beef against the professions would be the backlash right. We fight the impositions of the AMA and the Bar Association and all the rest of the bulwarks of middle-class power by railing against evolution, by decrying liberal bias in the news, and above all, by protesting abortion.

Its power as an anti-intellectual rallying point is one of the things that makes the anti-abortion crusade so central to contemporary conservatism. Free-market libertarians of a purist bent often express exasperation at the larger Republican embrace of the right-to-life crowd, seeing in the crusade to ban abortion a clear violation of the principles of privacy and limited government. There's nothing more private, they figure, than individual choices concerning our own bodies.

But it is important when trying to understand the pro-life movement to keep in mind that, whatever else the 1973 *Roe v. Wade* decision might have been, it was also a monument to the power of the professions. In fact, according to the sociologist Kristin Luker, almost the entire history of abortion law can be understood in the context of medical professionalization. Just as the nineteenth-century laws banning the procedure were passed at the behest of physicians just then establishing their own expertise, so the wave of reforms that unbanned the procedure in the sixties and seventies reflected the profession's changing views of itself. Abortion law remained tangled with medical professionalism right to the end: the list of groups that submitted amicus briefs to the Supreme Court in favor of abortion rights in 1973 reads like a veritable Who's Who of the nation's medical hierarchy. Furthermore, the justice who wrote the *Roe* decision, Harry Blackmun, had spent his legal career as the attorney for the Mayo Clinic, and, according to two journalists who have studied the controversy, it was the "rights of the physician" to treat his patient "according to his best professional judgment" that was foremost in Blackmun's mind in *Roe,* not the rights of the pregnant woman.[6]

Roe v. Wade also demonstrated in no uncertain manner the power of the legal profession to override everyone from the church to the state legislature. The decision superseded laws in nearly every state.* It unilaterally quashed the then-nascent debate over abortion, settling the issue by fiat and from the top down. And it cemented forever a stereotype of liberalism as a doctrine of a tiny clique of experts, an unholy combination of doctors and lawyers, of bureaucrats and professionals, securing their "reforms" by judicial command rather than by democratic consensus. When Antonin Scalia accused his Supreme Court colleagues in 2003 of striking down state sodomy laws more out of deference to "the law profession's anti-anti-homosexual culture" than respect for any particular provision of constitutional law, he was invoking this stereotype. As was Ann Coulter when she drew a similar line between judges and the media, arguing only

---

*Four states had legalized abortion altogether before *Roe v. Wade,* while thirteen others, including Kansas, had passed legislation recommended by the American Law Institute and the AMA in which a number of doctors had to agree on the procedure and then could only authorize it in order to protect the life or health of the woman, because of a fetal deformity, or in cases of rape or incest.[7] Under *Roe v. Wade* these medical limitations were largely swept away; abortion became available for almost any reason in the early stages of pregnancy. However, since the early nineties, state legislatures have passed numerous nonmedical restrictions on abortion, including parental notification for minors, counseling and waiting periods, and bans on state funding, all three of which are in effect in Kansas today.

semifacetiously that liberals were interpreting the constitution willy-nilly "so as to better reflect the storylines in this week's episode of *Ally McBeal.*"[8] And as were conservatives generally when the rumor went around in the summer of 2003 that certain Supreme Court justices were now skipping the Constitution altogether and looking to the legal traditions of other, more sophisticated countries when striking down the laws of heartland communities like Kansas and Missouri.

Making *Roe v. Wade*'s legal, medical, and governmental impositions seem even more monstrous was the field in which the liberal elite was apparently interfering: the very definition of human life. With jurisdiction over such a fundamental philosophical matter claimed by doctors and lawyers, the anti-abortion movement found it easy to convince itself that further degradation lurked around the corner. Movement literature now abounds in lurid tales of the medical profession gone mad, of doctors giving the thumbs-up to infanticide and euthanasia, of abortionists trafficking in fetal body parts, and of deranged scientists manufacturing embryos from which stem cells can then be harvested. The Nazi eugenics programs, they will even tell you, were sanctioned by the German medical community, the flower of European professional rectitude. "Where the destruction will end depends only on what a small scientific elite and a generally apathetic public will advocate and tolerate," wrote Dr. Everett Koop and the theologian Francis Schaeffer back in 1983. "Any hope of a comprehensive standard for human rights has already been lost."[9]

Each aspect of the backlash nightmare seems to follow a similar path. Overweening professionals, disdainful of the unwashed and uneducated masses, force their expert (i.e., liberal) opinions on a world that is not permitted to respond. Thus we read about church hierarchs decreeing that God has changed His mind about this sin or that and then using their episcopal authority to shut down or excommunicate congregations that don't agree. Thus we process endless complaints about scurrilous professors, answerable only to one another, rewriting history to suit their liberal preferences and pounding their thoughts into the heads of impressionable college students. And thus do we hear, over and over and over again, about the news media, staffed exclusively these days by graduates of journalism schools, ignoring critics and screening out stories that don't reflect their universally shared liberal views of the world.[10] Maybe what George Bernard Shaw once wrote is true: "All professions are conspiracies against the laity."

If so, it is only natural that education should become a major battleground in political wars like the one we see in Kansas. In Kansas as in many states, education is the largest discretionary item of the budget, the inevitable victim of the Cons' many rounds of tax cutting. As it happens, education is also what defines and unifies the Cons' enemies.

For the Johnson County Mods, many of them members in good standing of the professional middle class, education is largely a positive thing. They may be willing to mouth the standard denunciations of interfering experts that one hears in the business world, but education is also the basis of their own status, the source of all the JDs and MDs and MBAs and PhDs that make them an elite to begin with. Education is one of the things that distinguishes them from lesser mortals: It gives them expertise and credibility, it determines an individual's merit, and it links them to the larger world of the national elite.

The Mods respect public education; they support it virtually without reservation. The public schools that they have built in Johnson County are first-class, routinely ranking among the best in the nation. Indeed, public-school excellence is one of Johnson

County's most basic raisons d'être. The schools keep up real estate values. They encourage families and companies to move to Overland Park instead of Kansas City, Missouri. They give suburban life meaning and purpose. Supplying the public schools with whatever they require is a fundamental article of moderate Republican faith.

Admission to a selective college, the ultimate goal of these fine public schools, is the object of a sort of cult in the affluent Johnson County suburbs. I suppose the same is true to some degree in any upscale American suburb, but out here the awesomeness of the Ivy League is magnified by Kansas's remoteness and by its great fear of the hick-stigma. I knew a person in high school who was able to recite the address of the Harvard admissions office from memory. To this day I can recall precisely which of my classmates got into which snob colleges, how they immediately accreted the various sweatshirts, notebooks, and other paraphernalia needed to tell the world about their feat, and how they developed an irritating, instant intimacy with the lore of the beloved institution. Meanwhile, the students' parents, the Mods (back then known simply as Republicans), would contentedly add another sticker to the rear window of the Buick. They would throw parties celebrating the glorious occasion. They would fly university flags.

College admission is an achievement that lasts a lifetime in the Mod world, often overshadowing what one does later in life. So important is it that within a few minutes of meeting a Mod you will invariably have been asked where you went to school or, conversely, have discovered that he is himself a Harvard man, but that he also got degrees from Yale and Oxford.

The Cons generally don't give a damn. Their rank and file— and also certain of their leaders, including their candidate for governor in 2002—typically have no college degrees at all. For many of them, higher education is part of the problem, the institution that generates all these damnable know-it-alls in the first place.

Leftists like to explain the disaffection of working-class people with public education as a natural reaction to the patriotism, conformity, and civility pushed by what they call the "ideological state apparatus." The object of education, according to this view, is to police class boundaries by transforming most kids into unquestioning drones while selecting a small number of others for management positions. Kids from blue-collar homes are supposed to know intuitively that this is the case, and they respond accordingly, cutting class and getting high and listening to *The Wall* over and over again. A more nuanced version of this critique, the 1995 book *Lies My Teacher Told Me,* points out that high school American history textbooks give "a Disney version of history": heroic, egalitarian, jam-packed with progress, and almost entirely free of class conflict. Teaching such an "Officer Friendly" account of reality, the author concludes, is merely to "make school irrelevant to the major issues of the day."[11] The kids know bullshit when they see it.

The disaffection of the Kansas conservatives with public education is almost precisely the opposite. They do not have a problem with the idea that schools should be designed to churn out low-wage workers; indeed, Kay O'Connor told me that was a worthy goal. The Cons are pissed off because they think the schools don't provide *enough* Disney, *enough* Officer Friendly.

For the fancy colleges so venerated in Mission Hills and Leawood, the Cons have only contempt. Universities, in today's conservative mythology, are not so much founts of useful knowledge as they are playgrounds of political correctness, dens of sedition where tenured radicals revile our nation and brainwashed students march and chant. The treason of the intellectuals is such a hardy backlash perennial that there are entire Web sites dedicated to the plen-T-plaint on campus, to documenting each unpatriotic utterance by a professor or outrageous incident of offense-taking by a thin-skinned minority group. A hundred years ago Harvard students earned the enmity of the working class by scabbing the jobs of strikers just for fun. Today, the right tells us, students at that same bastion of privilege thumb their noses at workers by cheering for the very scum that guns down the sons of blue-collar Boston when they fight for freedom on foreign shores.

Education at the K–12 level, meanwhile, is the main place where average Kansans routinely encounter government, and for the Cons that encounter is often frustrating and offensive. School is where big government makes its most insidious moves into their private lives, teaching their kids that homosexuality is OK or showing them their way around a condom. Cons find their beliefs under attack by another tiny, insular group of arrogant professionals—the National Education Association—that stands above democratic control, and they look for relief in vouchers, homeschooling, or private religious schools.

Ask Con leaders publicly how they feel about the state's public schools, and they will insist that they love education as much as the next guy, that they are proud of Johnson County's high test scores and the state's fine basketball teams. They have nothing against public schools. God forbid! And how dare the Mods imply that they are anything less than 100 percent on this matter.

But read the screeds they circulate privately to one another, and their loathing of public education comes out in the open. When a high-profile court case ended in June 2003 with the removal of the Ten Commandments from an Ohio public school, the Kansas Conservative Listserv exploded in outrage. Public schools were "snakepits," declared a former county GOP chairman, and the authorities that caused the Commandments to be removed were "totalitarian liberal judges," "crypto-Nazis" who longed to "ghettoize" Christians. Another participant objected to the very term *public schools,* calling them "government schools" and later upgrading that to "government indoctrination centers." A third helpfully pointed out that "Christian children in public schools are deliberately subjected nearly daily to the leftist pro-homosexual pro-evolution pro-abortion propaganda of the leftist socialist NEA." The consensus eventually reached was that con-servatives should have no dealings with public schools at all, although one participant gamely suggested that the kids ought to go as "warriors" against the satanic regime.

An even more powerful condemnation of public education, by virtue of its lurid (but imagined) specifics, comes up in Jack Cashill's account of the nightmarish year 2006. It is only five years into the Al Gore administration, but education has already become a baroque exercise in p.c. horror. Cashill's hero attends a high school graduation ceremony at which two "diver-sity trainers" in bizarre indigenous-person costumes mount the stage and lecture the audience contemptuously about "the nation's original sin," that is, slavery. The diplomas they hand out are said to represent the students' "new understanding of 'our shameful history and our hereditary responsibility for it. Each of our graduates has submitted to rigid self-criticism and is purer for it.' "[12] *Hey, teacher, leave those kids alone!*

O̲f the many barking idiocies to which Kansas proudly affixed its good name over the last decade and a half, the most memo-rable by far was the 1999 decision by the State Board of Educa-tion to delete references to macroevolution and the age of the earth from the state's science standards.* So perfectly did the

---

*As in other places, the State Board of Education in Kansas sets broad "stan-dards" for what is supposed to be taught and learned in its public schools. These standards are not mandatory directives, dictating precisely what goes on in the classroom, but they do determine the content of the state's assess-ment tests, by which it judges the progress being made by students at differ-ent grade levels. And since teachers inevitably focus on what is on the tests, the standards gradually make their influence felt.

move fit the larger cultural set piece of Rubes versus Reality that the national media could not resist. They descended on the state in multitudes and commenced immediately to file stories alternately deploring and scolding. The cynical mocked Kansas on the late-night talk shows. The moralistic reprimanded Kansas on the editorial pages. The contemplative found in Kansas a timeless illustration of fundamentalism's tragic inability to accept or understand our advanced secular world.

As every high schooler knows, fundamentalism had taken this route before. The nation had laughed Nebraska Democrat William Jennings Bryan into the grave for it after the Tennessee "Monkey Trial" in 1925. Embracing biblical creationism has been synonymous with backwoods cluelessness ever since. "It is not often that a single state can make a whole continent ridiculous," wrote George Bernard Shaw after the trial, "or a single man set Europe asking whether America has ever really been civilized. But Tennessee and Mr. Bryan have brought off this double event."

To ask for a rematch on this battlefield was to embrace a legacy of folly, ignorance, and humiliation. For let's say the opposing team granted the Cons' request, allowed the rematch, agreed to let their doctrine—"young-earth creationism," "Intelligent Design," whatever it was—take the field against the massed critical scrutiny of professional science. All the Cons had to look forward to in such a case was certain, humiliating defeat.[13]

That prospect did not deter the Cons. For them the importance of the evolution issue arose not so much from the possibilities it offered to change the way Americans thought as from the allegorical resonance of the gesture. And like the abortion controversy or the jihad against gangsta rap, the battle over evolution seems almost to have been designed to keep Kansas polarized, keep its outrage levels high and its Con pot boiling, while changing the way things are actually done not a bit. The combat was purely symbolic; the board only changed high school standards, the general guidelines for teaching science. At no point did the board outlaw evolution or mandate the teaching of creationism.

It was symbolic combat, however, of the most momentous kind. To read through the conservatives' materials on the subject, you'd think the assault on evolution was the greatest and noblest culture-cause of them all. Evolution, one of them claims, is nothing less than a part of a sinister "war against God." Another maintains that evolution is a "pagan religion" masquerading as science that exists to legitimate materialism and teach "that there is no meaning to life, no inherent value in humans and no absolute source of moral authority."

> If it feels good . . . Do it! If it is inconvenient to have a baby . . . kill it . . . we get rid of spare cats, why not spare kids? If it's inconvenient to have a wife, get rid of her . . . neither marriage vows, nor their participants have any intrinsic value.

Getting down to hideous specifics is the creationist text that blames "naturalistic evolutionary teaching in our schools" for "teen drug use, the rampant spread of sexually transmitted diseases, despair and suicide in teens as well as youth violence."[14] That is why a concentrated attack on evolution is the thing that will put God back in charge, pull the rug out from under socialism, abortion, divorce, et cetera, and solve all the teen troubles listed above. With this one silver bullet we will fix it all.*

The Cons know, even as they make these claims, that this is

---

*Ironically, William Jennings Bryan hoped to accomplish exactly the opposite by defeating evolution. In his mind evolution led irresistibly to social Darwinism and the savagery of nineteenth-century capitalism; undermining it would make the country *less* capitalist, not *more*.

one silver bullet they will never be allowed to fire. The real object of their anti-evolution gambit, I believe, was not getting Kansans right with God but getting themselves reelected. As we have seen, conservatives grandstand eloquently on cultural issues but almost never achieve real-world results. What they're after is cultural turmoil, which serves mainly to solidify their base. By deliberately courting the wrath of the educated world with the evolution issue, the Cons aimed, it seems, to reinforce and to sharpen their followers' peculiar understanding of social class. In a word, it was an exercise in anti-intellectualism.

Anti-evolution strategists are no doubt aware that if you put aside all the scientific squabbles surrounding evolution (as 99 percent of observers surely do), the issue can be easily transformed into a moral battle between the democratic impulses of the common people and the hardest-core of the liberal elite—the intellectuals. Polls show that vast majorities of Americans support the teaching of "both theories" (evolution and creationism), but conservatives know that any effort to put such a scheme into practice will automatically trigger a forceful smackdown from the science establishment. And here is the key: this science establishment may be the most turf-conscious, credential-flaunting, undiplomatic bunch of pedagogues in all of academia. Provoke them, and they inevitably pull rank on you. Get them to do their high-hat, critic-squashing routine against some nice, unassuming Kansans—just as they did against old Doc Brinkley in the thirties—and you've set up a war pitting humble, God-fearing, blue-collar folk against an arrogant intellectual elite; a populist melodrama where the victims can't lose.

On the right, the class-based interpretation of the evolution controversy is a common one. David Brooks, for example, understands the popularity of those little "Darwin" fishes that people put on their cars as nothing but upper-crust boastfulness, just a way for elitist smarty-pants "to show how intellectually superior to fundamentalist Christians they are."[15] Turning specifically to the Kansas events, Jack Cashill once attacked a moderate, pro-evolution school board candidate by informing readers of the *Weekly Standard* that she was popular in Mission Hills, where she gave comfort to "the rich and the scared." The incumbent conservative, who had led the board in its famous stand against evolution, was said to be a hero to residents of "more modest quarters."[16]

According to *Kansas Tornado,* a right-wing narrative of the evolution controversy, the whole thing started with a humble "Prairie Village homemaker,"* who decided to get involved in formulating the science standards by which the progress of the state's public school students is evaluated. However, the committee charged with writing the standards, she found, was taking its cues from distant, elitist professional associations like the National Academy of Sciences. It wasn't interested in hearing the opinions of regular people, and so our unpretentious homemaker called a meeting of the alienated at the home of a prominent local creationist and set up what they called the Citizen's Writing Committee. This group produced much of the language that the state school board later adopted, to the scandalized horror of the entire world.

But the housewife and her citizen's crusade are just there to lend drama to our populist parable. The real subject of conservative anti-evolution literature is the "experts" on the other side of the battlefield and, more important, their expertise. "Should we 'leave it to the experts?' " asks *Kansas Tornado.* Obviously we should not. The scientists who showed up for the Kansas board hearings, the pamphlet goes on to assert, were petulant and selfish,

---

*Despite its name, Prairie Village is one of the more comfortable Johnson County suburbs and, coincidentally, the town where my high school was located.

demanding "special treatment" during the board's hearings as though they were a notch above the average run of citizens. Their strategy for dealing with the board was not democratic; it was "to engage in name-calling" and "to invoke the authority of the scientific establishment." They showed "disrespect for the board and contempt for any who would oppose them." The scientists' version of the standards, if adopted, would have made believers into "second-class citizens" who were not to be educated so much as indoctrinated.[17]

It is fortunate for historians that the fulminating John D. Altevogt was writing his short-lived column for the *Kansas City Star* at the time the evolution decision was handed down. In Altevogt's seething prose we can make out the inverted populist mentality at the very end of its tether, perpetually offended, raging against this or that elitist slight and storming at "liberal science and liberal reporting," those partners in deception. After the school board had taken its stand against evolution and the laughter of the nation had duly commenced, Altevogt raised his voice to condemn "the arrogant authoritarianism that just drips from many of those who oppose the board's new standards."

> If they can't have their way through an elected body, they'll get rid of the board and appoint one. Better yet, they'll sue the board. They don't know for what, but hey, get a liberal judge and this is not a problem either.

In Altevogt's view class arrogance was the *real* problem, the unmoved mover behind this charade. The liberals and evolutionists simply believe that they were born to rule everyone else, and they just will not allow things to be any other way. Their claims of expertise are merely a means to this aristocratic end. Two months after the controversy hit the front pages Altevogt had a run-in with one of the offenders, an evolution-believing science teacher from one of the prized Johnson County schools, and he proceeded to inform readers of the *Star* that although this teacher was unable to answer science questions dreamed up by Altevogt himself, he persisted in believing that "the science curriculum should be determined by his group, not by elected officials." Such arrogance! But Altevogt had news for this nabob: "Our country is governed by elected representatives, not groups of self-proclaimed 'experts.'"[18]

By sidestepping the scientific issues involved and keeping strictly to this narrative of intellectual snobs lording it over the common people, the Cons were then able to go down the list of fundamentalism's supposed offenses against democracy and turn each one back against their opponents. For example, Kansas's anti-evolution crusaders insist that it is the science community—not the fundamentalists—that is trying to impose its religious views on everyone else; that it is the science community—not the fundamentalists—that engages in "censorship of contrary evidence"; that it is the science experts who are "dogmatic" and "narrow-minded"; that it is these same experts who are irrational and emotional, unable to face reality; and that the reason no articles refuting evolution are ever published in professional, peer-reviewed journals is that those journals are biased.[19] (This last, incidentally, was a line once used to defend Dr. Brinkley from the professional inquisitors of the AMA.) What's more, these arbiters of professional rectitude wanted no backtalk. "Once you weren't supposed to question God," wrote Gregg Easterbrook of *The New Republic,* clearly caught up in the Kansas spirit. "Now you're not supposed to question the head of the biology department."[20] Sometimes the Cons were even moved to declare that it was the damnable scientists, in their megalomaniac desire to impose their obscene views on the rest of the world, who started the Kansas fight in the first place.[21]

Having provoked the inevitable reaction, the Cons promptly

began to scream "religious persecution," recasting themselves as the victims of a secular world's determination to stamp out the godly. Just as the small-minded hillbillies in *Inherit the Wind* persecute the high school science teacher for his views,* so the Cons carefully totted up each bit of criticism that was leveled at the Kansas board by the national media and imagined themselves nailed to the cross. All the ridicule, they believe, is merely the followers of "naturalism" expressing their irrational hatred for "people of faith." The Cons are thus, in their own minds, victims of bigotry as surely as any of the usual populations of the discriminated-against—the "people of color."

Altevogt, for one, saw the Inquisition coming only weeks after the decision, warning in the *Kansas City Star* of a "Christian-bashing chorus of lies and distortions" that would bring the Holocaust itself to mind. Later he claimed that the reason so many news stories didn't get the precise wording of the Kansas School Board's decision exactly right (for example, the board didn't strike Darwin from textbooks although early reports claimed it did) is that "the truth would have failed to generate the hatred for conservative Christians and public outrage sought by our liberal media establishment."[22] An even weirder expression of conservative persecution mania surfaced during the 2000 election campaign, when many of the board members who had made the now-infamous decision came up for reelection. It is a flyer showing Linda Holloway, a member of the State Board of Education from the Johnson County suburb of Shawnee, seated and smiling pleasantly, and surrounded by a halo of epithets in boldface type. This is a flyer *promoting* Holloway's reelection, mind you, and it is doing so by reminding you

---

*Contemporary anti-evolution literature returns again and again to the 1960 movie *Inherit the Wind* (a dramatization of the Monkey Trial starring Spencer Tracy) and the need to reverse the "paradigm" that this movie supposedly established.

that she has been called "Pond scum," "Pinhead," "Fanatic," and "Neanderthal."* All that, just for standing up to the "liberal academic establishment" and its drive to "silence any voices that challenge their atheistic orthodoxy." Ah, it's so unfair.[24]

Let us pause for a moment to assess the delusions of martyrdom that all this requires the Cons to embrace. What they mean by *persecution* is not imprisonment or excommunication or disfranchisement, but *criticism,* news reports that disagree with them: TV anchormen shaking their heads over Kansas, editorials ridiculing creationism, Topeka columnists using the term *wingnut.* This from the faction given to taunting their opponents as "pro-aborts," "totalitarians," "Nazis." The disproportion between dish-it-out and take-it is positively staggering.

The flip side of the Cons' persecution mania is a gleeful sense of subversiveness. Even while they cry about rude words from KU science professors and moan over a world that is coming apart, Con leaders like Jack Cashill are capable of backing the evolution decision because it causes headaches for what he calls "the country club cognoscenti."[25] Cons also provide a lively market for T-shirts proclaiming that students who pray are "a Real Menace to Society," and even for T-shirts screaming "Subvert the Dominant Paradigm" under a picture of Charles Darwin.

I saw the latter for sale at the second annual Darwin, Design,

---

*The Moderates, for their part, fell back on precisely the opposite theme. For them the denunciation of the outside world had summoned the dread specter of embarrassment—what Jack Cashill calls "the big E"—and they exhorted voters to oust the Cons from whatever positions they held on the grounds of status anxiety alone. *Don't let them think Kansas is a hick state!* So great was the perceived crisis in status that this theme spilled over from school board elections into all manner of other contests. A moderate Republican running for Congress from Johnson County even aired radio commercials that quoted from the East Coast editorials mocking Kansas and erected a billboard reading, simply, "Embarrassed?"[23]

and Democracy Symposium, a get-together at Rockhurst College in Kansas City. Modeled after an academic conference, the keynote speeches and panel discussions all aimed to publicize the much-ballyhooed theory of Intelligent Design. The inevitable Jack Cashill kicked things off with a denunciation of Hollywood for accepting a God-free vision of the universe. He kept things lively by showing clips from sinful films supposedly influenced by the doctrines of Darwin, such as *Hud* and *High Plains Drifter*. Cashill was followed, however, by an Intelligent Design theorist who lectured monotonously on the faked evidence supposedly used by evolutionists, and heads began to nod. To everyone's relief, the speaker finally yielded the stage to the Mutations, "three fine Christian ladies" in pink dresses who strutted and whirled like an early-sixties girl group and proceed to sing "Overwhelming Evidence," a ditty set to the pulsing beat of "Ain't No Mountain High Enough." Comically assuming the voice of the arrogant science establishment, the women pretend-derided the audience, singing that "the truth is what we say" and that, as professional scientists, "we don't have to listen to you!" The audience had plainly been bored by the preceding recitation of science's errors, but this lighthearted bit of persecuto-tainment hit exactly the right note, and sent everyone home with a smile on his or her face.[26]

Chapter Eleven

Antipopes Among Us

There are sober, sociological explanations for Kansas's penchant for martyrdom: the puritan background of the original settlers, say, or the Pentecostal traditions of the people who moved here in the forties and fifties. I personally prefer the more romantic notion that the extremity of the land itself accounts for the bumper crops of martyrdom-minded folks that Kansas so reliably produces. Most of the state is an empty place, a featureless landscape capable of quickly convincing anyone of their own cosmic insignificance. For this reason it has often been compared to the Holy Land, where a similarly blank vista generated an endless stream of prophets who descended on the cities to preach "world-worthlessness," as T. E. Lawrence once summarized the creed of the desert: "bareness, renunciation, poverty."[1]

Anyone who lives here very long gets used to the fact that their state is a magnet for the preternaturally pious, for every stripe of Christian holy man from the hermetic to the prophetic to the theocratic. It was not a roll of the dice that convinced

Sinclair Lewis back in the twenties to choose Kansas City as the place to observe the preacherly arts in person. And what a time Lewis would have here today! The zealots have come pouring out of their churches and into politics, seeking a transcendence here on earth that they once found only in the realm of the spirit.

Political or not, Kansas has always been in the first rank as a religious innovator. Kansas is to ghostly matters what Silicon Valley is to tech startups, or Seattle to alt-rock bands. Topeka was the home of the Congregationalist minister who, though he was pro-evolution and something of a radical on social issues, coined the phrase that has since become the watchword of smug fundamentalists nationwide: "What would Jesus do?" Kansas City is the headquarters for the Church of the Nazarene, the Unity movement, and the Reorganized Church of Latter Day Saints. We have our own schismatic branch of the Nation of Islam, and a band of charismatic testifiers known variously as the Kansas City Prophets, the Friends of the Bridegroom, or Joel's Army. One of Kansas City's run-down Missouri suburbs is believed by many in the Mormon faith to have been the original site of the Garden of Eden, as well as the place where Jesus will return to earth. One of the city's upscale Kansas suburbs is the headquarters of a powerful Christian radio network, on which you can hear pro-life leaders discuss their next move against the "abortion industry" and average people condemn liberal politicians for throwing off the Lord's timeline for the Rapture by trying to make peace between Israel and the Arab nations. (In Topeka, meanwhile, a group lays plans to speed up the Lord's end-times schedule by finding oil at a spot in Israel indicated by prophecy, thereby precipitating war with the Arabs, and thereby bringing on You Know What.) The Johnson County suburb of Olathe houses such a heavy concentration of fundamentalists, homeschoolers, and merchants of God-products that locals call it "the holy city."

For the most part this great bubbling Crock-Pot of Godliness takes a distinctly Protestant flavor, both formally and in a more general, lowercase-*P* sense. This is Christianity in revolt, railing against haughty establishments and dried-out formalism. It gravitates to the outrageous trappings of "alternative" youth culture as naturally as does Madison Avenue. "Equipping for extravagant worship, radical lifestyles and the great commission," blares a 2003 announcement for some Xtremely Xian enterprise of the Kansas City Prophets. A Christian office supply store that I visited stocked an impressive array of clothes for the tuned-in fundamentalist, T-shirts mimicking the logos for hip products and cool movies: Adidas, the *Matrix, S.W.A.T.*, Abercrombie & Fitch, and even the Powerpuff Girls (this last bearing the legend "Jesus Chick").

Other faith-choices available here express the universal dissatisfaction with the modern, liberal world by clinging to tradition more tenaciously than ever. Preeminent among these is the Society of Saint Pius X (SSPX), the "traditionalist" Catholic group founded by the excommunicated French archbishop Marcel Lefebvre that rejects the reforms instituted by the Second Vatican Council in the sixties. In addition to its national headquarters in Kansas City, the society operates a college and academy in St. Marys, Kansas, which has made that tiny town northwest of Topeka a beacon for alienated Catholics nationwide.

With the SSPX and the rest of the traditionalists the concern isn't speaking your heart, or grooving to the rhythm of the street, but in doing just the opposite: speaking Latin, stifling the groove altogether, reserving the pants for men only, performing the mass exactly as it was before Vatican II, and honoring to the letter the teachings of centuries of scholastic theologians.

Naturally, there is considerable overlap between Catholic traditionalism and the backlash right. Both movements originally arose in response to the great liberalization of the sixties, and in places like St. Marys, Kansas, the SSPX coexists with militia enthusiasts and Posse Comitatus types.[2] Were they bold enough to take on the mighty Catholic Church, American conservatives could well make Vatican II into the ultimate example of how the liberal elite pushes revolution from the top down: a ready-made parable of common people betrayed by an educated hierarchy more interested in the UN and folk music and nicey lovey togetherness than in carrying on its God-appointed duties.

For some decades now the American priesthood has been more or less liberal, both theologically and socially. A generation of priests—numerically the last big cohort—came of age in the era of Vatican II and enthusiastically accepted its values of progressivism, reform, and sensitivity to changing times. However, the sixties generation of priests, like their analogs in secular society, have come in for bitter recrimination in the era of the backlash. During the pedophilia scandals of recent years, conservative Catholics could be heard blaming the problem on the mood of liberalism that Vatican II inspired. A new movement for liturgical tradition has arisen—led largely by the laity, who seek order and stability instead of the drift they ascribe to Vatican II.

Where this craving for continuity and unity and orthodoxy has led, ironically, is to endless hairsplitting and quarreling and schism. The SSPX, for its part, declares Vatican II heretical and denounces the vernacular mass, but remains nominally loyal to the pope. (The Vatican regards the SSPX as schismatic.) This in turn strikes other traditionalists as insufficiently traditional; you're either with the Vatican II organization (whatever it is) or with the true Catholic Church, they reason, and they have split off from the SSPX and formed factions like the Mount Saint Michael's Community and the Society of Saint Pius V (SSPV!). At the end of this sectarian progression lies *sedevacantism*, the notion that, thanks to the manifold heresies of the church since the sixties, there is no one occupying the papal throne.[3]

The way David Bawden pronounces the word, in his heavy Oklahoma accent, it comes out "sadie-vaKONtist." For all I know, that's the right way to say it. Bawden is an expert, after all, a sedevacantist's sedevacantist. He spent years examining the options open to a true-believing Catholic and rejecting each one. Finally, he felt he had to take the ultimate step. He called a papal election, and he got himself chosen pope: Pope Michael I. Pope Michael of Kansas.

Pope Michael told me the whole story one chilly January morning in his family's isolated, ramshackle farmhouse about twenty miles outside St. Marys. He received me amid the sagging bookcases and icons of the family's living room, dressed in a homemade white vestment, dirty around the hem, that he wore over gray sweatpants and house slippers. Here Bawden, accompanied by his mom, explained to me his growing estrangement from the Vatican II church over the years and the thinking that led him to make a claim to the papal throne.

I should pause here to address your natural suspicion that this fellow is quite mad. He sure didn't seem so to me. He had a curious backwoods accent, a way of laughing that made me think of a character actor assigned to play "the nerd," and he lived in a place most unlike the Castel Gandolfo—in fact, it reeked of breakfast sausage the morning I was there—but he was clearly intelligent and most definitely in earnest. He appeared to have spent a lifetime studying canon law and Catholic theory of the old school—the legalistic, scholastic reasoning that mainstream church thinkers produced until Vatican II—and had worked out every angle of the situation, could tell you precisely why this concern or that was unfounded, why this critic or that was disqualified and had no right to criticize.

The Bawden family was initially drawn to St. Marys to join the SSPX back in 1980. David was even a student for a while at Lefebvre's seminary in Ecône, Switzerland. He didn't last long there, however, and his family eventually broke with the SSPX, denouncing it to a reporter from the *Kansas City Star*.[4] None of this deterred Bawden from his quest for the true Catholicism, though. He continued to study in his personal library of religious books, and at some time in the mid-eighties, he says, he "figured out that John Paul the Second was not pope." This was the epiphany. Before, Bawden had merely been unhappy with the practices of the modern church, but now he understood that the officer at its head was not legitimate either, thanks to that individual's own multiple heresies and the countless heresies of his predecessors, John XXIII and Paul VI. "How can a man be head of the church of which he is not a member?" Pope Michael reasons. "Because heretics depart from the church." (And heresy is just for starters: according to Pope Michael's Web site, Paul VI was the antichrist.)

The SSPX isn't too much better. "The problem with Lefebvre," Pope Michael declares, is that "he accepts John Paul the Second as pope, or he did when he died, and his organization still does. Well, if you accept a heretic antipope as your pope, then you're part of *his* church, not the Catholic Church." Then Pope Michael goes further. Lefebvre was not only not rebellious enough; he wasn't a real rebel at all. His whole uprising was a charade designed ultimately to bolster the corrupt Vatican II church. "They knew there were going to be people, when they put in the vernacular mass, who would head for the exits," Pope Michael surmises. "And so Lefebvre was there to catch them."

In the late eighties Bawden decided to commit his thoughts on all these subjects to paper. Accordingly, he wrote, along with a colleague, a nearly five-hundred-page tract titled *Will the Catholic Church Survive the Twentieth Century?* A work of medieval reasoning published in Kansas in 1990, it scolds Catholics everywhere for their ignorance of the endlessly complicated provisions of church law. The Vatican II church is, of course, the worst of the bunch; it is in the throes of "the Great Apostasy." Traditionalists like SSPX are an improvement, but only slightly. They, too, are tripped up by legal slackness and are repeating this or that forgotten heresy in apparent ignorance of the clearly stated proclamation of Pope Whatsis in his infallible papal bull Whatever. Everywhere one looked, souls were in peril of damnation thanks to the insufficiently rigorous scholarship of the clergy.

This sort of reasoning had the power to terrify in the Middle Ages. Powerful popes used it to overawe entire kingdoms: earthly rulers were putting their very souls in peril—plus those of all their subjects—by failing to heed some minute technicality in this or that bit of Latin legalese. Pope Michael merely shows us what this species of disputation looks like in the hands of a free-lancer. Nobody is pure enough; everybody manages to disqualify themselves sooner or later. Bawden uses the method on everyone. Your priest, with his years of seminary training, disagrees with Pope Michael, you say? Well, since your priest is a priest, he accepts the doctrines of Vatican II, and hence is a heretic, and hence is in error, and hence really isn't an expert after all.

Oddly enough, this is a style of argument that I have only seen used in my lifetime by the extreme left, zealously excommunicating one another and purifying their movement and holding eternal grudges against one another for this or that bit of heresy or thought-error. Pope Michael, though, seems to have derived it from the exact opposite end of the political spectrum.

This becomes clear as he attributes more and more events to conspiracy. He was thrown out of Lefebvre's seminary, he says, not because of any failing on his part, but because he "knew the faith too well. The ones they kept were the ones who didn't know the faith." Their sinister purposes were thus revealed by their preferences for weak-minded students. Then, apropos of nothing, the pope's mom mentions her dissatisfaction with the

John Birch Society, the fanatical anticommunist organization of the sixties. All they do, she says, is "Meet, eat, and retreat." Pope Michael chimes in: "They don't *do* anything."

Before long Pope Michael has broached the subject of the Masons and their nefarious doings. I make some idle remark about the many U.S. presidents who have been Masons, and the Bawdens pounce. "Do you believe in the conspiracy theory?"

Which one? I inquire, innocently.

"Of history."

"Things don't happen accidentally," continues the pope's mom. "Well, I mean, someone is trying to rule the world, and they're doing a pretty darn good job of it. And they are working with Satan." The Council on Foreign Relations comes up, as do the other usual suspects: your Bilderbergers, your Trilateral Commission.[5] The pope applies the idea to the recent history of the Catholic Church and concludes that, "basically, the communists, Masons, whatever, they're running the Vatican II church now."

As documentation of the charge, the two produce a hymnal from 1959 that includes a line (an incorrect translation from the Latin, they insist) that was *later incorporated in the new mass* by Vatican II. They also know someone who was told by a Jesuit *in the fifties* that the mass would be in English someday. Some people—the liberal elite—were in the know, while the rest just dumbly followed orders.

Having figured all this out, in 1990 David Bawden sent out invitations to a papal election to sedevacantists worldwide. Five of them showed up: his parents, his coauthor, and two friends of the family. They gathered in the thrift store owned by David's dad—both mother and son love thrift stores and garage sales, they tell me—and they got down to business and they elected David pope. Mom produces the family scrapbook and shows me the newspaper stories about the event: the *St. Marys Star* covered it, as did the *Topeka Capital-Journal*. There is also a page from a 1990 calendar, the sort that's illustrated with photos of healthy puppies, the kind of thing they hand out for free at the veterinarian's office, with the words *elect pope* in neat cursive on the square for July 16.

Please don't laugh. There is something about this conjunction of spiritual grandiosity and humble surroundings that's distinctively, quintessentially American. It is even more distinctively Kansan. People in this empty land have been calling the world back to the paths of self-denying righteousness for over a century now, always imagining themselves closer to God by virtue of their distance from civilization. And here is Pope Michael, rebuking the world from his remote farmhouse, and solving all by himself the great problem that seems to vex so many out here—the world's sheer gone-to-hellness since the sixties. In tackling this obsessive issue he does not turn to secular scholarship, to academic history or sociology or political economy. The Kansas mind holds those to be inadmissible, woefully compromised by their liberalism or their implication in the conspiracy. Instead the answers must be sought exclusively among foundational church texts, the way others out here look exclusively to the Constitution or the Bible. And thus are even the brightest driven back—whether they are searching for certainty and holiness, or simply for an explanation of what has happened to their world—to the crudest theories of liberal conspiracy.

So Pope Michael stands defiantly outside the great liberal organization, denouncing it for the most outrageous crimes. But he doesn't identify himself with the little guy, with the downtrodden, any more than the state's conservative Republican leaders genuinely care about the fate of the farmers and the small towns. On the contrary; the side he takes is that of the most overbearing traditions of the church itself, its medieval popes, its nineteenth-century Spanish priests. It is these that he believes to have been left unfairly behind, that need to be defended. He lines up with the big guys; indeed, even as he walks the aisles of the local thrift store he dreams of being the biggest guy of them all.

Chapter Twelve

Performing Indignation

Spin the spiritual dial a little farther, and the religiosity of credulous Kansas can start to seem downright loony. In addition to its heartfelt soul-savers, Kansas is a renowned haven for charlatans, for that variety of spiritual swindler who has discovered what pleasing earthly results he can achieve by posing as an intimate confidant of the Almighty. In this category falls that classic Kansas type, Elmer Gantry, as well as a host of rank-and-file hypocrites, with which the Franks, thanks to my father's kindheartedness, are more familiar with than most. My dad is an inveterate benefactor of self-described Christians who are down on their luck, hiring them to do some work around the house. Invariably do they disappoint him, botching the job in some spectacular manner, or goldbricking conspicuously, or just walking off for no good reason, or writing him bad checks, or stealing his lawn mower. But before they make their exit, each of these people, regardless of the reason he's been hired and independently of the others, has seen fit to while away the workday alternately praising Jesus and grumbling bitterly to anyone who will listen (usually me) about the hopeless liberal depravity of everyone else in the world.

Perhaps all this is just another aspect of our middle-American condition. Way back in 1940, the newspaperman W. G. Clugston insisted that susceptibility to even the most hypocritical Jesus-slingers has always marked Kansas's peculiar form of idealism. Where the trick really mattered, though, was in the realm of the political. And here the charlatans aren't just the occasional itin-erant housepainter; they are the state's governing class. Instead of dealing with its economic problems as material issues, Clugston wrote, the state persistently chose to elect a series of prayerful scoundrels, "leaders who had failed them in everything except pretended piety and good intentions." The state's ruling clique was constantly inventing new crusades against sin (the main example being Prohibition) because "unless they could find some new emotional appeal with which to keep the people's attentions centered upon a battle with 'The Evil One,' they could stay in office only by promoting material advantages for the peo-ple to enjoy."[1] And they sure as hell weren't going to do that. What would ConAgra say?

The Kansas conservatives, it seems to me, can be divided into two basic groups. On one side are the true believers, the average folks who have been driven into right-wing politics by what they see as the tyranny of the lawyers, the America-haters at Harvard, the professional politicians in Washington, or the eviction of God from public space. These kinds of Con will throw them-selves under the wheels of an abortion doctor's car; they will go door-to-door and spend their life savings for their causes; they will agitate, educate, and organize with a conviction that anyone who believes in democracy has to admire.

On the other side are the opportunists: professional politi-cians and lawyers and Harvard men who have discovered in the great right-wing groundswell an easy shortcut to realizing their ambitions. Many of them once aspired to join—maybe even did join—the state's moderate Republican insider club. Rising up that way, however, would take years, maybe a lifetime, when by mouthing some easily memorized God-talk and changing their position on abortion—as Brownback[2] and other leading Cons have done—they could instantly have a *movement* at their back, complete with superdedicated campaign workers they wouldn't have to pay and a national network of pundits and think tanks and talk-show hosts ready to plug them in.

Kansas's bright young Republicans know which way the wind is blowing. The old Mod machine, they can tell, is tired and aging and clearly out of step with the national trend to the right. Bob Dole and Nancy Kassebaum are long gone, while Brownback, Tiahrt, and company promise to be with us for decades to come. The state's smart young lawyers these days all become Con men, as do its Harvard grads and its Rhodes scholars.

I met one of these promising young fellows at a reception for Sam Brownback in 2003. As we watched the windburned farmers in clip-on ties shake the hand of their hero, this fledgling power broker—a banker's son in an expensive-looking suit and an even more expensive East Coast education—informed me in that classic D.C. simper that he doesn't return phone calls from the press (meaning me), no matter what they are about. An unremarkable specimen of the familiar eastern *Preppius filius,* I thought, as I walked away. That he might be a person of rare spirituality never crossed my mind. And yet when the young man who seemed so effete and so cynical to me was profiled by the Topeka newspaper, he emerged as a figure of almost Christlike humility, insisting that his aim in Washington is only to be "useful to God" and dropping such juicy personal tidbits as his feeling that working as chief of staff in Brownback's office is "where God wants [him] to be right now."

. . .

El Dorado, Kansas. Deepest July 2002. I am here to try to witness the interaction between opportunist and believer firsthand, to see what makes the Kansas equation work. There are no clouds in the vast Kansas sky, and the temperature hovers around one hundred degrees, as it has for a week. The town's nineteenth-century main street is, of course, empty. The only going concern appears to be the obligatory secondhand store, and I appear to be the only customer. Not a welcome one, either. The scowling proprietor will have no small talk. She keeps an eye on me as I walk up and down the aisles. She can plainly see that I'm up to no good.

Out at Lake El Dorado, the woman at the gateway complains about the heat. Everyone who works there with her, she says, is either diabetic or hyperglycemic, and the heat is driving their blood-sugar levels to intolerable highs.

The lake itself is a man-made affair built in the eighties. The remains of a dead forest jut through its surface, but along the shoreline there are only a few trees here and there, and virtually no shade for the dying grass—it's just prairie-meets-water under the relentless Kansas sun.

The Kansas Vietnam Veterans are holding their annual reunion here in a campsite that they have dubbed Firebase Shady Creek. They've brought all the usual things one would expect at such a gathering: beer and charcoal grills, camo netting and Winnebagos, tents and lawn chairs. They are regular folks from Wichita and Towanda and Hutchinson, getting together with old friends and watching fireworks and boating on the lake.

They are not having a good time in the ordinary, untroubled sense, however. In addition to all the conventional outdoor fun, the vets have gathered here in the dazzling heat to remind themselves that they are the victims of one of American history's cruelest episodes. In this they are assisted by a platoon of traveling trinket vendors peddling images of anguish and vengeance: T-shirts showing a GI crucified on a bamboo cross, T-shirts of an eagle chained to a map of Southeast Asia, a wishing well consecrated to the release of the prisoners that many believe Vietnam still holds. In the vengeance category fall such items as the Jane Fonda urinal target and the Vietnam flag doormat.

In the seventies, and especially while the war was still going on, the victimhood of Vietnam vets often had a leftist cast to it. The vets saw themselves as victims then because their love for their country had been manipulated in the service of a pointless and even an obscene cause. The Johnson administration's "best and brightest," drafted from the corporate world, were manufacturing corpses the way they made cars or appliances, and selling the slaughter with a form of patriotism as hollow as the TV commercials of the fifties.

Like everything else, however, the political valence of Vietnam-related martyrdom has been switched. What you hear more commonly today is that the soldiers were victimized by betrayal, first by liberals in government and then by the antiwar movement, as symbolized by the clueless Fonda. The mistake wasn't taking the wrong side in the wrong war; it was letting those intellectuals—now transformed from cold corporate titans into a treasonable liberal elite—keep us from prevailing, from unleashing sufficient lethality on the Vietnamese countryside. Conservatives like Barry Goldwater made this argument at the time, of course, but it took decades for the idea to win the sort of mainstream audience it has today. This may be conservatism's most striking cultural victory of all, a perfect inversion: the fifties-style patriotism that was once thought to have *victimized* the Vietnam generation is today thought to be a cause that is *sanctified* by their death and suffering. What their blood calls out for is not skepticism but ever blinder patriotism.[3]

In the seventies conservatives came to believe that the legacy of Vietnam was the "Vietnam syndrome," a debilitating fear of sending in the troops lest lives (and votes) be lost. A more obvious legacy these days is the ferocious new militarism in which setbacks in the field are routinely blamed on liberals in Congress and in the media, and in which it is thought to be socially acceptable for old soldiers to revel in their brutalization and even to boast about their personal kill-skills. (Example: the popular "sniper" bumper sticker that threatens, "Don't run, you'll only die tired.")

All that a soldier wants to do is fight, according to this understanding, and the more violently the better. Training him and sending him off to battle isn't a hideous imposition; it is natural and even noble. To support our men in uniform is to let them see combat. Such a viewpoint denies the age-old conflict between officers and enlisted men that is documented by every war novel ever written, and instead identifies the lowliest of foot soldiers unproblematically with their commanders, who assuredly do pine to give their soldiers that chance to fight. Applied to the historical Vietnam War itself, this way of thinking implies that the army suffered no disobedience, no griping, not even any of the jolly countercultural troublemaking seen in feel-good war films like *Good Morning Vietnam*. Dissent was the sole province of the hippie traitors at home.

We need only return to our Kansans at Lake El Dorado to see that the soldier/hippie divide was hardly that clear. True, the proprietor of the barbecue stand has posted a sign in which Maxine, the cranky but lovable Hallmark Cards granny, says, "Hey! It's either 'One Nation Under God' or bite my ass and just leave!" but otherwise the get-together is swimming in the rebel culture of the sixties: piercings, beards, long hair, even tie-dye. The hardest-rocking music of the Vietnam era wafts over the assemblage, pumped from gigantic, military-looking amplifiers: Cream, the Doors, the Rolling Stones, Deep Purple—the untroubled authenticity of the days when the vets were a *genera-tion* and the world trembled before their strong music. All of which is today—thanks to the many generations of manufactured rebellion that have followed—no more menacing than the power-chord theme song from *Bob the Builder*. The once-famous guitar solo from "Cinnamon Girl" that everyone here has heard ten thousand times blinks harmlessly in and out on the baking, unmoving air. The vets even hoist a PBR to "Eve of Destruction," the original antiwar song.

Eventually, the time comes to turn down the rock, take a seat under the camo netting, and pay attention to Phill Kline, the promising young Con who is campaigning for the Republican nomination for Kansas attorney general. Kline warms up the audience with a gruesome tale of the abuse of POWs by the North Vietnamese, who taunted their prisoners between beatings by telling them that "America has forgotten you," that "America no longer cares. America will not come to get you."

Kline is a powerful and even a hypnotic speaker, his talents honed by the years he's spent doing the local-Limbaugh routine on a Kansas City radio station. I have no doubt that I am hearing the hundredth iteration of a standard campaign speech; in fact, I will hear pieces of it many more times before the year is out. But each time Kline manages to give the impression that what he is telling us is urgent news for us alone. He stands slightly hunched over on the temporary stage, no jacket, his yellow tie loosened with the effort of his oration, his voice slightly hoarse and occasionally cracking with emotion. Kline's eloquence is world-class, the best Kansas has to offer. Of course, he knows this; Kline has spent the last few years doing nothing but running for office. And while his neat haircut and rimless spectacles recall Alf Landon, his message is pure contemporary backlash.

Kline somehow makes the transition from a gulag in North Vietnam to the frustrating cultural issues of today. While the

232 • What's the Matter with Kansas?

POWs then risked torture to say the Pledge of Allegiance, today we live in a society that has, at the behest of a circuit court in crazy San Francisco, purged the Pledge from the classroom. A vet hollers out his own angry verdict on the infamous decision: "*bull shit!*" Kline knows that the California court decision does not apply in Kansas, but he keeps it coming, winding them up. "And that was one month after another federal court in Pennsylvania ruled that pornography has to be provided to our children in the classroom," an apparent reference to a decision restricting Internet filters. "So from one coast we hear that the Pledge is unconstitutional, and from the other coast we hear that pornography must be provided to children, because that is mandated by the Constitution." The good people of Middle America are spit on again, victimized by the daft fashions of the snobs on the coasts as surely as those soldiers were in a Vietnamese prison camp thirty years previous.

And Phill Kline is there with us, suffering as we do while the high and mighty in government try to tame the people of Kansas. "The genius of America, folks," he says, "is not found in the halls of power. Government is not the repository of wisdom. The genius of America is found at our kitchen tables, and our living rooms, and our places of worship." Kline is sprinting now, setting himself up for the great Jacksonian moment, his rhythm that of a charismatic preacher nearing his metaphysical climax. "Government is formed not to create special privileges, not to listen to the loudest voice, not to pay attention to those who write the biggest checks: it is to protect our inherent rights."

A few days later I meet with a member of Kline's campaign to find out what Kline meant by that "biggest checks" business. Kline's reputation, from his days in the Kansas house, is that of a fanatical tax-cutter; for those who can write big checks he has done massive favors over the years. The answer surprises even cynical old me. What Kline was referring to, his press secretary tells me, is the Microsoft antitrust suit. Kansas, he informs me, is one of only a handful of states that still hasn't settled with the software monopolist, hinting that this is because the outgoing attorney general (a Mod) received campaign money from Oracle and various other Microsoft competitors. Kline's campaign, meanwhile, understands that this antitrust suit is obviously without merit and is, in fact, merely a political shakedown: the Clinton Justice Department "threatened this enterprise with extinction unless they basically give in to the demands of the executive branch. Same as tobacco litigation: Executive branch threatens a business with extinction unless they give money to the legislative branch so they can fund pet projects." The logic is convoluted and conspiratorial, but it gets a Republican where he needs to be: Kline would serve the state's poorest and weakest by letting Microsoft off the hook.

Another thing this spokesman tells me is that more Kansans need to go to jail. In Kansas, he says, the "rate of incarceration went up forty-four percent in the nineties. In the rest of the nation, it went up 71.7 percent. So we are not putting people in jail" at the same rate as other states. Our relative level of guilt is not in question; it's the state's slack punishment that is causing us to fall behind, that is embarrassing us before the nation. We need to get tough, make up for lost time, fill existing prisons, and build new ones. A little while later the spokesman reminds me that Kline is a Christian, that he is a member of the Nazarene faith, that he reads the Bible every day, and, sure enough, some months afterward, I see a newspaper story about Kline, now the attorney general of Kansas, delivering a sermon in a Dodge City church.

What percentage, I wondered as I read that story, would Jesus jail?

. . .

The man Phill Kline was running against that dizzying summer day in El Dorado was a prominent moderate Republican from Leawood, one of the more exclusive Johnson County suburbs. Although Kline also comes from Johnson County, the battle between the two quickly snapped into the familiar symbolic framework: Kline was the candidate of the common man; the other guy the representative of the elite. Kline proclaimed himself the choice of the "barbecue and beer Republicans." Newspaper profiles pointed out that "he isn't wealthy and doesn't pretend to be." The modest house he lived in soon made its appearance, plus references to the depth of his religious faith, and then the reporter would mention Kline's cars, his Buick and his well-worn Crown Vic.[4] There is a great symbolism in those cars: When I spoke to Kline's press secretary, I was told that his opponent, by nefarious contrast, was a "country-club Republican" who ran his elitist errands in a *Volvo*.

Stick with Phill Kline for very long, though, and you start to suspect that all this workerist talk is just the contrivance of a very shrewd political mind. While the state's right-wing populists constantly revile professional politicians driven by ambition, they rarely stop to consider that their hero, Phill Kline, might be exactly that. He is always running for something. He was the head of the College Republicans when a student at KU, he ran for Congress while he was still in law school, he made his name in the nineties as a fierce tax-cutter in the Kansas house, then he ran for Congress again, then he got himself nominated to be U.S. attorney for Kansas, and then, when I met him, he was running for attorney general—which position he finally won. Nor have the requirements of that post caused him to cease campaigning. The cases Kline has chosen to emphasize are precisely the sort of culture-war outrages (underage sex, homosexual rape) that will rally his followers and keep him in the backlash spotlight. Less than a year into his job Kline had already appeared on *The O'Reilly Factor,* getting indignant along with Bill over the bad values of the ACLU.

It was clear to me that Kline had shaped his populist persona with considerable care. People who have known the man for years insist that his conservatism is something of a pose. Of course I don't know about that, but I can say that Phill Kline is one of the maybe five people I have ever met in Kansas who even knows that there is a difference between what today's journalists call "populism" and the leftist, nineteenth-century original. Once, when I told him where I had gone to high school, his initial reaction was to perform one of those friend-making stunts that accomplished politicians do so well: he summoned up out of some distant mental warehouse the exact score of a football game between my school and his in the seventies. But then, seeming to remember something, he snapped back into proletarian character and responded to some generic lament of mine about my high school friends moving away by laughing that they were probably all out on the golf course. Or in Bermuda.

The deafness of the conservative rank and file to the patent insincerity of their leaders is one of the true cultural marvels of the Great Backlash. It extends from the local level to the highest heights, from clear-eyed city council aspirant to George W. Bush, a man so ham-handed in his invocations of the Lord that he occasionally slips into blasphemy.[5] Indeed, even as conservatives routinely mock Democrats for faking their religious sentiment, they themselves plainly feel so exempt from such criticism that they wander blithely in and out of the land of hypocrisy, never pausing to wonder if their followers might be paying attention. Laura Ingraham, a right-wing pundit renowned for appearing on the cover of the *New York Times Magazine* in a sexy miniskirt ten years ago, today denounces Hollywood elites for wanting to tear down "traditional values."[6] Ann Coulter poses as a journalist.[7] Bill O'Reilly poses as a proletarian. Hawkish politicians great and small pose as hardened war veterans, while dovish politicians who are actual war veterans are accused of weakness. Rush Limbaugh, that unwavering scourge of the drug addict, turns out to be one himself. The careers of Newt Gingrich, Henry Hyde, Bob Barr, and Enid Waldholtz are all tainted by revelations of foulest hypocrisy. And yet the suspicions of the rank and file are not aroused. The power of their shared vision of martyrdom is sufficient to overcome any set of facts that are merely material, merely true.

Epilogue

In the Garden
of the World

In 1965, the year I was born, my family still lived in the blue-collar Kansas City suburb of Shawnee, a modest settlement on the westernmost perimeter of town, out beyond the tracks of the Santa Fe Railroad. It was a place where the city faded slowly into country, and the subdivisions were checkerboarded with soybean fields, and there were no trees tall enough yet to obscure the vast blue sweep of the Kansas sky. It was a "workers' paradise," my dad remembers now, a place where the ranch homes and split levels housed the families of appliance salesmen, auto mechanics, and junior engineers at the giant Bendix plant just across the state line: upbeat people, guys with GI Bill educations and color TVs in massive fake-mahogany cabinets. The world had not gone sour for them yet; had you told them then that they would one day be devoted to something like Fox News, a network that offers its viewers nothing but torture—endless images of a depraved world that, it tells them, they are powerless to correct—they would have questioned your sanity.

Shawnee today has the feel of a place whose energy has been spent, whose time has come and gone, like one of those dead towns built in the western half of the state in some burst of inexplicable optimism in the 1880s. When I visit the old neighborhood now, I am the only pedestrian on the streets, a spectacle so odd that people slow their cars down in order to get a better look at me. The elementary school my brother attended in the crewcut days—B-47s roaring overhead as he capered on the jungle gym—is in the process of closing for good. There is not a trace of the armies of kids that used to chase one another up and down the blocks. Nor would those armies of kids be welcome in this new Shawnee, with its occasional heaps of rusting junk and its snarling rottweilers and its testy "No Trespassing" signs. The Lutheran church down the street that impressed five-year-old me with its daring sixties modernism looks today like a home-built A-frame, laughably shoddy, forlorn in a treeless lawn of knee-high weeds, its paint peeling. The shopping mall they were constructing the summer my family moved to Mission Hills has now passed through all the stages of retail life and is sinking irreversibly into blight, its storefronts empty except for a pool hall, a karate studio, and the obligatory "antique" store.

The implacable ideological bitterness that one finds throughout the state has here achieved a sort of saturation. The eastern part of Shawnee is still a blue-collar suburb, but after three decades of deunionization and stagnant wage growth, blue-collar suburbs like this one look and act very differently than before. Shawnee today burns hotter than nearly any place in the state to defund public education, to stamp out stem-cell research, to roll back taxes, and to abase itself before the throne of big business. The suburb is famous for having sent the most determined of the anti-evolutionists to the State Board of Education and for having chosen the most conservative of all Kansas state legislators, a woman who uses her hard-knock life story to dress up her constant demands that the state do whatever is necessary to lessen burdens on corporate enterprise. The offices of Kansans for Life, Tim Golba's old group, occupy a storefront in that dying mall, and the headquarters of the Phill Kline campaign are here too, in a glorified Quonset hut squatting on a weed-covered lot three blocks from the former Frank residence.

A while back the *Wall Street Journal* ran an essay about a place "where hatred trumps bread," where a manipulative ruling class has for decades exploited an impoverished people while simultaneously fostering in them a culture of victimization that steers this people's fury back persistently toward a shadowy, cosmopolitan Other. In this tragic land unassuageable cultural grievances are elevated inexplicably over solid material ones, and basic economic self-interest is eclipsed by juicy myths of national authenticity and righteousness wronged.

The essay was supposed to be a description of the Arab states in their conflict with Israel, but when I read it I thought immediately of dear old Kansas and the role that locales like Shawnee play in conservatism's populist myth. Conservatism's base constituent, the business community, is the party that has gained the most from the trends that have done such harm out here. But conservatism's house intellectuals counter this by offering an irresistible alternative way of framing our victimhood. They invite us to take our place among a humble middle-American *volk,* virtuous and yet suffering under the rule of a snobbish elite who press their alien philosophy down on the heartland.

Yes, the Cons will acknowledge, things have gotten materially worse on the farms and in the small towns, but that's just business, they tell us. That is just the forces of nature doing their thing. *Politics* is something different: Politics is about blasphemous art and crazy lawsuits filed by out-of-control trial lawyers and smart-talking pop stars running down America. Politics is when the people in the small towns look around at what Wal-Mart and ConAgra have wrought and decide to enlist in the crusade against Charles Darwin.

But the backlash offers more than this ready-made class identity. It also gives people a general way of understanding the buzzing mass-cultural world we inhabit. Consider, for example, the stereotype of liberals that comes up so often in the backlash oeuvre: arrogant, rich, tasteful, fashionable, and all-powerful. In my real-world experience liberals are nothing of the kind. They are an assortment of complainers—for the most part impoverished complainers—who wield about as much influence over American politics as the cashier at Home Depot does over the company's business strategy. This is not a secret, either; read any issue of *The Nation* or *In These Times* or the magazine sent to members of the United Steelworkers, and you figure out pretty quickly that liberals don't speak for the powerful or the wealthy.

But when you flip through *People* magazine, you come away with a very different impression of what liberals are like. Here you read about movie stars who go to charity balls for causes like animal rights and the "underprivileged." Singers who were big in the seventies express their concern with neatly folded ribbons for this set of victims or that. Minor TV personalities instruct the world to stop saying mean things about the overweight or the handicapped. And beautiful people of every description don expensive transgressive fashions, buy expensive transgressive art, eat at expensive transgressive restaurants, and get edgy with an expensive punk sensibility or an expensive earth-friendly look.

Here liberalism *is* a matter of shallow appearances, of fatuous self-righteousness; it *is* arrogant and condescending, a politics in which the beautiful and the wellborn tell the unwashed and the beaten-down and the funny-looking how they ought to behave, how they should stop being racist or homophobic, how they should be better people. In an America where the chief sources of one's ideas about life's possibilities are TV and the movies, it's not hard to be convinced that we inhabit a liberal-dominated world: feminist cartoons for ten-year-olds are followed by commercials for nonconformist deodorants; entire families of movies are organized around some transcendent dick joke; even shows for toddlers have theme songs about keeping it real.

Like any industry, though, the culture business exists primarily to advance its own fortunes, not those of the Democratic Party. Winning an audience of teenagers, for example, is the goal that has made the dick joke into a sort of gold standard, not winning elections for liberals. Encouraging demographic self-recognition and self-expression through products is, similarly, the bread and butter not of leftist ideology but of consumerism. These things are part of the culture industry's very DNA. They are as subject to change by an offended American electorate as is the occupant of the Danish throne.

Never understanding this is a source of strength for the backlash. Its leaders rage against the liberalism of Hollywood. Its voters toss a few liberals out of office and are surprised to see that Hollywood doesn't care. They toss out more liberals and still nothing changes. They return an entire phalanx of pro-business blowhards to Washington, and still the culture industry goes on its merry way. But at least those backlash politicians that they elect are willing to do one thing differently: they stand there on the floor of the U.S. Senate and shout *no* to it all. And this is the critical point: in a media world where what people shout overshadows what they actually do, the backlash sometimes appears to be the only dissenter out there, the only movement that has a place for the uncool and the funny-looking and the pious, for all the stock buffoons that our mainstream culture glories in lampooning. In this sense the backlash is becoming a perpetual alter-ego to the culture industry, a feature of American life as permanent and as strange as Hollywood itself.

Even as it rejects the broader commercial culture, though, the backlash also mimics it. Conservatism provides its followers with a parallel universe, furnished with all the same attractive pseudospiritual goods as the mainstream: authenticity, rebellion, the nobility of victimhood, even individuality. But the most important similarity between backlash and mainstream commercial culture is that both refuse to think about capitalism critically. Indeed, conservative populism's total erasure of the economic could only happen in a culture like ours where material politics have already been muted and where the economic has largely been replaced by those aforementioned pseudospiritual fulfillments. This is the basic lie of the backlash, the manipulative strategy that makes the whole senseless parade possible. In all of its rejecting and nay-saying, it resolutely refuses to consider that the assaults on its values, the insults, and the Hollywood sneers are all products of capitalism as surely as are McDonald's hamburgers and Boeing 737s.

Who is to blame for this landscape of distortion, of paranoia, and of good people led astray? I have spent much of this book enumerating the ways in which Kansas voters choose self-destructive policies, but it is just as clear to me that liberalism deserves a large part of the blame for the backlash phenomenon. Liberalism may not be the monstrous, all-powerful conspiracy that conservatives make it out to be, but its failings are clear nonetheless. Somewhere in the last four decades liberalism ceased to be relevant to huge portions of its traditional constituency, and we can say that liberalism *lost* places like Shawnee and Wichita with as much accuracy as we can point out that conservatism won them over.

This is due partially, I think, to the Democratic Party's more-

or-less official response to its waning fortunes. The Democratic Leadership Council (DLC), the organization that produced such figures as Bill Clinton, Al Gore, Joe Lieberman, and Terry McAuliffe, has long been pushing the party to forget blue-collar voters and concentrate instead on recruiting affluent, white-collar professionals who are liberal on social issues. The larger interests that the DLC wants desperately to court are corporations, capable of generating campaign contributions far outweighing anything raised by organized labor. The way to collect the votes and—more important—the money of these coveted constituencies, "New Democrats" think, is to stand rock-solid on, say, the pro-choice position while making endless concessions on economic issues, on welfare, NAFTA, Social Security, labor law, privatization, deregulation, and the rest of it. Such Democrats explicitly rule out what they deride as "class warfare" and take great pains to emphasize their friendliness to business interests. Like the conservatives, they take economic issues off the table. As for the working-class voters who were until recently the party's very backbone, the DLC figures they will have nowhere else to go; Democrats will always be marginally better on economic issues than Republicans. Besides, what politician in this success-worshiping country really wants to be the voice of poor people? Where's the soft money in that?

This is, in drastic miniature, the criminally stupid strategy that has dominated Democratic thinking off and on ever since the "New Politics" days of the early seventies. Over the years it has enjoyed a few successes: the word *yuppie,* remember, was coined in 1984 to describe followers of the presidential candidate Gary Hart.[1] But, as political writer E.J. Dionne has pointed out, the larger result was that *both* parties became "vehicles for upper-middle-class interests" and the old class-based language of the left quickly disappeared from the universe of the respectable. The Republicans, meanwhile, were industriously fabricating their own class-based language of the right, and while they made their populist appeal to blue-collar voters, Democrats were giving those same voters—their traditional base—the big brush-off, ousting their representatives from positions within the party and consigning their issues, with a laugh and a sneer, to the dustbin of history. A more ruinous strategy for Democrats would have been difficult to invent.[2] And the ruination just keeps on coming. However desperately they triangulate and accommodate, the losses keep mounting.

Curiously enough, though, Democrats of the DLC variety aren't worried. They seem to look forward to a day when their party really is what David Brooks and Ann Coulter claim it to be now: a coming-together of the rich and the self-righteous. While Republicans trick out their poisonous stereotype of the liberal elite, Democrats seem determined to live up to the libel.

Such Democrats look at a situation like present-day Kansas and rub their hands with anticipation: Just look at how Ronald Reagan's "social issues" have come back to bite his party in the ass! If only the crazy Cons push a little bit more, these Democrats think, the Republican Party will alienate the wealthy suburban Mods for good, and we will be able to step in and carry places like Mission Hills, along with all the juicy boodle that its inhabitants are capable of throwing our way.

While I enjoy watching Republicans fight one another as much as the next guy, I don't think the Kansas story really gives true liberals any cause to cheer. Maybe someday the DLC dream will come to pass, with the Democrats having moved so far to the right that they are no different than old-fashioned moderate Republicans, and maybe then the affluent will finally come over to their side en masse. But along the way the things that liberalism once stood for—equality and economic security—will have been abandoned completely. Abandoned, let us remember, at the historical moment when we need them most.

There is a lesson for liberals in the Kansas story, and it's not that they, too, might someday get invited to tea in Cupcake Land. It is, rather, an utter and final repudiation of their historical decision to remake themselves as the *other* pro-business party. By all rights the people in Wichita and Shawnee and Garden City should today be flocking to the party of Roosevelt, not deserting it. Culturally speaking, however, that option is simply not available to them anymore. Democrats no longer speak to the people on the losing end of a free-market system that is becoming more brutal and more arrogant by the day.

The problem is not that Democrats are monolithically pro-choice or anti–school prayer; it's that by dropping the class language that once distinguished them sharply from Republicans they have left themselves vulnerable to cultural wedge issues like guns and abortion and the rest whose hallucinatory appeal would ordinarily be far overshadowed by material concerns. We are in an environment where Republicans talk constantly about class—in a coded way, to be sure—but where Democrats are afraid to bring it up.

Democratic political strategy simply assumes that people know where their economic interest lies and that they will act on it by instinct. There is no need for any business-bumming class-war rhetoric on the part of candidates or party spokesmen, and there is certainly no need for a liberal to actually get his hands dirty fraternizing with the disgruntled. Let them look at the record and see for themselves: Democrats are slightly more generous with Social Security benefits, slightly stricter on environmental regulations, and do less union-busting than Republicans.

The gigantic error in all this is that people *don't* spontaneously understand their situation in the great sweep of things. They don't just automatically know the courses of action that are open to them, the organizations they might sign up with, or the measures they should be calling for. Liberalism isn't a force of karmic nature that pushes back when the corporate world goes too far; it is a man-made contrivance as subject to setbacks and defeats as any other. Consider our own social welfare apparatus, the system of taxes, regulations, and social insurance that is under sustained attack. Social Security, the FDA, and all the rest of it didn't spring out of the ground fully formed in response to the obvious excesses of a laissez-faire system; they were the result of decades of movement building, of bloody fights between strikers and state militias, of agitating, educating, and thankless organizing. More than forty years passed between the first glimmerings of a left-wing reform movement in the 1890s and the actual enactment of its reforms in the 1930s. In the meantime scores of the most rapacious species of robber baron went to their reward untaxed, unregulated, and unquestioned.

An even more telling demonstration of the importance of movements in framing people's perspectives can be found in the voting practices of union members. Take your average white male voter: in the 2000 election they chose George W. Bush by a considerable margin. Find white males who were union members, however, and they voted for Al Gore by a similar margin. The same difference is repeated whatever the demographic category: women, gun owners, retirees, and so on—when they are union members, their politics shift to the left. This is true even when the union members in question had little contact with union leaders. Just being in a union evidently changes the way a person looks at politics, inoculates them against the derangement of the backlash. Here values matter almost least of all, while the economy, health care, and education are of paramount concern.[3] Union voters are, in other words, the reverse image of the Brownback conservative who cares nothing for economics but torments himself night and day with vague fears about "cultural decline."

Labor unions are on the wane today, as everyone knows, down to 9 percent of the private-sector workforce from a high-water mark of 38 percent in the fifties. Their decline goes largely unchecked by a Democratic Party anxious to demonstrate its fealty to corporate America, and unmourned by a therapeutic left that never liked those Archie Bunker types in the first place. Among the broader population, accustomed to thinking of organizations as though they were consumer products, it is simply assumed that unions are declining because nobody wants to join them anymore, the same way the public has lost its taste for the music of the Bay City Rollers. And in the offices of the union-busting specialists and the Wall Street brokers and the retail executives, the news is understood the same way aristocrats across Europe greeted the defeat of Napoleon in 1815: as a monumental victory in a war to the death.

While leftists sit around congratulating themselves on their personal virtue, the right understands the central significance of movement-building, and they have taken to the task with admirable diligence. Cast your eyes over the vast and complex structure of conservative "movement culture," a phenomenon that has little left-wing counterpart anymore. There are foundations like the one operated by the Kochs in Wichita, channeling their millions into the political battle at the highest levels, subsidizing free-market economics departments and magazines and thinkers like Vernon L. Smith. Then there are the think tanks, the Institutes Hoover and American Enterprise, that send the money sluicing on into the pockets of the right-wing pundit corps, Ann Coulter, Dinesh D'Souza, and the rest, furnishing them with what they need to keep their books coming and their minds in fighting trim between media bouts. A brigade of lobbyists. A flock of magazines and newspapers. A publishing house or two. And, at the bottom, the committed grassroots organizers like Mark Gietzen and Tim Golba and Kay O'Connor, going door-to-door, organizing their neighbors, mortgaging their houses, even, to push the gospel of the backlash.

And this movement speaks to those at society's bottom, addresses them on a daily basis. From the left they hear nothing, but from the Cons they get an explanation for it all. Even better, they get a plan for action, a scheme for world conquest with a wedge issue. And why shouldn't they get to dream their lurid dreams of politics-as-manipulation? They've had it done to them enough in reality.

American conservatism depends for its continued dominance and even for its very existence on people never making certain mental connections about the world, connections that until recently were treated as obvious or self-evident everywhere on the planet. For example, the connection between mass culture, most of which conservatives hate, and laissez-faire capitalism, which they adore without reservation. Or between the small towns they profess to love and the market forces that are slowly grinding those small towns back into the red-state dust—which forces they praise in the most exalted terms.[4]

In this onrushing parade of anti-knowledge my home state has proudly taken a place at the front. It is true that Kansas is an extreme case, and that there are still working-class areas here (Wyandotte County, parts of Topeka) that are yet to be converted to the Con gospel. But it is also true that things that begin in Kansas—the Civil War, Prohibition, Populism, Pizza Hut—have a historical tendency to go national.

Maybe Kansas, instead of being a laughingstock, is actually in the vanguard. Maybe what has happened there points the way in which all our public policy debates are heading. Maybe someday soon the political choices of Americans everywhere will be whittled down to the two factions of the Republican Party. Whether the Mods still call themselves "Republicans" then or have switched to being Democrats won't really matter: both groups will be what Kansans call "fiscal conservatives," which is to say "friends of business," and the issues that motivated our parents' Democratic Party will be permanently off the table.

Sociologists often warn against letting the nation's distribution of wealth become too polarized, as it clearly has in the last few decades. Societies that turn their backs on equality, the professors insist, inevitably meet with a terrible comeuppance. But those sociologists were thinking of an old world in which class anger was a phenomenon of the left. They weren't reckoning with Kansas, with the world we are becoming.

Behold the political alignment that Kansas is pioneering for us all. The corporate world—for reasons having a great deal to do with its corporateness—blankets the nation with a cultural style designed to offend and to pretend-subvert: sassy teens in Skechers flout the Man; bigoted churchgoing moms don't tolerate their daughters' cool liberated friends; hipsters dressed in T-shirts reading "FCUK" snicker at the suits who just don't get it. It's meant to be offensive, and Kansas is duly offended. The state watches impotently as its culture, beamed in from the coasts, becomes coarser and more offensive by the year. Kansas aches for revenge. Kansas gloats when celebrities say stupid things; it cheers when movie stars go to jail. And when two female rock stars exchange a lascivious kiss on national TV, Kansas goes haywire. Kansas screams for the heads of the liberal elite. Kansas comes running to the polling place. And Kansas cuts those rock stars' taxes.

As a social system, the backlash *works*. The two adversaries feed off of each other in a kind of inverted symbiosis: one mocks the other, and the other heaps even more power on the one. This arrangement should be the envy of every ruling class in the world. Not only *can* it be pushed much, much further, but it is fairly certain that it *will* be so pushed. All the incentives point that way, as do the never-examined cultural requirements of modern capitalism. Why shouldn't our culture just get worse and worse, if making it worse will only cause the people who worsen it to grow wealthier and wealthier?

Should you ever happen to take the tour of Kansas City, Kansas, that is prescribed by the 1939 WPA guide, you will notice a peculiar thing: many of the features it highlights are no longer there. You will find no trace of the tower billed as the tallest in the city. Or the "elaborate Italian Renaissance architecture" of the public library. Or the city's many meatpacking plants. Or even the "panoramic view" of the bend in the Missouri where Lewis and Clark landed: the spot where the visitor was supposed to stand has been leveled by the confused, coiling ramps of an interstate highway.

This disfigured landscape is a large part of my father's Kansas City: From a childhood spent riding the now vanished streetcars, he knows where each once-grand avenue in the old metropolis will take you, what businesses used to occupy each abandoned building, what each erased neighborhood was called and precisely where it stood. He remembers the big bands playing at the now demolished Pla-Mor ballroom, and the proud newspaper pictures of the Wichita machinists pasting dollar bills on their thousandth B-29, and the packinghouse workers streaming on foot across the now disused James Street Bridge, a form of transportation as inconceivable here today as are the urban neighborhoods in which those workers once lived.

As you cast your eyes back over this vanished Midwest, this landscape of lost brotherhood and forgotten pride, you can't help but wonder how much farther it's all going to go. How many of those old, warm associations are we willing to dissolve? How much more of the "garden of the world" will we abandon to sterility and decay?

My guess is, quite a bit. The fever-dream of martyrdom that Kansas follows today has every bit as much power as John Brown's dream of justice and human fraternity. And even if the state must sacrifice it all—its cities and its industry, its farms and its small towns, all its thoughts and all its doings—the brilliance of the mirage will not fade. Kansas is ready to lead us singing into the apocalypse. It invites us all to join in, to lay down our lives so that others might cash out at the top; to renounce forever our middle-American prosperity in pursuit of a crimson fantasy of middle-American righteousness.

Notes

Interviews

State Sen. David Adkins, Prairie Village, Kansas, April 29, 2003

David Bawden, Delia, Kansas, January 27, 2003

Michael Carmody, Wichita, May 4, 2003

Alan Cobb, Topeka, July 24, 2002

Mary Kay Culp, Shawnee, September 23, 2002

Jill Docking, Wichita, May 1, 2003

Jose Flores, by telephone, January 30, 2003

Mark Gietzen, Wichita, August 25, 2003

Dan Glickman, by telephone, September 20, 2002

Tim Golba, Olathe, September 2, 2002

Bud Hentzen, Wichita, May 1, 2003

Wes Jackson, Salina, May 2, 2003

Steve Kraske, Kansas City, Missouri, September 4, 2002

Chuck Kurtz, by telephone, September 28, 2002

State Rep. Bruce Larkin, by telephone, January 29, 2003

Jim Lawing, Wichita, May 1, 2003

Sue Ledbetter, Wichita, September 4, 2002

Professor Burdett Loomis, by telephone, July 17, 2002

State Rep. Rocky Nichols, Topeka, January 27, 2003

State Sen. Kay O'Connor, Olathe, November 21, 2002

Judy Pierce, Wichita, September 5, 2002

Arturo Ponce, by telephone, May 9, 2003

Carol Rupe, Wichita, April 30, 2003

Penny Schwab, Garden City, May 3, 2003

Professor Donald Stull, by telephone, January 29, 2003

Dwight Sutherland, Jr., Prairie Village, December 22, 2002

State Rep. Dale Swenson, by telephone, February 8, 2003

Donn Teske, by telephone, January 30, 2003

Frank Velazquez, by telephone, July 1, 2003

State Sen. Susan Wagle, Andover, May 5, 2003

Professor Bill Wagnon, Topeka, July 24, 2002

Whitney Watson, Shawnee, July 21, 2002

Duane West, by telephone, May 8, 2003

Bob Wood, Wichita, September 4, 2002

Introduction

1. I am referring to McPherson County, Nebraska, but there are several counties in that state where extreme poverty coincides with extreme Republicanism—just as there are in Kansas and the Dakotas. My source for the county poverty rankings is "Trampled Dreams: The Neglected Economy of the Rural Great Plains," a study by Patricia Funk and Jon Bailey (Walthill, Neb.: Center for Rural Affairs, 2000), p. 6.

2. Ben J. Wattenberg, *Values Matter Most: How Republicans or Democrats or a Third Party Can Win and Renew the American Way of Life* (New York: Free Press, 1995). Like many backlash thinkers, Wattenberg was briefly caught up in New Economy boosterism in the late nineties.

3. This persistent failure is discussed by the liberal *Washington Post* columnist E. J. Dionne in *Why Americans Hate Politics,* but it is also a point of great annoyance among conservatives themselves. David Frum, for example, complains that Ronald Reagan could have abolished affirmative action "with a few signatures." But he never did. Frum, *Dead Right* (New York: Basic Books, 1994), p. 72. Reagan's betrayal on the abortion issue is even more of a sore point with the conservative hard core. See Christopher Lasch, *The True and Only Heaven: Progress and Its Critics* (New York: Norton, 1991), p. 515.

4. Indeed, repealing the twentieth century is, broadly speaking, the stated objective of the Intelligent Design movement, which has set about accomplishing this goal by assailing Darwinian evolution. The movement's notorious "wedge" document, produced in 1999 by the Discovery Institute's Center for the Renewal of Science and Culture, asserts that "the social consequences of materialism have been devastating." As examples the document lists "modern approaches to criminal justice, product liability, and welfare," in addition to "coercive government

programs." These can all be destroyed, the authors suggest, with a strategic attack on evolution. As the document goes on to explain, "We are convinced that in order to defeat materialism, we must cut it off at its source. That source is scientific materialism. This is precisely our strategy. If we view the predominant materialistic science as a giant tree, our strategy is intended to function as a 'wedge' that, while relatively small, can split the trunk when applied at its weakest points. . . . Design theory promises to reverse the stifling dominance of the materialist worldview, and to replace it with a science consonant with Christian and theistic convictions." The wedge document can be found in numerous places on the Internet; one such is: http://www.discovery.org/csc/TopQuestions/wedgeresp.pdf.

Chapter One: The Two Nations

1. The red-state/blue-state narrative drew heavily on *One Nation, Two Cultures,* a culture-warring book brought forth in 1999 by the neoconservative doyenne Gertrude Himmelfarb, wife of Irving Kristol and mom of Bill Kristol, editor of the *Weekly Standard.*

2. See, for example, David Frum's account of the Bush White House, *The Right Man* (New York: Random House, 2003), p. 36, or the story by James Harding in the *Financial Times* for May 20, 2003. In the latter, the Bush strategist Karl Rove was reported to be reading a biography of McKinley and speaks of the Republican Party winning a grand realignment just as McKinley did.

3. I am referring here to the county-by-county results, in square miles. Bush won the votes of counties occupying 2,427,039 square miles, while Gore only took the votes of 580,134 square miles.

   You think this is so obviously irrelevant no one in their right mind would ever bring it up? Think again. An article that appeared on *National Review Online* a year after the election used this fact to show that Bush's vote was more "representative of the diversity of the nation" than Gore's: "A look at the county-by-county map of the United States following the 2000 vote shows only small islands (mostly on the coasts) of Gore Blue amid a wide sea of Bush Red. In all, Bush won majorities in areas representing more than 2.4 million square miles, while Gore was able to garner winning margins in only 580,000."

4. The "two Americas" was, for the most part, a pop narrative generated by conservatives. As far as I have been able to determine, there were only a few attempts to define the red-state/blue-state divide in a liberal manner, the most notable being Paul Krugman's effort to stand the narrative on its head by depicting red Americans as freeloaders, living off

the tax money (i.e., farm subsidies) of wealthy blue America. Needless to say, this viewpoint was not widely embraced, even though, by the definitions of the "two Americas" narrative, blue-state people are supposed to dominate the nation's media and constantly to distort the news to depict themselves in a favorable light.

5. My roundup of the red-state/blue-state literature incorporated the following, listed in chronological order: David Broder, "Burying the Hatchet," *Washington Post*, November 10, 2000; Robert Tracinski, "Rural Individualists," *National Post*, November 30, 2000; Matt Bai, "Red Zone vs. Blue Zone," *Newsweek*, January 1, 2001; Newt Gingrich, "Two Americas," *Chief Executive*, February 1, 2001; John Podhoretz, "The Two Americas: Ironic Us, Simple Them," *New York Post*, March 13, 2001; Michael Barone, "The 49 Percent Nation," *National Journal*, June 9, 2001; Andrew Sullivan, "Lizzie Crashes into America's Class War," *Sunday Times* (London), July 29, 2001; David Brooks, "One Nation, Slightly Divisible," *The Atlantic*, December 2001; "Sons of Liberty," *Wall Street Journal*, December 7, 2001; James Poniewozik, "The NASCAR of News," *Time*, February 11, 2002; Jill Lawrence, "Values, Votes, Points of View Separate Towns," *USA Today*, February 18, 2002; Blake Hurst, "The Plains vs. the Atlantic," *The American Enterprise*, March 1, 2002; Ronald A. Buel, "Winning over Oregon," *Portland Oregonian*, March 17, 2002; Paul Krugman, "Those Farm Subsidy Blues: Blame It on the Red States," *Milwaukee Journal-Sentinel*, May 9, 2002; Doug Saunders, "Caught in the Crossfire of the 'Two Americas,'" *Toronto Globe and Mail*, October 12, 2002; Roy Huntington, "The Insider," *American Handgunner*, January–February 2003; Steve Berg, "The Red and the Blue," *Minneapolis Star Tribune*, February 9, 2003.

6. Disingenuously adopting the voice of the hated liberal Other is a not-uncommon rhetorical device among conservative commentators. In 2002 it was used by Peggy Noonan, who claimed to speak for the spirit of just-departed Minnesota Democrat Paul Wellstone in order to scold Wellstone's still-living supporters.

In Brooks's case, though, the device proved just a bit too tricky for his readers. Conservatives across the country apparently believed that Brooks meant it about being "more sophisticated and cosmopolitan" than people in the red states, and they raced to their keyboards to complain. A Missouri farmer named Blake Hurst was even moved to write a three-thousand-word article for *The American Enterprise* magazine flogging Brooks for his elitist blue-state pretensions and, bizarrely, taking Brooks's many passages of straightforward praise for red America as concessions wrung from a dedicated foe. These passages Hurst then proceeded to expand upon (that's right, we *are* more humble than you), effectively making his article a mirror image of Brooks's own.

Ordinarily it would be an embarrassing mistake for a magazine to publish an essay based on a misunderstanding that a sixth-grader should have been able to catch, but instead Hurst's article was celebrated widely among right-wingers on the Internet as a thundering riposte to Brooks, who was now (despite his years of contributions to conservative publications) thought to be a liberal-elitist devil-figure. Hurst's essay was reprinted on the *Wall Street Journal Online* and numerous farm publications, incidentally helping to validate one of the stereotypes that both he and Brooks had set out to dismiss: that Middle Americans are dopes.

Among the many who misunderstood Brooks's use of the second person, the most amusing response came from Phil Brennan, a conservative of the old school, who took to the right-wing Web site NewsMax.com to charge Brooks with "insufferable elitism as displayed in his look at an America neither he nor his fellow snobs pretend to understand." Brennan went on to find confirmation in Brooks's article of a rather curious theory of the decline of journalism. In the old days, he tells us, journalists "were a manly sort, utterly devoted to heterosexual activity, who fully understood who and what they were. And their reporting reflected that. And because of that self-knowledge there wasn't an elitist among them." http://www.newsmax.com/archives/articles/2002/2/20/15555.shtml.

7. I am referring to Wyandotte County, where Kansas City, Kansas, is found. It went for Gore by 67 percent to 29 percent. *Kansas Statistical Abstract 2001*, Thelma Helyar, ed. (Lawrence, Kans.: Policy Research Institute, 2002). Income statistics are from 1999 and can be found on p. 320, election results on p. 180. Wyandotte does produce some of the best barbecue in America, but call someone there a "bobo" or an "elitist," and you'd be asking for a fight.

Since the Republican–NASCAR connection figures so prominently in contemporary populist fantasies, it is worth pointing out that conservative Republicans are by no means universal fans of NASCAR. Indeed, the populist conservatives of Kansas vigorously opposed the construction of the Kansas Speedway on the grounds that it was corporate welfare, which it may well have been. (Some of them don't like Branson either, but we'll have to save that for another book.) John Altevogt, a newspaper columnist who was for a time the chairman of the Wyandotte County Republican Party, has even written that he and his neighbors "do not consider NASCAR a 'good corporate neighbor' "; indeed, they "consider it to be little more than a nuisance and a giant eyesore." *MetroVoice News* (Kansas City), March 5, 2001.

8. Consider the snowmobile dilemma: As in one of those "You might be a redneck if . . ." books, David Brooks insists in the above-mentioned *Atlantic* article that one can trace the red-state/blue-state divide by determining whether a person does outdoor activities with motors (the good old American way) or without (the pretentious blue-state way): "We [blue-state people] cross-country ski; they snowmobile." And yet in *Newsweek*'s take on the blue/red divide, a "town elder" from red America can be heard railing against people who drive snowmobiles for precisely the opposite reason: snowmobiles signal big-city contempt for the "small-town values" of Bush country!

How are the bold sociologists of politics to resolve this vexing matter of the snowmobile? What does snowmobiling truly signify? Populism or elitism? Conservatism or liberalism? Arrogance or humility? Perhaps the answer lies not in a yes-snowmobile or a no-snowmobile verdict but in a more subtle parsing of the snowmobile signifier, one that takes into consideration the long-simmering feud between the rival snowmobile brands—a feud that is of paramount importance in certain reaches of the Upper Midwest (even ranking above the various NASCAR controversies) but with which Brooks is probably unfamiliar because he is such a "sophisticated" blue-state dude.

To wit: The Polaris is a distinctly Republican brand of snowmobile, humble yet martial in its red, white, and blue color scheme. Democrats, on the other hand, do their proud prowling on Arctic Cats, a brand of snowmobile that has taken as its colors the show-off and suggestively third-worldish combination of green, purple, and black.

9. In the selection printed above, Brooks tosses off a few names from the conservative political world as though they were uncontroversial folk heroes out in the hinterland, akin to country music stars or favorite cartoonists. But the real reason liberals don't know much about James Dobson or Tim LaHaye is not because they are out of touch with America but because both of these men are far-right ideologues. Those who listen to Dobson's radio program or buy LaHaye's novels, suffused as they are in Bircher-style conspiracy theory, tend to be people who agree with them, people who are conservatives, people who voted for Bush in 2000.

10. Brooks asserts at one point in his *Atlantic* essay that "upscale areas everywhere" went for Gore in 2000. While the phenomenon of well-to-do Democrats is interesting and worth considering, as a blanket statement about the rich—or, by extension, about corporate America,

the system that made them rich—this is not even close to correct. Bush was in fact the hands-down choice of corporate America: according to the Center for Responsive Politics, Bush raised more in donations than Gore in each of ten industrial sectors; the only sector in which Gore came out ahead was "labor." In fact, Bush raised so much money from wealthy contributors (more than any other candidate in history, a record that he then broke in 2003), he established a special (and notorious) organization for them: the Pioneers.

Nor is Brooks's statement valid even within its limited parameters. When he says "upscale areas everywhere" voted for Gore, he gives Chicago's North Shore as an example of what he means. In fact, Lake Forest, the definitive and the richest North Shore burb, chose the Republican, as it always does, by a whopping 70 percent. (According to the official election results of Lake County, Illinois.) Winnetka and Kenilworth, the other North Shore suburbs known for their being "upscale," went for Bush by 59 percent and 64 percent respectively. (According to the official election results of Cook County, Illinois.)

And there were obviously dozens of other "upscale areas" where Bush prevailed handily: Morris, Somerset, and Hunterdon Counties, New Jersey; Fairfax County, Virginia (suburban D.C.); Cobb County, Georgia (suburban Atlanta); DuPage County, Illinois (more of suburban Chicago); Chester County, Pennsylvania (suburban Philadelphia); and Orange County, California (the veritable symbol of upscale suburbia), to name but a few. Or, keeping within the parameters of this book, there's Mission Hills, Kansas, by far the wealthiest town in the state, which chose Bush over Gore by 71 percent to 25 percent. Johnson County, Kansas, the most upscale county in the state, also gave Bush a lopsided victory, choosing him over Gore by 60 percent to 36 percent. (According to the official election results of the State of Kansas.)

11. In *The New York Times* for October 21, 2003, Brooks writes that of all the Democrats then vying for their party's presidential nomination, John Edwards offers the most "persuasive theory" of Democratic decline: "that the Democrats' besetting sin over the past few decades has been snobbery."

12. Richard Hofstadter's thoughts on the Populist language of the "two nations" is particularly compelling given the current circumstances. See *The Age of Reform: From Bryan to F.D.R.* (New York: Knopf, 1955), chap. 2. The quote from Jerry Simpson can be found on p. 64.

Dos Passos's famous "two nations" passage can be found in *The Big Money,* the third volume of the *U.S.A.* trilogy (New York: Harcourt, Brace and Company, 1937), pp. 462–3.

all right we are two nations
America our nation has been beaten by strangers who have
bought the laws and fenced off the meadows and cut down the
woods for pulp and turned our pleasant cities into slums and
sweated the wealth out of our people and when they want to
they hire the executioner to throw the switch.

13. "The people who lift 'things' (the . . . RAPIDLY . . . declining fraction)
are the new parasites living off the carpal-tunnel syndrome of the computer programmers' perpetually strained keyboard hands," screeched
Tom Peters in 1997. (*The Circle of Innovation: You Can't Shrink Your
Way to Greatness* [New York: Knopf, 1997]), p. 8.) He wasn't alone.
"The rich, the former leisure class, are becoming the new over-
worked," declared *Wired* magazine in its January 1998 issue. "And
those who used to be considered the working class are becoming the
new leisure class."

14. This is not the first time conservatives have rediscovered the virtues of a
conservative working class after a period of overheated reverence for the
creative white-collar type. As Barbara Ehrenreich points out in chap. 3
of *Fear of Falling: The Inner Life of the Middle Class* (New York:
HarperCollins, 1990), the same thing happened at the tail end of the sixties, the decade that introduced so many of the business-revolutionary
fantasies that came to flower in the New Economy nineties.

15. See Blake Hurst, "In Real Life," *The American Enterprise*, November–
December 1999.

16. Brooks's inventive explanation for the red-staters' complete comfort with
free-market capitalism is that they don't know need or envy. "Where
they live," he writes, "they can afford just about anything that is for
sale." On the other hand, blue-state people are reminded constantly that
there are people higher than they on the social ladder, simply because of
the spatial dynamics of the city. Evidently, there are no other grounds for
disgruntlement at all, which leads to the clear conclusion that no one
would ever complain about free-market capitalism—that many of the
revolutions and wars and social welfare schemes of the last century could
have been avoided—if only the rich would hide themselves better.

17. Indeed, Brooks himself seems undecided as to whether the cafeteria
metaphor describes reality or describes conservative ideas about reality.
In his 2001 red/blue story in the *Atlantic Monthly*, which is quoted
here, the cafeteria metaphor is presented as an objective observation
about American life. This cafeteria business is just the way life is.
Brooks repeats the argument on *The New York Times* op-ed page on

January 12, 2003, only now as something that "most Americans" agree with and understand instinctively.

Chapter Two: Deep in the Heart of Redness

1. George Gurley, "Coultergeist," *New York Observer,* November 11, 2002. A short while later in the interview, Coulter offered a measure of her respect for common sense by telling Gurley that she wished Timothy McVeigh, the Oklahoma City bomber, had blown up *The New York Times* building.

2. John Gunther, *Inside USA* (New York: Harper and Brothers, 1947), p. 259.

3. See Judy Thomas, "Kansas Ranks Dead Last in New Vacation Survey," *Dallas Morning News,* December 3, 1995. In 2003 the number-one tourist attraction in the entire state of Kansas was a sporting goods store in Kansas City, Kansas.

4. Fast food looms so large in the Kansas self-image that there is a sizable exhibit on the subject in the state historical museum in Topeka. In addition to the restaurants named above, the mall in Kansas City where I wasted many hours as a teenager housed the world's first TJ Cinnamon, the pioneer in cinnamon-roll franchising. Kansas was also the birthplace of the Harvey Houses, one of the earliest chain restaurants, which grew up alongside the Atchison, Topeka, and Santa Fe Railroad.

5. The Kansas journalist W. G. Clugston, in *Rascals in Democracy* (New York: Richard Smith, 1940), points out that each of the elections from 1928 to 1936 featured a Kansan on one of the national tickets: in 1928 and 1932 the Republicans ran the veteran Kansas senator Charles Curtis for vice president, and in 1936 they nominated Kansas governor Alf Landon to carry the banner against Roosevelt. Earl Browder, who headed the Communist ticket in 1936 and 1940, was a native of Wichita. Dwight D. Eisenhower was also a Kansan, as is, of course, Bob Dole.

6. For the characterization of Kansas as a "freak state," I am indebted to Craig Miner, *Kansas: The History of the Sunflower State, 1854–2000* (Lawrence: University Press of Kansas, 2002).

7. Debs's speech can be found at http://douglassarchives.org/debs_a80.htm. Roosevelt's Osawatomie address, in which he introduced his "New Nationalism," strikes some ironic notes given today's circumstances. In it he denounced "corruption in business on a gigantic scale," called for the regulation of corporations and the purging of corporate money from politics. He also announced his support for a graduated income tax and the inheritance tax, both of which had originally been proposed by the Populists and were soon enacted under the Wilson administration.

And both of which are today targets of Kansas's right-wing populists, who are in turn fed and funded by business interests.

8. "What's the Matter with Kansas?" has been reprinted numerous times. One place to find it is in White's *Autobiography* (New York: Macmillan, 1946), p. 280.

9. Elizabeth Barr, "The Populist Uprising," in *A Standard History of Kansas and Kansans,* William Connelley, ed. (Chicago: The Lewis Publishing Co., 1918), vol. 2, p. 1148.

10. Ingalls's famous assessment of his home state is quoted in Walter Prescott Webb, *The Great Plains* (New York: Ginn, 1931), p. 502.

11. For reasons understood only by the strategic geniuses of the New Economy, what Western decided to acquire was home security companies—several of them. It then launched a hostile takeover bid (the first one *ever* in this field, Wittig enthused) for the nearby Kansas City Power and Light Company. And then, when that gambit failed, it immediately turned around and prepared *itself* to be taken over.

12. Privatizing the gains while socializing the debt was a consistent strategy of the nation's energy companies in the post-Enron age. Westar may have been among the most notorious offenders, but it was hardly alone. See Rebecca Smith, "Beleaguered Energy Firms Try to Share Pain with Utility Units," *Wall Street Journal,* December 26, 2002.

13. Westar Energy, Inc., *Report of the Special Committee to the Board of Directors,* April 29, 2003, p. 333. The report is available online at http://media.corporate-ir.net/media_files/nys/wr/reports/custom_page/WestarEnergy.pdf.

14. For details of the Aquila catastrophe, see: Steve Everly, "Major Shareholder Criticizes Management of Utility Company Aquila," *Kansas City Star,* January 22, 2003; Diane Stafford, "Hockaday Defends Service on Boards of Embattled Sprint, Aquila," *Kansas City Star,* March 2, 2003; Edward Iwata, "Scandal Jolts Energy Traders," *USA Today,* January 21, 2003; and Mark Davis, "Former, Current Employees of Aquila Inc. Hurt by Company's Problems," *Kansas City Star,* October 20, 2002.

15. According to Nomi Prins's account of the telecom meltdown for *Left Business Observer* (see http://www.leftbusinessobserver.com/Telecoms.html), only 5 percent of all the fiber-optic cables in the world are today being used for anything. In the telecom collapse, some $2.8 trillion in capitalization was wiped out.

16. For details of the tax troubles faced by Esrey and LeMay and the failed WorldCom merger, see: Simon Romero, "For Sprint Chief, a Hard Fall From Grace," *The New York Times,* February 12, 2003;

and Rebecca Blumenstein, Shawn Young, and Carol Hymowitz, "More Sprint Officials Used Questionable Shelters," *Wall Street Journal*, February 6, 2003.

On the national media's adulation of Esrey, see the October 5, 1999, Associated Press profile of the man that begins with the words "Visionary. Dedicated. Focused." The Kansas City media, meanwhile, had been showering the man with praise for years. See the June 9, 1991, *Kansas City Star* profile of Esrey that carries the words "driven, bright, daring" in the headline.

17. Jerry Heaster, "Such a Gem We Have in Sprint," *Kansas City Star*, October 6, 1999.

18. According to 2000 census data for cities of more than one thousand people, Mission Hills is the fourth-richest city in the country, measured by median household income.

19. According to the Web site of the Center for Responsive Politics. See http://www.opensecrets.org/states/presmap.asp?State=KS. The zip code for Mission Hills is 66208.

20. So closely was Mission Hills identified with Kansas City, Missouri, in those days that photos of the place are included in the WPA guide to Missouri, not the one for Kansas.

21. The Eskimo Pie inventor was, of course, Russell Stover. Details about the house come from Bill Norton, "The Beast of Mission Hills," *Kansas City Star Magazine*, August 2, 1987.

22. Although Wichita (pop. 340,000) is larger than any single suburb of Kansas City, Johnson County's total population surpassed that of Sedgwick County, where Wichita is located, in 2002. The Kansas City metropolitan area includes about 1.8 million people.

23. Kansas City has a population density about one-tenth that of Chicago. It is number five on the Sierra Club's list of "Sprawl-Threatened Large Cities." See http://www.sierraclub.org/sprawl/report98/kansas_city.html.

24. According to the U.S. Bureau of Economic Analysis, the per capita personal income of Johnson County in 2000 was $43,200; that of Sedgwick County, where Wichita is located, was $28,200; for Kansas as a whole, it was $27,400, which puts the state almost exactly in the middle of the pack.

25. Rhodes's essay, "Cupcake Land," was originally published in *Harper's* magazine in 1987; you can also find it in the revised version of *The Inland Ground: An Evocation of the American Middle West* (Lawrence: University Press of Kansas, 1991), Rhodes's collection of essays having to do with the area around Kansas City.

26. Lourdes Gouveia and Donald Stull, "Dances with Cows," in *Any Way You Cut It: Meat Processing and Small-Town America,* ed. Stull, Broadway, and Griffith (Lawrence: University Press of Kansas, 1995), p. 85.

27. Garden City's per capita income, as a percentage of the state per capita income, has dropped consistently since the packers came to town in the early 1980s. Donald Stull and Michael Broadway, " 'We Come to the Garden' . . . Again," *Urban Anthropology,* vol. 30, no. 4 (winter 2001), p. 278. On public health in Garden City, see p. 288.

28. Ibid, p. 295.

29. According to the anthropologist Robert J. Hackenberg, the Garden City saga bespeaks "the acceptance of a marginal class, and passive exploitation of it, as a permanent feature of the social system by a nation's middle and upper classes." "Joe Hill Died for Your Sins," in *Any Way You Cut It,* p. 261. Also, see Gouveia and Stull, "Dances with Cows," p. 102.

30. See, for example, Craig Miner's *Wichita: The Magic City* (Wichita: Sedgwick County Historical Museum Association, 1988), which tells the town's history as a progression from one booster-made boom to another. Among other things, the book is a treasure trove of nineteenth-century town slogans and Babbittesque business poetry. One rhyme published in the *Wichita Eagle* in the 1890s and unearthed by Miner could well stand as a motto of our own time: "Those of faith who reason least / Obtain the fattest of the feast."

    An exhibit I saw in 2003 at the Wichita Historical Museum, also called "The Magic City," strikes the same chord. "This is the story of a city," the introduction explains, "a special place that—from the very beginning—has attracted successful entrepreneurs, seekers of wealth with an optimistic spirit who knew that here everything is possible. This is Wichita, the Peerless Princess of the Plains—THE MAGIC CITY."

31. See White's famous essay, "What's the Matter with Kansas?" *Autobiography,* p. 280. White's views changed rather dramatically later on.

32. This unhappy fact is included in A. V. Krebs's *Agribusiness Examiner,* May 16, 2003, issue 248.

33. Heffernan's percentages are estimates, he notes, because accurate figures have "become more difficult to obtain. Trade journals have come under pressure to not publish some of this information and government agencies often say that to reveal the proportion of a market controlled by a single firm in such a concentrated market is revealing proprietary information." See *Consolidation in the Food and Agriculture System,* a

report to the National Farmers Union, February 5, 1999, p. 2. For a few sectors, Heffernan has published more up-to-date figures; these appear in Heffernan and Mary K. Hendrickson, "Multi-National Concentrated Food Processing and Marketing Systems and the Farm Crisis," a paper presented at the annual meeting of the American Association for the Advancement of Science, Boston, Mass., Feb. 14, 2002. Both papers are available online at: http://www.foodcircles.missouri.edu/consol. htm.

34. See James B. Lieber, *Rats in the Grain* (New York: Four Walls Eight Windows, 2000), epigraph; and Kurt Eichenwald, *The Informant* (New York: Broadway Books, 2000), p. 303.

35. I am relying for this description on Daryll E. Ray, "The Failure of the 1996 Farm Bill: Explaining the Nature of Grain Markets," in *A Food and Agriculture Policy for the 21st Century*, ed. Michael Stumo (Lincoln, Neb.: Organization for Competitive Markets, 2000), pp. 85–94.

36. *Kansas Farm Facts 2002* (Topeka: Kansas Department of Agriculture, 2002), p. 95.

37. Ask a free-market economist about all these goings-on, and he or she will tell you that what happens to the farmers doesn't matter as long as consumers get cheap beef, bread, and potatoes. The problem, however, is that when an industry becomes so concentrated that its component companies have unchallenged market power (as is clearly the case with the food trust), there is nothing forcing them to pass along the savings to the consumer. So while the farmers work themselves into an ever deeper hole, prices in supermarkets remain roughly the same. According to the findings of one professor of agriculture, food prices for consumers have grown by 2.8 percent since 1984 while the prices that farmers receive for producing the same food have *fallen* by 35.7 percent. The middlemen keep the difference. These figures were given at Senate Agriculture Committee hearings in 1999 by C. Robert Taylor, a professor of agriculture and public policy at Auburn University. I am quoting them as they appeared in an article by A. V. Krebs, the editor of the *Agribusiness Examiner*. This particular article appeared in the *Progressive Populist*, April 1, 2002, p. 7.

38. "This policy of all-out production, with no regard for market needs, is a boon for users of grain and other crop," writes Daryll Ray of the University of Tennessee Agricultural Policy Analysis Center. "Crop agriculture is providing integrated livestock producers, millers and other processors, and importers with one of their most important raw-material inputs at a 40 to 50 percent discount with Uncle Sam picking

up the difference" (Daryll Ray, "Current Commodity Programs: Are They for the Producers or the Users?" Article dated October 31, 2003. Available on the Web site of the University of Tennessee's Agricultural Policy Analysis Center: http://www.agpolicy.org/weekcol/169.html).

39. A. V. Krebs, *Agribusiness Examiner,* July 28, 2003, issue 273. Issues of *Agribusiness Examiner* are archived on Krebs's Web site, http://www.ea1.com/CARP.

40. I am referring here to the rise of the contract system under which an increasing percentage of farm products are now delivered to the processor. In some areas of farm production, in fact, actual markets—in which cattle or hogs, say, are bid up or down by competing buyers—have almost completely disappeared. Farmers are merely "growers" now, workers who provide labor and land to produce some commodity that is under contract from start to finish to the conglomerate.

In the sixties and seventies my father designed steel-frame cattle auction markets for towns across the Great Plains. Only a few of them are still used for that purpose today, he says. The market for cattle simply does not exist anymore; the animals are raised by contract with the all-powerful meatpackers, a price agreed upon long before the creature changes hands.

On the transformation of farmers into "growers," see Heffernan and Hendrickson, "Multi-National Concentrated Food Processing and Marketing Systems and the Farm Crisis," p. 5. On the prevalence of contracts over markets in the pork industry, see the USDA's publication *Food and Agricultural Policy: Taking Stock for the New Century,* September 2001, p. 19. It estimates that hogs sold under contract account for about 65 percent of the animals slaughtered in the year 2000, while open markets make up only about 30 percent, down from 95 percent in 1970. The remainder are hogs owned directly by the packer.

Sharecropper is the term actually used to describe what has happened to farmers by Ronald Cotterill, director of the Food Marketing Policy Center at the University of Connecticut, in "A Critique of the Current Food System," *A Food and Ag Policy for the 21st Century,* p. 39.

Chapter Three: God, Meet Mammon

1. In fact, Bush prevailed in every single ward in Garden City, while a handful of neighborhoods here and there in Johnson County went for Gore.

2. In 1996, when he was but a congressman, Brownback said: "Mr. Speaker, as I travel my district in eastern Kansas and talk to people back home, I ask them, do they think the biggest problems we face as a nation, are they moral or are they economic? Are they the problems associated

with the economy or problems associated with values? And I will get in almost every crowd 8 or 9 to 1 that will say the problems are moral rather than they are economic we are facing. They are problems with family and a disintegration of the family. They are problems with drugs. They are problems with crime. They are problems with people not willing to work. They are problems with people willing to do things that if they would think about it or if their own moral compass was a little better set, they would not do at all." This was part of a speech saluting Congress for giving a medal to Billy Graham, January 24, 1996.

Brownback's thoughts about the metaphysical origins of poverty can be found in an essay he wrote about William Booth, founder of the Salvation Army. See *Profiles in Character: The Values That Made America* (Nashville: Thomas Nelson, 1996), p. 14.

Several times, in speeches to the U.S. Senate, Brownback has expressed a desire to measure culture the way we do the economy. In a March 5, 1997, speech he referred to our "gross domestic piety," and in a May 1, 1997, speech he described a study of American culture that showed, as Brownback put it, a decline "from, in 1970, a 73 percent objective number to a 38 percent objective number—in half, the cultural decline in America, in a period—look at the time period we are talking about here—twenty-five years. Is this incredible?"

3. Tiahrt: *Wichita Eagle,* May 7, 1996. Anti-abortion leader: David Gittrich, *Wichita Eagle,* November 10, 1994. David Miller: quoted in Allan J. Cigler and Burdett A. Loomis, "After the Flood: The Kansas Christian Right in Retreat," *Prayers in the Precincts: The Christian Right in the 1998 Elections,* ed. John C. Green, Mark J. Rozell, and Clyde Wilcox (Washington, D.C.: Georgetown University Press, 2000), p. 232. Brownback: quoted in Linda Killian, *The Freshmen: What Happened to the Republican Revolution?* (New York: Westview Press, 1998), p. 176.

4. Dennis Farney, "Religious Right," *Wall Street Journal,* April 10, 1995.

5. God's wishes regarding Ryun are mentioned on p. 14 of the pamphlet Ryun wrote for the National Republican Congressional Committee, *America Strong: George W. Bush's Plan* (Ottawa, Ill.: Green Hill, 2001). The exact date of his conversion is given in *Insight* magazine (the Sunday supplement of the *Washington Times*), March 31, 1997. Speaking in tongues: Fred Mann, "Jim Ryun: Running on Faith," *Wichita Eagle,* December 29, 1996. Courtship: the article was written jointly by Ryun and his wife, Anne, and published in *Focus on the Family,* a publication of the James Dobson empire, November 1995, pp. 11–12.

6. Church-based campaigning: see the story by Timothy J. McNulty, "Vote in Kansas Shows the Power of Grassroots Organizing," that

originally appeared in the *Chicago Tribune* but was widely reprinted (my copy of it comes from the *Wichita Eagle,* November 25, 1994). "What it's all about": Suzanne Perez Tobias, "Tiahrt Found His Voice Slowly but Surely," *Wichita Eagle,* December 4, 1994.

7. I am not exaggerating. The daily life and beliefs of the Family are described in chilling detail by the religion writer Jeffrey Sharlet in an essay called "Jesus Plus Nothing" that was published in the March 2003 issue of *Harper's* magazine. Sharlet supplies more details about the organization's connections with dictators in an interview published on Alternet (http://www.alternet.org/story.html?StoryID=16167).

When I asked Sharlet about the frequent and alarming references to Hitler that Family members make in his essay, he elucidated as follows: "The Family views Hitler's ideology not as a philosophical model, but as an organizational schema. Members ignore the fact that 'organization,' in its most degraded sense, was the core of Hitler's fascism, preferring to emphasize the 'fellowship' Hitler fostered within his elite cadres. The Family aspires to the same bond: throughout its rhetoric, references to the 'vision' Hitler had for Germany are extremely common, with the caveat that it's worth examining for its roots in a band of brothers dreaming in the back of a Bavarian beer hall. So might one of the Family's small prayer cells of business, military, and political leaders transform America, the Family hopes."

Brownback is not mentioned in Sharlet's *Harper's* story, but his residence in the Family's town house was widely reported in April 2003. The foot-washing incident was reported by the Associated Press in November 1998, immediately after Brownback had been reelected for the first time. Brownback's conversion to Catholicism by McCloskey was reported by the *Washington Post* on July 22, 2002.

8. Roger Allison, "The Problem Is Corporate Agribusiness, Not the Estate Tax," *In Motion,* June 2001. See http://www.inmotionmagazine.com/ra01/ratax.html. Also, see United for a Fair Economy's summary of the subject at http://www.ufenet.org/estatetax/ETFarms.html.

9. All of these views are found in Ryun's pamphlet, *America Strong: George W. Bush's Plan,* which was distributed by the National Republican Congressional Committee before the 2002 election. The passage quoted here appears on p. 81.

10. Laurie Kalmanson, "Abortion Question Divides GOP Hopefuls," *Wichita Eagle,* July 19, 1992. This article was published before Tiahrt was first elected to the state legislature.

11. Jim Cross, "Koch Employees Put Money on Tiahrt," *Wichita Eagle,* July 28, 1996.

12. The herbicide was atrazine. As ag secretary, Brownback made restrictions on the use of atrazine voluntary, obviously placing the convenience of big farmers above the health of everyone else. See James Kuhnhenn, "Topeka Republican Is Making His Mark in Congress's Freshman Class," *Kansas City Star,* February 23, 1995.

    The lawsuit was *Hellebust v. Brownback,* and it ended with the U.S. District Court for Kansas ruling the Kansas Department of Agriculture in violation of the Fourteenth Amendment's one person, one vote provision. Brownback and company appealed the decision in 1994 to the U.S. Circuit Court, but they lost again.

13. The faction of the freshmen that Brownback led was known as the New Federalists. On his Spartan lifestyle and determination to get money out of politics, see Killian, *The Freshmen,* and Mike Hendricks's profile of Brownback for the *Kansas City Star,* October 27, 1996. On ambition, see Brownback's contribution to *Profiles in Character,* a book made up of essays written by members of the House freshman class, p. 18.

14. The reception, paid for by what was then known as the U.S. Telephone Association, is described by Steve Kraske in the *Kansas City Star,* May 25, 1998. Brownback's opposition to McCain-Feingold is also discussed in the article.

15. See the official transcript of the hearing: United States Senate Committee on Commerce, Science, and Transportation, *Hearing on Media Ownership,* January 30, 2003.

16. Here is Brownback's statement on this matter: "I am, however, concerned with 'increased coarseness' as a societal concern. No one segment of our nation is responsible, but all of us, as a society and a community, are responsible. I will not support efforts to use our mutual and legitimate concerns over indecency or increased coarseness in our society as a ruse to push forward damaging regulatory competition policies, such as national ownership limitations in the radio market, or restraints on converged ownership between various forms of media where such arrangements do not implicate antitrust law."

17. Photocopy of 1998 Kansas Republican Party platform, dated January 31, 1998, collection of the author. This platform was a controversial document, drafted by the party's conservative faction and denounced by the then-governor of Kansas, moderate Republican Bill Graves. What's more, the man responsible for having it drafted, state party chairman David Miller, went down to defeat in a race against Graves later that year. Today's Kansas Republican Party, controlled by moderates, has no copies of the document. The platform remains, nevertheless, a concise expression of the political vision of right-wing populism.

Chapter Four: Verns Then and Now

1. Vernon L. Parrington, *The Beginnings of Critical Realism in America,* vol. 3 of *Main Currents in American Thought* (New York: Harcourt Brace, 1930), pp. 262, 266.

2. Literary naturalism of the early twentieth century was in fact the target of a keynote lecture I saw at an anti-evolution get-together in Kansas City in the summer of 2002.

3. MRI: as reported by the Associated Press in 2000, http://more.abc-news.go.com/sections/living/dailynews/mri_love001108.html. Government bungling and federal poverty programs: Kevin McCabe and Vernon Smith, "Who Do You Trust?" *Boston Review,* December 1998–January 1999. National parks: Terry L. Anderson, Vernon L. Smith, and Emily Simmons, "How and Why to Privatize Federal Lands," *Policy Analysis,* November 9, 1999. (In this article Smith and company also equate the national parks with Soviet Communism.) Electricity privatization: Vernon L. Smith, "Regulatory Reform in the Electric Power Industry," http://www.stoft.com/e/lib/papers/Smith-1995-History.pdf and also Stephen J. Rassenti, Vernon L. Smith, and Bart J. Wilson, "Turning Off the Lights," *Regulation,* fall 2001. Hardwired: Vernon L. Smith, "Reflections on *Human Action* After 50 Years," *Cato Journal,* fall 1999. *Regulation* and *Cato Journal* are both publications of the Cato Institute.

4. Smith's *Journal* article was published on October 16, 2002. A week later, economist Lester Telser of the University of Chicago corrected Smith, pointing out that, thanks to the particulars of the electricity industry, a seller "resembles more closely a discriminating monopolist than the firms in a competitive industry." Which is an accurate description of what actually took place in California. "Selling Electricity Is Easy; Then Comes the Hard Part," Letter to the Editor, *Wall Street Journal,* October 23, 2002.

   Smith's *Journal* essay, for its part, doesn't even mention the corporate energy traders (Enron being the preeminent example) who played the market in California so lucratively. Instead, Smith's proposed solution to the disaster is to deregulate all the way, to pass the costs of power directly to consumers and let them deal with the problem by changing the way they behave. (Thanks to Gene Coyle for bringing this to my attention.)

5. See "Officials Discuss Selling Turnpike," *Topeka Capital-Journal,* June 13, 2003, and the paper's editorial response, "Kansas Turnpike—Not for Sale," June 22, 2003. The most prominent proponent of privatizing public highways is, naturally, the libertarian Reason Foundation, which is supported by Koch money.

6. http://www.rppi.org/vernonsmithteaches.html.

7. Koch quoted in the *Benefactor,* a publication of George Mason University, fall 2002, http://www.gmu.edu/development/pubs/benefact/fall02/pages/nobel.html. Smith and Koch both sit on the board of the Mercatus Center, where they are joined by the free-market culture theorist Tyler Cowen. The list of "scholars and fellows" at Mercatus includes familiar New Economy figures like Larry Kudlow (listed as a "distinguished scholar") and washed-up right-wing political types like Wendy Gramm and J. C. Watts. Mercatus, unsurprisingly, was also funded by money from Enron.

8. Statistics from the *Kansas Statistical Abstract 2001,* op. cit., and the Environmental Working Group farm subsidy database: http://www.ewg.org/farm/region.php?fips=20097.

9. On Ulysses, see *Kansas: A Guide to the Sunflower State* (New York: Viking, 1939), p. 438; Daniel Fitzgerald, *Ghost Towns of Kansas* (Lawrence: University Press of Kansas, 1988); and the *Grant County Republican,* March 20, 1909. I am grateful to Tad Kepley for bringing the latter two sources to my attention.

10. Read them at http://www.boeing.com/commercial/7e7/criteria.pdf.

11. See, for example, the Web site of Washington State's organization for winning the work: "Action Washington: Working TOGETHER for the Boeing 7E7," http://www.actionwashington.com.

12. See the *Wall Street Journal*'s "RealEstateJournal" Web site for June 13, 2003: http://homes.wsj.com/propertyreport/propertyreport/20030613-siteselection.html.

13. As the *Wichita Eagle* pointed out, the bond issue was fifty times larger than the next largest bit of corporate welfare issued by the state, and it would have increased the state's bonded debt by almost 20 percent. *Wichita Eagle,* April 2, 2003.

14. Lieutenant governor's remarks: See Molly McMillin, "7E7 Bond Gave State Favorable Profile," *Wichita Eagle,* December 12, 2003. Parentheses in original. Possible sale of Boeing–Wichita: See the editorial "Stunning" in the January 26, 2004, issue of the *Wichita Eagle.*

Chapter Five: Con Men and Mod Squad

1. This phrase has been used on the floor of Congress by the Wichita Republican Todd Tiahrt, as well as at the great 1991 Wichita rally discussed later in this chapter. Tiahrt: Associated Press story dated April 6, 2000; Wichita rally: see the Norman and Hirschman story referenced in note 4. On Kansas abortion law, see Miner, *Kansas: The History of the Sunflower State,* pp. 388–89.

2. A detailed account of the Kansas legislature in the late eighties can be found in Burdett Loomis's book *Time, Politics, and Policies: A Legislative Year* (Lawrence: University Press of Kansas), 1994.

3. See the account of the Summer of Mercy in James Risen and Judy L. Thomas, *Wrath of Angels: The American Abortion War* (New York: Basic, 1998), pp. 323–24. Thomas covered the anti-abortion movement for the *Wichita Eagle*.

4. See the account of the event by Bud Norman and Bill Hirschman in the *Wichita Eagle*, August 26, 1991.

5. Although he apparently wrote it himself, this line is in fact one of the epigraphs to Goodwyn's famous book, *Democratic Promise: The Populist Moment in America* (New York: Oxford University Press, 1976).

6. It is also worth pointing out that on the final day of the Summer of Mercy, people from the farm towns surrounding Wichita drove their tractors and pickups, decorated for the occasion with posters decrying abortion, in a giant parade through the city. This is described at http://www.forerunner.com/forerunner/X0494_Wichita_Kansas.html.

7. Tim Golba: interview with the author. Mark Gietzen: Timothy J. McNulty, "Tiahrt's Win Grew from Grass Roots," *Wichita Eagle*, November 25, 1994. See also Risen and Thomas, *Wrath of Angels*, p. 334.

8. Jon Roe, "The People Are Fed Up," *Wichita Eagle*, March 22, 1992. See the op-ed piece by Denney Clements on March 27, 1992, in which these populist demands are applied to those who defeated the abortion bill.

9. During the election of 1992, the story was told how a moderate state legislator from Wichita one day learned that her most dedicated campaign volunteer was in reality a spy for the fundamentalists. When asked to comment on the story, this volunteer declared (from a jail cell to which she had been sentenced after blocking an abortion clinic), "This is the Lord at work." See Judy Lundstrom Thomas, "Rallying the Faithful Politically," *Wichita Eagle*, September 20, 1992.

10. Judy Lundstrom Thomas, "Protest Sets Tiller Off on GOP," *Wichita Eagle*, August 20, 1992. In a story published a month later, Thomas reported that 83 percent of the new precinct committee people were "abortion foes and members of the religious right."

11. Judy Lundstrom Thomas, "GOP Leader Quits After Contentious Vote," *Wichita Eagle*, August 14, 1992.

12. See Connie Bye, "Johnson County GOP Veers Right," *Kansas City Star*, November 19, 1992. The columnist was Myrne Roe. "And they hate" appeared in the *Wichita Eagle* for September 24, 1992; the quote

about white gloves, which was a response to the national Republican convention, was published on August 27, 1992.

13. It's called the Kansas Republican Assembly. The group's Web site (http://www.ks-ra.org/Who.htm), ironically, warns against fake Republicans who are said to be dividing the party and turning it away from tradition.

14. According to Jim Sullinger of the *Kansas City Star,* only 10 precinct positions in Johnson County were contested in 1990. In 1996, 343 of the positions were contested. "GOP Candidates Set Filing Record," *Kansas City Star,* Johnson County edition, June 15, 1996.

15. The candidate lost.

16. Norquist on the Mods: Lloyd Grove, "Reliable Source," *Washington Post,* November 7, 2002.

17. "If we're $700 million in the red," the conservatives think, according to Burdett Loomis, a professor of political science at the University of Kansas, "we'll just have to cut $700 million, and government will just have to do less bad things." See also the Steve Rose editorial in the *Johnson County Sun* for March 1, 2002. The state's fiscal crisis, Rose writes, "was no accident. And it was not negligence. It was even stupidity. This was a deliberate, tactical, well-orchestrated effort on the part of conservatives to make certain that we would be in the pickle we are in, a pickle they think is a banana split."

18. This is the explanation advanced by Peter Beinart, editor of the *New Republic,* who visited Olathe and wrote one of the most thoughtful articles to appear in the national press about the Kansas war: "Battle for the 'Burbs," *New Republic,* October 19, 1998.

Beinart offers an insightful description of the way fundamentalists react to the modern culture that surrounds them, and he gives dozens of colorful examples of the reach of evangelical Christianity in Kansas life. The trouble arises when he tries to downplay the class differences between the Cons and other Kansans, a move typical of liberal commentary on the backlash (see Lasch, *The True and Only Heaven,* p. 479). Beinart points out that Olathe, the hotbed of Johnson County conservatism, is a growing place with prosperous businesses, as indeed it is. What he overlooks is that, for all its apparent prosperity, Olathe is in fact decidedly *less* affluent than other parts of Johnson County. There are also class differences *within* Olathe that are not examined. As it happens, Olathe has a few moderate Republicans in addition to the delegation of wild conservatives for which it is famous, and each of the Olathe Mods that I met was a member of the white-collar or professional class, just like Mods from elsewhere in Johnson County.

Each of the Olathe conservatives I spent time with, though, was either a blue-collar worker or married to one.

Having dismissed class, Beinart goes on to propose that what really differentiates Cons from Mods is the Cons' relative newness to Kansas City. Coming as so many of them do from farm communities in rural Kansas, a migration he implies began with the construction of the interstate highway system, these transplanted farm folks try to re-create small-town life by organizing themselves around their (funda-mentalist) churches. And they are shocked and horrified by the things they encounter in the city: homosexuality, abortion, and so on. So they move to the right.

A problem with this thesis is that Kansas City had served as a clearing-house for people from the rural Midwest (such as my grandparents) for a hundred years before the 1990s without suffering such a spectacular right-wing revolt. Once upon a time, in fact, KC had quite a reputation for doing what Beinart describes, namely, introducing the innocent to the sinfulness of the big city. (See, for example, Theodore Dreiser's *An American Tragedy*, Edward Dahlberg's *Bottom Dogs*, or William Allen White's *Autobiography*.) But that era is over. Kansas City has repressed its once-famous seamy side in favor of Cupcake Land. Furthermore, when Kansas City was at its most wicked—that is, in the 1930s—it was also at its most liberal. Today's right-wing politics and right-wing religion did not start until after the cleanup squads had done their work.

Even more damaging to Beinart's theory is the fact that many of the conservatives that I studied for this book (Tim Golba, Mary Pilcher Cook, Phill Kline, Jim Ryun, Jack Cashill, and others) are not migrants from rural or small-town America at all; they grew up either in John-son County, Wichita, Topeka, or in some other urban area. Nor does the opposite implication—that small towns make one a conservative—hold true. The most rural of the state's four congressional districts (the first, covering western Kansas) is also the least conservative, producing traditional pragmatic Republicans like Pat Roberts and Jerry Moran. Furthermore, many Mod leaders have solid rural credentials: Dennis Jones, for example, the current (moderate) chairman of the Kansas Republican Party, is from the small western Kansas town of Lakin. Bill Graves and David Adkins both come from Salina. And, of course, there is Bob Dole, who grew up in the tiny town of Russell. (Or, going back even further, you have the ultimate Republican moderate, Dwight Eisenhower of Abilene.)

19. Wallace quoted in Michael Kazin, *The Populist Persuasion* (New York:

Basic Books, 1995), p. 221. On the role of class in the backlash, see Lasch, *The True and Only Heaven,* chap. 11; Ehrenreich, *Fear of Falling;* and Kazin, *The Populist Persuasion,* chap. 9.

20. The "two Johnson counties" is a theme Rose has returned to a number of times over the years. See his *Johnson County Sun* columns for December 5, 2002, and August 4, 2000. About Rose himself and his connections to the Johnson County in-crowd, see Kendrick Blackwood, "Mr. Johnson County," *Pitch Weekly,* November 14, 2002.

21. In his *Sun* column for December 5, 2002, Rose does propose a series of explanations for the "disconnect" of Olathe from moderate Johnson County, but these are obviously facetious: Could it be Olathe's separate water system? he wonders. Its separate school system? Its different cable TV provider? Its electric power company? The big Nazarene church out there?

22. Using census data from 1999, I generated median housing value and per capita income maps of Johnson County. Although the county as a whole is considerably wealthier than the rest of Kansas, the following electoral wards, in comparison to the surrounding county, had relatively low housing values and/or per capita incomes: Lenexa Ward 4; Merriam Ward 1; Olathe Wards 1, 3, and 4; Overland Park Ward 1; Shawnee Wards 2 and 4. I used the following electoral wards to test for relatively high housing values and/or per capita incomes: Fairway Ward 3, Leawood Wards 2, 3, and 4; and Mission Hills.

   I then examined the electoral results of each of these wards in the following races, in which the choice between Mod and Con was particularly clear-cut: U.S. Senate, Republican primary, 1996 (Sam Brownback vs. Sheila Frahm); U.S. Congress, Kansas District 3, Republican primary, 1996 (Vince Snowbarger vs. Ed Eilert); Kansas attorney general, Republican primary, 2002 (Phill Kline vs. David Adkins). In each of these races, the lower-income wards as identified above generally chose the more conservative Republican candidate, whereas the higher-income wards almost always chose the more moderate candidate. I also examined the results of the Republican primary for Kansas governor in 1998 (Bill Graves vs. David Miller), but in that race, the moderate candidate won every incorporated ward in the county. (Miller did win a number of precincts in Olathe, however, and if you break down the vote by state legislative districts instead of wards, the only district Miller won in the entire state is the fourteenth district in Olathe.)

23. The 1964 presidential election between Lyndon Johnson and Barry Goldwater was one of only six times in the state's history when Kansas has gone Democratic (the others were 1896, 1912, 1916, 1932, and

1936). In 1964, every Shawnee ward and four of the five Olathe wards cast majorities for Johnson, while the wealthy suburbs as identified above all went for Goldwater. Mission Hills went for Goldwater by 74 percent to 26 percent.

24. This unfortunate line appeared in a list of electoral tips printed in the June 1996 issue of Mainstream's *Messenger* newsletter.

25. The scene is described by Thomas Edsall in "GOP Moderates Poised for a Resurgence in Kansas," *Washington Post,* August 3, 1998.

26. The KCCC made national headlines in the early nineties when it rejected a prominent Jewish businessman who had applied for membership.

Chapter Six: Persecuted, Powerless, and Blind

1. Michael Barone: "The divide is not economic, but cultural." John Podhoretz: "The divide is not racial or economic."

2. *Arrogance* is even the title of a liberal-bashing 2003 book by Bernard Goldberg.

3. See, for example, the examination and demolition of the idea of a "new class" in Ehrenreich's 1989 book, *Fear of Falling,* chap. 4, and the parallel takedown in Lasch's *True and Only Heaven,* pp. 509–22. The most glaring problem with the idea of a "new class" is that it applies only to liberals; conservatives who work in the various fields that are identified with the "new class" are automatically excused from membership.

4. G. Gordon Liddy, *When I Was a Kid, This Was a Free Country* (Washington, D.C.: Regnery, 2002), pp. 26–27.

5. Ann Coulter, *Slander: Liberal Lies About the American Right* (New York: Crown, 2002), pp. 29, 27.

6. Coulter says this in the *New York Observer* interview quoted in chapter two. All other quotes from Coulter in this paragraph are from *Slander.*

7. Ironically, the sole recent conservative victory in the culture wars—forcing CBS to cancel the broadcast of an unflattering Ronald Reagan drama—was also an opportunity for conservative pundits to admit how unsuccessful they've been over the years. "We hit a milestone in the culture wars last week," wrote Robert Bartley of the *Wall Street Journal* on that occasion. "For once, perhaps for the first time, one of our pre-eminent cultural institutions conceded that the great unwashed had it right." "The Culture Wars Reach the Culture," *Wall Street Journal,* November 10, 2003.

8. Sean Hannity, *Let Freedom Ring: Winning the War of Liberty over Liberalism* (New York: Regan Books, 2002), p. 43.

9. See, for example, www.tonguetied.us, which is excerpted on the Web site of the Fox News Channel.

10. Goldberg: *Bias* (Washington, D.C.: Regnery, 2002), chaps. 1 and 3. Tyrrell: *Boy Clinton: The Political Biography* (Washington, D.C.: Regnery, 1996), pp. 169–71. On the peculiar research strategies of the many books on the liberal media, see Chris Lehmann, "The Eyes of Spiro Are Upon You," *Baffler* 14 (2001).

11. In November 2002, I attended a gathering of Kansas conservatives who voted to have a copy of this original Clinton-bashing text sent to a library being opened in a nearby neighborhood, even though Clinton had left the national stage almost two years previously.

12. David Brock, the author of *The Real Anita Hill* and a self-confessed "right-wing hit man," describes this conservative fatalism as it appeared in Wlady Plesczynski, deputy editor of the *American Spectator,* in its heyday. "Wlady," he writes, was "typical of the conservatives in his fatalism. As he saw it, the liberal culture . . . coddled the Dems and tore down the Republicans at every turn. Certain that we were losers no matter what we did, destined to remain on the fringes of respectable debate, Wlady encouraged taking potshots at the enemy. For Wlady, accepting what I wrote about his political foes, no matter how unflattering or unbelievable, was simply a matter of faith." Brock, *Blinded by the Right: The Conscience of an Ex-Conservative* (New York: Crown, 2002), p. 86.

13. In her newspaper column for December 30, 2003, Ann Coulter writes:

> Apparently the only thing standing between a government of laws and total anarchy is the fact that conservatives are good losers. If we don't give liberals everything they want, when they want it, anarchy will result. We must obey manifestly absurd court rulings, so that liberals obey court rulings when they lose.
>
> Point one: They almost never lose. Point two: They already refuse to accept laws they don't like. They do it all the time— race discrimination bans, bilingual education bans, marijuana bans.

14. In denying its own agency, as well as in many other ways, the backlash is a precise mirror image of the pseudo-leftist academic discipline known as cultural studies. According to this theoretical tendency, the most banal and routine culture-products are intensely political and subversive; the left is constantly but silently winning the war over everyday life; and even the lowliest of consumers are endowed with massive quantities of agency, with a stupendous power to exert their radical will in the world. For the backlash, on the other hand, nobody

has agency except for people on the left. We, the Middle Americans, are utterly powerless to change our culture—to ban abortion or outlaw sodomy or build Ten Commandments monuments—or to prevent the left from wrecking daily life. And yes, the backlash agrees, everything *is* politicized—the way you mow your lawn, the color you paint your house, whether or not you ride a bicycle—but politicized negatively. Everything offends; everything is calculated to advance liberalism's plot to make the culture more to its liking. Backlashers are, in fact, just about the only people in the world who would agree with the professors who find all sorts of subversiveness in Madonna and Britney and Christina Aguilera. A final, telling commonality: neither movement bothers seriously to consider the role of business in American life or culture.

15. Mark Lilla, "A Tale of Two Reactions," reprinted in *Left Hooks, Right Crosses,* ed. Christopher Hitchens and Christopher Caldwell (New York: Nation Books, 2002), p. 262. My emphasis.

16. Coulter makes this assertion several times in *Slander,* each time without explanation. See, for example, p. 122, where she describes Enron as "some stupid, meaningless phrase" that is pointlessly repeated by the liberal media. I confess that I do not understand Coulter's objection; the Enron bankruptcy was an important news item regardless of one's political views. For the press to take her advice and ignore the Enron story would have carried it far beyond "bias" and into the realm of Soviet-style manipulation.

17. On advertising's tendency to "obfuscate the work process," see Stuart Ewen, *Captains of Consciousness: Advertising and the Social Roots of the Consumer Culture* (New York: McGraw-Hill, 1976), chap. 4. On professional journalism's attitude toward business news, see Robert McChesney, *The Problem of the Media: U.S. Communications Politics in the Twenty-first Century* (New York: Monthly Review Press, 2004), chap. 2.

18. In a much-quoted passage, Gary Aldrich described the Clintonoids among whom he worked as "girlie men." "There was a unisex quality to the Clinton staff that set it far apart from the Bush administration. It was the shape of their bodies. In the Clinton administration, the broad-shouldered, pants-wearing women and the pear-shaped, bowling-pin men blurred distinctions between the sexes. I was used to athletic types, physically fit persons who took pride in body image and good health." *Unlimited Access,* p. 30.

19. Gold's savage but famous 1930 attack, "Wilder: Prophet of the Genteel Christ," can be found in Michael Folsom, ed., *Mike Gold: A Literary*

Anthology (New York: International Publishers, 1972), pp. 197–202.

20. Tyrrell, *Boy Clinton,* pp. 164, 167.

21. "A country's action is directed by its intellectuals," Peikoff declares. And "three generations of crusaders, moved by the power of German philosophy, had sought to refashion America's political institutions in the image of Europe's." Peikoff, *The Ominous Parallels: The End of Freedom in America* (New York: Meridian, 1993), p. 274. *The Ominous Parallels* was first published in 1982 and is volume 3 in "the Ayn Rand Library."

Chapter Seven: Russia Iran Disco Suck

1. Liddy's list of vanished freedoms is a masterpiece of the plen-T-plaint, but he never explains why it is these very particular freedoms, rather than, say, the ready availability of crystal meth, or the right to race nitrous-burning dragsters on city streets, that makes a place a "free country." Nor do his particular plaints hold up on close inspection. Leaf burning: Burning leaves is indeed illegal in many places, but this is because of state law and local ordinance and only rarely because of onerous federal command. In fact, people in rural areas and small Kansas towns burn leaves all the time. Maybe Liddy should move there. Shooting birds: Bird hunting has been regulated since long before G. Gordon Liddy was born. Crows that are damaging crops, which is the example Liddy gives of a bird it is illegal to shoot, are specifically *not* protected by federal law. Carrying guns: Many cities, including Dodge City in Kansas, had laws restricting the carrying of guns within the city limits long before Liddy was born. Liddy's suggestion that firearms are now difficult to obtain is ludicrous on its face. Fireworks: The regulations vary from state to state. I know for a fact that firecrackers are readily available in Indiana and Wisconsin, since I nearly blew my finger off with one a few years ago.

   If allowing each of these things everywhere in the land without any restriction at all—leaf burning, bird killing, tree chopping, gun carrying, fireworks purchasing—is the measure of whether a country is free or not, there are no free countries on earth, nor have there ever been.

2. In *The Positive Thinkers,* Donald Meyer comments extensively on positive thinking's understanding of the business civilization and extreme laissez-faire economics as the way of nature. (See in particular chap. 8.) As for its politics, Meyer points out that Norman Vincent Peale, the movement's greatest celebrity preacher, dabbled in right-wing Republicanism, and a famous positive-thinking Congregationalist church in California embraced the John Birch Society.

It is possible that the universal embrace of positive thinking by the bitter self-made men of my youth was a geographic coincidence, since Kansas City is home to one of the great powers of the positive-thinking world, the Unity Church. But I am inclined to think not. Positive thinking is today a nearly universal aspect of liberal Protestantism, traces of it appearing in the speeches of Ronald Reagan and the self-help entertainment of Oprah Winfrey. Donald Meyer, *The Positive Thinkers: Popular Religious Psychology from Mary Baker Eddy to Norman Vincent Peale and Ronald Reagan* (Middletown, Conn.: Wesleyan University Press, 1988).

3. Garry Wills, *Reagan's America: Innocents at Home* (Garden City, N.Y.: Doubleday, 1987), p. 305.

4. White, *Autobiography*, p. 217. The quote in the preceding paragraph is from p. 187 of the autobiography.

5. See especially chap. 23 of *The Positive Thinkers*, on the teachings of Norman Vincent Peale. "Think exclusively about yourself—that is, concentrate exclusively upon saturating your sub- (un-) conscious with the automatic power of positive thoughts," Meyer summarizes his thinking. "The world in which the subsequent automatic behavior took place need not be thought of, since it was already defined. The proper analogy here was—again, in echo of ancient business jargon—that of the 'game,' and once again Peale's prodigious mass-instruction service spelled it out" (p. 284).

6. Positive thinking has important similarities with management and motivational literature. In 1957 James Fifield, Jr., the positive-thinking leader of a Congregationalist church in California, wrote: "Have you ever noticed how friendly the top men in a business organization are? Did it ever occur to you that this friendliness emanated from a deep sense of Christian love toward their fellowmen? And that at the same time this profound good-fellowship was the best possible political weapon for getting to the top?" Quoted in Meyer, *The Positive Thinkers*, p. 283. The Unity School, based in Kansas City, used to publish a magazine called the *Christian Businessman*.

Chapter Eight: Happy Captives

1. Altevogt no doubt intends this as a grave insult. The founder of the Mainstream Coalition, the Reverend Robert Meneilly, is well-known locally for having been Johnson County's most prominent supporter of the civil rights movement back in the sixties. For area liberals he is something of a hero. Meneilly is not known, however, as a leader of the working class; his church is in fact located in an upscale part of the Johnson County suburbs.

2. Altevogt's most outrageous remarks appeared not in his *Star* columns but in a Christian newsweekly called *MetroVoice News*, where his thoughts have appeared since he left the *Star* in December 1999. Mainstream Coalition/Ian Paisley: "Translate This," *MetroVoice News*, March 5, 2002. Topeka reporter: "Kansas Conservatives vs. AP Bias," *Kansas City Star*, June 16, 1999. *Topeka Capital-Journal*: "Silly Media Tricks," *MetroVoice News*, February 4, 2002. Embarrassing news stories: "Is Ignorance Bliss at KCTV News?" *MetroVoice News*, February 22, 2002.

3. This rant appeared on the Kansas Conservative Network Listserv, January 3, 2004.

4. A fictional version of such a scheme can be found in Cashill's novel, *2006: The Chautauqua Rising* (Dunkirk, N.Y.: Olin Frederick, 2000). Another example came up at a meeting of Johnson County Cons that I attended in November 2002. While most of the people at the gathering wanted to spend the evening complaining about the perfidy of the Mods, Cashill stepped forward with a grand plan for retaking the offensive. The idea was to raise the funds sufficient for a sustained media barrage, and then to force the old reliable abortion debate—the same wedge issue that broke Wichita apart so effectively back in the summer of 1991—down the throats of everyone in the Kansas City metropolitan area, to make abortion the inescapable topic of local conversation regardless of how the powers-that-be would try to avoid it. "And the message goes to different groups in different ways," Cashill proposed, unveiling his scheme.

> To the conservative groups, we tell them, "Here are your arguments. Get out there and be an advocate. Don't keep your mouth shut any longer." And to the RINOs [i.e., Republicans in Name Only, aka the Mods] we say, "Here are the constitutional arguments. You can make a libertarian argument for abortion. You cannot make a constitutional argument for Roe versus Wade. It's an abomination, it's a disgrace, no Republican can support Roe versus Wade, period." To the larger audience, to the soft liberal Democratic kind of audience, . . . we say, "We don't expect you to convert, we just expect you to tolerate the people who feel this way. We just expect you to tolerate those people who think it's wrong to stick a scalpel in a baby's head just as it's being born."

For the Democrats at the top, however, the message would be decidedly unpleasant. The region's Catholic bishops, who evidently get to play the part of holy hoodlums in Cashill's script, strong-arm the liberals into giving up on their liberalness. "Because if this message gets out, if it works here," Cashill imagined them saying to the no doubt quivering elites, "it's all over for the Democratic Party."

5. The essay is chap. 9 of Cashill's essay collection, *Snake Handling in Mid-America: An Incite-ful Look at American Life and Work in the 90s* (Kansas City, Mo: Westport, 1991).

6. Jack Cashill, "On Power," *Ingram's*, April 1994, p. 35.

7. Someone fired a bullet through the window of Blackmun's third-story apartment in February 1985, only months after a series of clinic bombings on the East Coast. The episode is described in Risen and Thomas, *Wrath of Angels*, pp. 3–4.

8. Jack Cashill and James Sanders, *First Strike: TWA Flight 800 and the Attack on America* (Nashville: WND Books, 2003), pp. 118, 88. Cashill and Sanders argue that the FBI and the National Transportation Safety Board would not admit that the airplane was shot down by a missile because the White House thought that knowledge of a terrorist attack might make Bill Clinton unpopular with voters and cause Bob Dole to be elected president. And therefore the truth was covered up. The media, for its part, is said to have gone along with this scheme because, among other reasons, "the last thing that any two key people in any major newsroom wanted was a scandal that would give Newt Gingrich a Republican president."

9. Secretive former communist: *Ingram's*, April 2000.

10. Benedict Arnold: *Ingram's*, July 2003. Traffic tickets: *Ingram's*, November 2002.

11. While Golba does work at a bottling plant, it is not a Pepsi plant. Steve Rose, "Golba's Politics vs. Our Schools," *Johnson County Sun*, June 5, 2002.

12. When asked why Golba had taken Mainstream's name, Dwight Sutherland, who is Golba's lawyer in addition to being a conservative leader in his own right, said, "It has the disco beat, and the kids all love it." Grace Hobson, "Activist Appropriates Political Group's Name," *Kansas City Star*, December 19, 2003.

   According to the *Kansas City Star*, during the 2000 races for the Kansas house, Golba recorded a phone message that suggested citizens should vote for a candidate his group did not endorse if they wanted "unborn babies to continue to die in Kansas." Jim Sullinger, "Anti-Abortion Group Launches Campaign by Phone," *Kansas City Star*, July 25, 2000.

13. O'Connor denies that she said women should not vote, and obviously

she votes herself. The remarks appeared in Associated Press dispatches as well as a *Kansas City Star* story; see John Hanna, "Female State Legislator Attempts to Clarify Remarks on Women's Suffrage," Associated Press, September 28, 2001.

14. Beer containing less than 3.2 percent alcohol is one of the constant reminders of the Prohibition years in Kansas. Prohibition began in Kansas by constitutional amendment in 1881, but in 1937 the state legislature declared beer with less than 3.2 percent alcohol to be a "cereal malt beverage," not an "intoxicating liquor," and hence legal. Proper liquor was not permitted in Kansas until 1948, and even then it could only be dispensed from liquor stores and, later, private clubs. What few taverns you found in Kansas when I was in college sold only the three-two stuff.

    In the seventies, Attorney General Vern Miller went to outrageous lengths to remind the world that prohibition was still largely in effect in Kansas, once even raiding an Amtrak train for serving liquor as it traveled through the state. Airlines, too, were required to stop serving drinks when in Kansas airspace. In 1987, the state constitution was finally amended to permit the full-blown saloon, vending its dreaded "liquor by the drink," but plenty of laws still complicate the sale of liquor in Kansas. To this day grocery stores, for example, can only stock the watery three-two beverage. Read up on the fascinating, perplexing history of Kansas liquor law at http://skyways.lib.ks.us/ksleg/KLRD/Kansas_liquor_laws_2003.pdf.

15. If you do an Internet search of the exact words in the headline of O'Connor's poster—"What Has Happened Since Christian Principles Were Removed from Public Life Starting in 1962?"—you will suddenly find yourself in a world where Masons conspire to dominate humanity and Christians are persecuted by sinister Illuminati.

16. It's called Parents in Control, and you can read O'Connor's thoughts on the subject on its Web site, parentsincontrol.org.

17. It is important to note that the Republican trend was already under way before the Summer of Mercy. Republicans were the majority party in Sedgwick County in 1990, by 38 percent to 32 percent of voter registrations. What happened in the nineties is that the gap between the two parties widened dramatically. In 1994 it was 41 percent to 34 percent; in 1998 it was 42 percent to 31 percent; and in 2003 it was 47 percent to 30 percent.

18. Mark Gietzen, *Is It a Sin for a Christian to Be a Registered Democrat Voter in America Today?* (Pittsburgh: Dorrance, 2001), pp. 67–68.

Chapter Nine: Kansas Bleeds for Your Sins

1. The classic text on this aspect of the backlash is Thomas and Mary Edsall's *Chain Reaction: The Impact of Race, Rights, and Taxes on American Politics* (New York: Norton, 1992).

2. Altevogt comparing himself to Jackie Robinson: "A Year of Fresh Perspectives," *Kansas City Star*, November 3, 1999. Altevogt on outreach to black voters: "Investing in the Future of the Black Community," *Metro Voice News* (Kansas City), July 11, 2001. Altevogt writes of that Virginia election: "Virtually every attempt by one candidate to insert race into this election made news. We on the other hand, gleefully and, at times, obnoxiously, inserted race into the election. We didn't just insert race into the process, we flatulently filled the airwaves of black radio with it, every spot a whoopee cushion of controversy. And not one article. Black radio simply appears to be off the radar of the dominant media establishment."

   A year later, however, Altevogt would have reason to eat his words. During the 2002 elections, a black-oriented radio station in Kansas City began running commercials comparing Social Security to "reverse reparations." The commercials' sponsor, GOPAC, quickly withdrew the spots under nationwide criticism. The producer responsible for the commercials was revealed to be Rich Nadler, one of the people identified by Altevogt as a colleague in his Virginia outreach effort. See Jim Sullinger, "Republicans Pull 'Reverse Reparations' Ad from KC Radio Station," *Kansas City Star*, September 13, 2002.

3. A refreshing demurral from the accolades with which Brownback is usually received on these issues comes from former Kansas City, Missouri, mayor Emanuel Cleaver, as reported in the *Kansas City Star* for April 21, 2003. "They've failed to understand that it's about policy," Cleaver said, referring to Brownback and Missouri Republican Jim Talent. "You can introduce legislation with [Georgia Democrat] John Lewis and still not get African-American votes back home because you go against things that are at the core of African-American survival in this country. Surely they've got to realize we're smart enough to see, on the key issues, they have not changed."

4. The Kansas newspaper columnist David Awbrey relates how he interviewed one of the NAACP lawyers years after the *Brown* decision and asked him why Topeka had been chosen as the target city for the famous lawsuit. "Kansas, with its free state past," Awbrey writes, "was selected to show that racial discrimination wasn't just a Southern problem, but a national shame. If Kansas treated blacks as second-class citi-

zens, the rest of the country had to take special notice." Awbrey, "Ghost of John Brown Is Very Angry," *Topeka Capital-Journal,* February 28, 2000.

This is not meant to let Kansas off the hook in any way. Obviously, Topeka was also a segregated city—that's why it drew the NAACP lawsuit in the first place. And no history of Johnson County, the wealthy suburban sprawl immediately adjacent to Kansas City, Missouri, should neglect to mention the white-flight factor in the area's spectacular growth, as well as the role of restrictive covenants, racist lending practices, and other forms of housing discrimination. In the early days, schools in Johnson County were segregated as well.

Another mark against the state is its momentary dalliance with the Ku Klux Klan in the 1920s. Fortunately for Kansas's fantasy of itself, the state's ruling Republicans put a quick stop to the Klan fad by revoking the organization's charter. In this act they were pushed by the famous Kansas newspaperman William Allen White, who crusaded against the Klan in 1924, calling them "moral idiots" and "an organization of cowards." On these matters, see Miner, *Kansas,* pp. 252–58.

5. In 2003 a KU historian published a book enumerating the various racist practices in which the state's early settlers engaged, despite their professions of tolerance. The book's appearance met with angry denunciation on the Kansas Cons' Listserv, where one poster described it as "typical of totalitarian liberalism's hate-America approach to scholarship."

6. The William Wilberforce Prize, I learned, has no connection to the British group Anti-Slavery International, with which the descendants of Wilberforce were connected. Still, Wilberforce remains a hero of considerable standing to the culture-war right. In *Profiles in Character,* the collection of essays by members of the 1994 congressional "freshmen," two of the twenty-eight congressmen included chose to write about Wilberforce.

7. Phelps's "Message to Topeka" appears on the Web site of the *Topeka Capital-Journal:* http://www.cjonline.com/webindepth/phelps/.

8. Indeed, the Civil War comparison is so commonplace as to be a cliché. James Risen and L. Thomas, in *Wrath of Angels,* describe the abortion controversy as "America's most volatile, most divisive, and most irreconcilable debate since slavery" (p. 5). Craig Miner, the author of *Kansas,* the definitive one-volume history of the state, describes the state's free-soilers as "a moral interest group, and like people impassioned on both sides of the abortion issue in the late twentieth century, focused on 'higher law'" (p. 56).

9. The equation of criticism with crime was a national phenomenon.

Indeed, Massachusetts senator Charles Sumner was beaten almost to death on the floor of the Senate by a southern congressman after delivering a speech called "The Crime Against Kansas."

10. Slavery theorists believed that the territory open to slave settlement needed constantly to increase; it couldn't remain static or confined by borders. Hence they viewed a slave Kansas as critical for the survival of the institution generally: it had to move farther west, and Kansas was the way westward. One reason for this emphasis on expansion was the environmentally rapacious agricultural practices of the South, which used up land quickly; another was that constant expansion meant constant demand for slaves, and hence high prices for slaveholders in the East. Without new markets for slaves, demand for slaves would collapse, and with it the paper value of the estates of the great planters.

   For these reasons, they were willing to overlook even the most outrageous crimes committed by the pro-slavery party in Kansas.

11. The bogus legislature made it legal for any male citizen of the United States (i.e., men from Missouri) to vote in Kansas provided they paid a poll tax. On the other hand, anyone who would not take an oath to sustain the Fugitive Slave Law (i.e., Free Soilers), even if they lived in the state, would be ineligible to vote.

12. T. H. Gladstone, *The Englishman in Kansas or, Squatter Life and Border Warfare* (New York: Miller, 1857), p. 43.

13. For a short summary of the historiographical issues involved, see Fawn M. Brodie, "Who Defends the Abolitionist?" in *The Antislavery Vanguard: New Essays on the Abolitionists* (Princeton, N.J.: Princeton University Press, 1965). This volume features essays by leftists Martin Duberman, Staughton Lynd, and Howard Zinn.

14. In fact, after I wrote this sentence, I went to the movies and found that the abolitionists *are* mocked in precisely this way in the 2002 film *Gangs of New York,* which depicts abolitionists as effete liberal-Protestant preachers and old-money WASP buffoons who are utterly ignorant of the *real* conflict in American life: the rise of the white ethnics, communicants of a fighting man's church. For the film's heroes, the fight to free the slaves is obvious bunk, some bullshit dreamed up by rich goo-goo liberals and their eternal friends the minorities. The New York draft riots are the natural result. Director Martin Scorsese and his admirers clearly believe that the film tells some sort of deep truth about American history, but the only historical episode it really illuminates is the antibusing riots of the seventies. In fact, the film's vision of American social conflict—rich, milquetoast Protestants

aligned with black people against the noble white ethnics—is nearly identical to the vision of social conflict held by the antibusing forces in Boston in 1972, as they are described in J. Anthony Lukas's famous account of the early years of the backlash, *Common Ground: A Turbulent Decade in the Lives of Three American Families* (New York: Knopf, 1985).

15. Writing in 1969, Kevin Phillips pointed out that, due to lingering bitterness over Quantrill's destruction of Lawrence, the county in which it was situated was for almost a century afterward the "most Republican county in Kansas." Phillips, *The Emerging Republican Majority* (New Rochelle, N.Y.: Arlington House, 1969), note, p. 383.

Once, when I asked an interview subject why Kansans disliked Democrats so much, he said: "I had a house in Lawrence that had two bullet holes in the front door, that Quantrill's people put in. And those were Democrats."

16. This is one recipient's recollection of the phone calls, as recounted in a press release issued by the National Jewish Democratic Council, dated June 19, 1998, and carried on the PR Newswire. In another part of the state, the calls took the form of a poll, in which the callers asked voters if they knew Jill Docking was Jewish.

Brownback has of course denied any connection to the anti-Semitic campaign, and the identity of the callers remains a mystery. Brownback has also built bridges to Jewish voters with his adamant support of Israel.

17. Alan Fram, "Kansas Senate Candidates Test Whether GOP Has Swung Too Far Right," Associated Press, October 15, 1996.

Chapter Ten: Inherit the Whirlwind

1. Brooks: *Bobos in Paradise: The New Upper Class and How They Got There* (New York: Simon & Schuster, 2000), p. 14. Limbaugh: David Brooks, ed., *Backward and Upward: The New Conservative Writing* (New York: Vintage, 1996), p. 308.

2. Whittaker Chambers, *Witness* (New York: Random House, 1952), p. 793. Chambers was himself an ex-Communist, and he returns to this inverted-Marxist sociological divide many times in his book. "From their roosts in the great cities, and certain collegiate eyries, the left-wing intellectuals of almost every feather (and that was most of the vocal intellectuals in the country) swooped and hovered in flocks like fluttered sea fowl . . . and gave vent to hoarse cries and defilements. I had accused a 'certified gentleman,' and the 'conspiracy of

gentlemen' closed its retaliatory ranks against me. Hence that musk of snobbism that lay rank and discrepant over the pro-Hiss faction" (pp. 789–790).

3. On the anti-intellectual history of evangelicalism, see Richard Hofstadter, *Anti-intellectualism in American Life* (New York: Knopf, 1963), chaps. 3–5.

4. Ehrenreich, *Fear of Falling*, p. 139.

5. For my description of Brinkley's doings, I am relying on R. Alton Lee, *The Bizarre Careers of John R. Brinkley* (Lexington: University Press of Kentucky, 2002—the quote can be found on p. 115), Clugston's *Rascals in Democracy,* and Francis W. Schruben, *Kansas in Turmoil: 1930–1936* (Columbia: University of Missouri Press, 1969).

6. Luker: See chaps. 2, 4 of Kristin Luker, *Abortion and the Politics of Motherhood* (Berkeley: University of California Press, 1985). On the list of groups submitting amicus briefs, see Luker, p. 142. Luker argues that abortion reform and *Roe v. Wade* effectively removed medical expertise from the abortion debate, making the issue a political competition between different non-elite constituencies, but the pro-life movement, as well we shall see, insists on magnifying the role of the various professions in the controversy. Two journalists who have studied: Risen and Thomas, *Wrath of Angels,* p. 34.

7. Risen and Thomas, *Wrath of Angels,* pp. 11, 14.

8. "Today's opinion is the product of a Court, which is the product of a law-profession culture that has largely signed on to the so-called homosexual agenda," Scalia wrote in his famous dissent in *Lawrence v. Texas,* "by which I mean the agenda promoted by some homosexual activists directed at eliminating the moral opprobrium that has traditionally attached to homosexual conduct. I noted in an earlier opinion the fact that the American Association of Law Schools (to which any reputable law school *must* seek to belong) excludes from membership any school that refuses to ban from its job-interview facilities a law firm (no matter how small) that does not wish to hire as a prospective partner a person who openly engages in homosexual conduct."

Coulter: This was in Coulter's column for December 3, 2003, putatively a response to the Massachusetts Supreme Court's decision legalizing gay marriage. In it she insists that liberals have essentially abandoned the rule of law, and she flat-out rejects the legal authority of the courts, writing that the Massachusetts chief justice "has as much right to proclaim a right to gay marriage from the Massachusetts Supreme Court as I do to proclaim it from my column." Coulter's columns are available at http://www.anncoulter.com/columns.html.

9. Everett Koop and Francis Schaeffer, *Whatever Happened to the Human Race?* revised edition (Westchester, Ill.: Crossway Books, 1983), p. 42. *Whatever Happened to the Human Race?* was one of the most influential anti-abortion tracts of the eighties. Its coauthor, Everett Koop, went on to become President Reagan's surgeon general. Among other things, the book is a meditation on the rightful role of the medical profession, which the authors believe has overstepped its field of expertise.

10. Indeed, the most convincing elements of Jack Cashill's study of TWA 800 are his attacks on the hypocrisies of journalistic professionalism. When Cashill's coauthor, independent investigator James Sanders, discovered what he believed to be evidence that a missile had struck the airplane, he was rebuffed by the mainstream media and, eventually, charged by the Justice Department with conspiracy to steal part of the wreckage. Although journalists are customarily highly protective of their First Amendment rights, on this occasion the profession did not rally around the accused. The obvious message is that those who are not part of the great news organizations are not worthy of even elementary levels of professional courtesy or respect. Another incident described in the book makes the point more chillingly. At an FBI press conference, a man described as "an unkempt figure among the reporters" asked a critical question, to which the FBI agent in charge responded by ordering flunkies to haul the man out of the room. "There was something very disquieting about the goonish tactics," writes a reporter who was there, but there is no mention of protest from the man's journalistic brethren. Cashill and Sanders, *First Strike*, pp. 205, 212, 137, 140, 89.

    Ironically, the rise of professionalism among journalists is also one of the cultural factors that has made possible the right's erasure of the economic. As the media scholar Robert McChesney has pointed out, professionalism's emphasis on legitimacy and expertise has caused mainstream journalism to define news almost exclusively as the doings of the state, government officials, and rival politicians; the corporate world is not considered a legitimate subject for critical inquiry or the attention of the general public. As McChesney points out, this lack of true journalistic scrutiny is what made possible such costly debacles as the Enron and WorldCom bankruptcies. McChesney, *The Problem of the Media,* chap. 2.

11. James W. Loewen, *Lies My Teacher Told Me: Everything Your American History Textbook Got Wrong* (New York: New Press, 1995), pp. 25, 288.

12. Cashill, *2006*, p. 84.

13. This is even the case for Intelligent Design, the doctrine widely believed by the Kansas Cons to be a valid, legitimate, academically accepted critique of evolution. Separated from the religious and political cant that always accompanies it, Intelligent Design falls apart when subjected to searching criticism. See, for example, paleontologist Kevin Padian's review of the anthology *Intelligent Design Creationism and Its Critics* in *Science* magazine, March 29, 2002.

14. "War against God": this line is found in a pamphlet distributed at the Intelligent Design Symposium in Kansas City that is described later in this chapter. John D. Morris, "The Dayton Deception," in *Scopes: Creation on Trial* (Green Forest, Ark.: Master Books, 1999), p. 31. The teachings of the "pagan religion" are from the flyer *Is Evolution Science?* that was written by Tom Willis, president of the Creation Science Association for Mid-America (dated October 10, 1995), a Missouri group that was instrumental in writing the Kansas science standards of 1999. Ellipses in original. See also the infamous "wedge" document, discussed in the introduction, note 4. "More and more commentators": Paul Ackerman and Bob Williams, *Kansas Tornado: The 1999 Science Curriculum Standards Battle* (El Cajon, Calif.: Institute for Creation Research, 1999), p. 6.

15. Brooks, "One Nation, Slightly Divisible." Brooks seems to base this pronouncement on his personal observation of Darwin-fish people. When they are actually asked why they put the Darwin-fish on their cars, though, they say they are doing it for precisely the opposite reason. A University of Georgia professor who has actually conducted a study of people who put Darwin-fishes on their cars finds that many of them see the fish as "a kind of defense, a way for persecuted atheists to fight back against the onslaught of religion." The newspaper story describing the Darwin-fish study does not mention anyone using the fish as a symbol of upper-class caste or as a put-down of intellectual inferiors. Carol Kaesuk Yoon, "Unexpected Evolution of a Fish Out of Water," *The New York Times*, February 11, 2003.

16. Cashill, "The Natural Selection Election," *Weekly Standard*, July 31, 2000.

17. Ackerman and Williams, *Kansas Tornado*, pp. 27, 15, 19, 15, 23.

18. *Kansas City Star*, columns by John Altevogt for August 25, 1999, and October 21, 1999.

19. Three of these allegations appear in *Kansas Tornado* (see pp. 11, 6, 7). *Dogmatic* and *narrow-minded* are terms used by Linda Holloway, the chairman of the State Board of Education when it made its historic decision. The item about the bias of peer-reviewed journals is a frequent plaint of the Intelligent Design movement, which sees itself as an aca-

demically respectable version of creationism. See Jonathan Wells, "Design Theorist Charges Academic Prejudice Is a 'Catch-23,'" *Research News & Opportunities in Science and Theology,* July–August 2002. See also the related article by Wells in the *American Spectator,* December 2000–January 2001.

20. Easterbrook apparently believes that the science community is trying to suppress doubts about itself because it is being genuinely challenged by Intelligent Design. "The New Fundamentalism," *Wall Street Journal,* August 8, 2000.

21. The reasoning goes like this: the science standards the state was considering before the Cons got into the act represented "an attempt . . . to establish the worldview of philosophical naturalism as the official, state-sanctioned belief for science education in Kansas," and that the good parents of Kansas simply said no to this outrageous imposition (Ackerman and Williams, *Kansas Tornado,* p. 21; see also p. 44). Others argue that liberals generally are responsible. John Altevogt, for example, said at a public forum discussing the school board's deed that "this has been one of the biggest nonoutrages that the left has ever tried to put together" (*Kansas City Star,* September 16, 1999).

   Although widely held among the Kansas Cons, the view that the whole evolution imbroglio was started by uppity scientists is contradicted by the fact that the Cons themselves had already declared their support for presenting "the scientific facts supporting creationism presented on an equal basis with evolution" in the 1996 Kansas Republican platform and had reaffirmed that stance in their 1998 platform. The school board's decision was not made until August 1999.

22. *Kansas City Star,* Altevogt columns for August 25, 1999, and September 8, 1999.

23. Cashill, "The State of Embarrassment," *Ingram's,* July 2000. Cashill, "The Natural Selection Election."

24. Holloway lost. The flyer I describe was accompanied by a letter noting that "there has been an overwhelming display of **bigotry and intolerance** by those who claim to be '**Moderate**'. Why is the **Sacred Cow of Evolution** guarded so closely by the Liberal Educational and political establishments? Truth to tell is that Evolution has more to do with the **Political correctness of Revolution, Socialism, and World government than it does Science!**" Sic sic sic sic sic. Both flyer and letter from the archives of the Mainstream Coalition.

25. Ironically, Cashill made this point to an audience of executives in *Ingram's,* the Kansas City business magazine, July 2000.

26. The full lyrics of "Overwhelming Evidence," as well as the description

of the Mutations as "three fine Christian ladies," can be found on the Web site of Phillip Johnson, one of the leaders of the Intelligent Design movement: http://www.arn.org/docs/pjweekly/pj_weekly_010702.htm.

Chapter Eleven: Antipopes Among Us

1. T. E. Lawrence, *The Seven Pillars of Wisdom* (Garden City, N.Y.: Doubleday, 1936), p. 39.
2. News stories on the SSPX community in St. Marys, Kansas, often mention the concentration of other right-wing groups in the area. See, for example, Dennis Farney, "Paranoia Becomes an Article of Faith in a Kansas Town," *Wall Street Journal,* August 17, 1995.
3. I am following the narrative of the sociologist Michael W. Cuneo, author of the insightful as well as entertaining book *The Smoke of Satan: Conservative and Traditionalist Dissent in Contemporary American Catholicism* (Baltimore: Johns Hopkins University Press, 1999), chap. 4.
4. The *Star* ran a page-one series on the bizarre goings-on at St. Marys in April 1982. In the stories, the Bawdens, along with a number of other families who had been drawn to the area, described their falling-out with the SSPX hierarchy. Among other things, the Reverend Hector Bolduc, then in charge of the St. Marys campus, reportedly banished the Bawdens from the grounds and told them they could not receive the sacraments from any priest other than himself. When the Bawdens then held a meeting of disgruntled SSPX followers, they were harassed with midnight phone calls and insulting, anonymous letters. David Bawden, later Pope Michael, is quoted as saying, "I know from long association with Father Bolduc, if I had done half of what he has, I would go straight to hell." Eric Palmer, "Traditional Catholics Seek Their Eden in Kansas," *Kansas City Star,* April 18, 1982; Eric Palmer, "Shadows Dim the Portrait of a Rebel Priest," *Kansas City Star,* April 19, 1982.
5. In Bawden's 1990 book, he even seems to give credence to that infamous hoax, *Protocols of the Elders of Zion,* comparing quotations from it to statements of the leaders of the Vatican II church, who are supposedly in thrall to the great conspiracy. T. Stanfill Benns and David Bawden, *Will the Catholic Church Survive the Twentieth Century?* (Belvue, Kans.: Christ the King Library, n.d. [1990]), pp. 122, 123.

Chapter Twelve: Performing Indignation

1. Clugston, *Rascals in Democracy,* pp. 20, 21.
2. " 'When he first ran, he [Brownback] took a pro-choice position,' said David Gittrich, executive director of Kansans for Life." Mike

Hendricks, "Politics Attracted Brownback Early," *Kansas City Star,* October 27, 1996.

In the early days of Brownback's career, he was usually identified as a traditional moderate Republican. When the lawsuit that would eventually oust him from the Kansas Department of Agriculture was filed in 1993, a story about Brownback appeared on page one of the reliably moderate *Topeka Capital-Journal* (a paper that was then owned by the family of Brownback's wife) suggesting that he had a bright future in politics. To establish Brownback's qualifications, the story included many flattering quotations from none other than Sheila Frahm, the moderate Republican whom Brownback would later demolish on his way to the U.S. Senate in 1996. (*Topeka Capital-Journal,* January 22, 1993.)

It should also be noted that when he first ran for Congress in 1994, Brownback refused to support the "Contract with America" and was hailed as being a sensible, moderate Republican for so refusing. (The *Wichita Eagle* even ran an editorial praising him for it on September 29, 1994.) Once in Washington, of course, Brownback staked out a position to the *right* of the contract, leading a group that called itself the "New Federalists."

3. "Remembered as a war that was lost because of betrayal at home," writes the sociologist Jerry Lembcke, "Vietnam becomes a modern-day Alamo that must be avenged, a pretext for more war and generations of more veterans." This analysis appeared on http://www.tompaine.com/feature2.cfm/ID/3600. Lembcke is the author of *The Spitting Image: Myth, Memory, and the Legacy of Vietnam* (New York: New York University Press, 1998), a book that debunks the familiar story of returning veterans being spat upon by antiwar demonstrators.

4. All quotes are from David Eulitt, "A Higher Principle: Kline: Legislators Should Look to Conscience," *Topeka Capital-Journal,* July 8, 2002

5. According to the Israeli newspaper *Ha'aretz* for June 26, 2003, Bush told the Palestinian prime minister, "God told me to strike at al-Qaida and I struck them, and then He instructed me to strike at Saddam, which I did, and now I am determined to solve the problem in the Middle East."

6. Conservatives mocking Democrats for faking religious faith: one more time, see the shameless Ann Coulter, who writes in "The Jesus Thing," her column for January 7, 2004: "Democrats never talk about believing in something; they talk about simulating belief in something. *Americans believe in this crazy God crap that we don't, so how do we hoodwink them into believing we believe in God?* It's part of the casual contempt Democrats have for the views of normal people." Laura Ingraham and Hollywood: see "David Frum's Diary" for September 22, 2003, on *National*

Review Online (http://www.nationalreview.com/frum/diary 092203.asp).

7. See the telling list of Coulter's errors compiled by Al Franken in *Lies and the Lying Liars Who Tell Them: A Fair and Balanced Look at the Right* (New York: Dutton, 2003), chaps. 2, 3.

Epilogue: In the Garden of the World

1. Ehrenreich, *Fear of Falling*, p. 196.

2. "The notion that an enlightened upper class could save liberalism," says E. J. Dionne, "was one of the liberals' gravest mistakes. This view ignored the most basic electoral fact: that upper-income voters tend to vote their economic interests and that most of them, most of the time, will support conservatives. Liberals simply could not expect to substitute the votes of lower-income whites with the ballots of a 'coalition of conscience'" (*Why Americans Hate Politics*, pp. 12, 89–90).

   Here is how Mike Royko, the Chicago newspaper columnist, put the same idea in 1972: "Anybody who would reform Chicago's Democratic Party by dropping the white ethnic would probably begin a diet by shooting himself in the stomach." Quoted in Mike O'Flaherty and Seth Sanders, "44,000,000 Ronald Reagan Fans Can't Be Wrong!" *Baffler* 15 (2002), p. 85.

3. Statistics on union voting patterns are from the "2000 Union Voter Survey," a study commissioned by the AFL-CIO and conducted by Peter D. Hart Research Associates. Union members said their least important election issues were, in descending order, moral values, taxes, and guns. Thanks to Jim McNeill for bringing this to my attention.

4. See David Brooks's many published meditations on the populist majesty of Wal-Mart, the retail force that is doing so much to push places like rural Kansas into poverty—destroying the small-town business districts, forcing down retail wages, crushing farm prices, and committing countless violations of labor law along the way. "Walk into one of those places," Brooks wrote in a June 9, 2002, *New York Times Magazine* story, referring to Wal-Mart and the other big-box discounters, "and you're in middle-American nirvana. You can get absolutely everything you need for a wholesome, happy life."

Acknowledgments

This book could not have been written without the kindness and understanding of my wife, Wendy Edelberg, and also of our daughter, Madeleine. To them I am grateful beyond words.

Big thanks are also due to my fellow Kansan Andrew Patzman, who first suggested that I look into the subject of populist conservatism, and to my father, Lloyd Frank, who accompanied me on so many of this book's expeditions and who sat patiently by while I explored mysterious grain elevators and gorged myself at the barbecue emporiums of Kansas City and the steak palaces of Topeka and Wichita. My brothers David and Nathan graciously read over the manuscript and helped me capture the feel of our particular 1970s.

Sara Bershtel, my editor at Metropolitan Books, did amazing things with the manuscript and was assisted in this by her colleague Riva Hocherman, while Shara Kay kept things organized. Joe Spieler, my agent, was encouraging and helpful throughout. As usual Team Baffler was a massive help, with George Hodak and David Mulcahey winning special thanks for their excellent edits. Jim Lawing did a great last-minute edit. Chris Lehmann and Ana Marie Cox also furnished crucial editorial advice.

My research assistants were of critical importance. Jenny Ludwig read several years' worth of *Wichita Eagles* on my behalf, while Andy Nelson spent many an hour at the Johnson County Courthouse in Olathe digging up obscure facts. Mike O'Flaherty helped with the broad theoretical framing of the project, offering fascinating accounts of the basic sociological texts on the backlash.

Gene Coyle, Doug Henwood, Jim McNeill, Nomi Prins, and Daryll Ray each helped me understand the particulars of the industrial fields discussed in the book. Liz Craig, Caroline McKnight, and Dwight Sutherland, Jr. guided me through the complexities of Kansas politics, while old friends Bridget Cain and Tad Kepley reminded me of what Kansas was like back in the day. All errors, of course, are my very, very own.

Index

About the Author

The founding editor of *The Baffler*, Thomas Frank is the author of *One Market Under God* and *The Conquest of Cool*. He writes frequently for *Harper's*, *The Nation*, and *Le Monde diplomatique*.